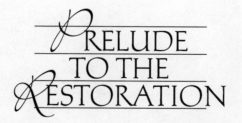

PRELUDE TO THE RESTORATION

Sidney B. Sperry

Other volumes in the Sperry Symposium Series
from Deseret Book Company

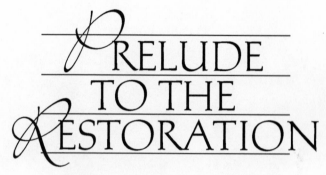

PRELUDE TO THE RESTORATION

FROM APOSTASY TO THE RESTORED CHURCH

THE 33RD ANNUAL
SIDNEY B. SPERRY SYMPOSIUM

DESERET BOOK
SALT LAKE CITY, UTAH

RELIGIOUS STUDIES CENTER
BRIGHAM YOUNG UNIVERSITY

Library of Congress Cataloging-in-Publication Data

Sperry Symposium (33rd : 2004 : Brigham Young University)
  Prelude to the Restoration : from Apostasy to the Restoration / the 33rd Annual Sidney B. Sperry Symposium.
     p. cm.
  Includes bibliographical references and index.
  ISBN 1-59038-329-X (hardback : alk. paper)
  1. Church history—Congresses. 2. Great Apostasy (Mormon doctrine)—Congresses. 3. Restoration of the gospel (Mormon doctrine)—Congresses. I. Title.
  BX8643.G74S64 2004
  270—dc22
                                                            2004011966

Printed in the United States of America   70582
Phoenix Color Corporation, Hagerstown, MD

10   9   8   7   6   5   4   3   2   1

CONTENTS

PREFACE

*I*n years past the Sperry Symposium has provided speakers and hearers, authors and readers a valued opportunity to engage one of the standard works of Latter-day Saint scripture. That esteemed tradition has been expanded recently to include reflections on the Church in the twentieth century. This volume looks forward to the two hundredth anniversary of the birth of Joseph Smith in 2005 by looking back to some of the events, processes, people, and ideas that set the stage for the marvelous Restoration begun by the Prophet.

Latter-day Saints acknowledge the hand of the Almighty in shaping history. Unsurprisingly, then, as the distinguished historian Gordon S. Wood wrote, the Restoration "appeared at precisely the right moment in American history" ("Evangelical America and Early Mormonism," *New York History,* October 1980, 381). One might add that, in anticipation of the Restoration, America appeared at precisely the right moment in world history. Indeed, because of the Restoration we know that the earth itself appeared in its proper time and season. This volume provides glimpses into the complicated choreography of history by which the world became ready for

Joseph Smith and the restoration of the Church of Jesus Christ. The complex processes at work between the Apostasy and the Restoration do not lend themselves to reduction or simplification, and this volume cannot impose unwarranted order on the chaos. Yet it identifies themes, movements, and people who participated in making the moment right for the Restoration, including some that are ignored or unknown by many Latter-day Saints. These deserve attention.

The theme of this year's Sperry Symposium was influenced by a devotional address Elder M. Russell Ballard delivered to the student body at Brigham Young University–Hawaii ("What Price Religious Freedom," November 2, 2001): "I had prepared a talk, written it, and had it prepared to give to you by the teleprompter," he said, but "in the middle of the night I had the impression that I was to set that aside and speak to you from my heart, as a father would speak to his children, on a matter that the Lord apparently wants someone here to hear and to understand." He then quoted the first nine verses of Mark 12, the parable of the wicked husbandman, "a scripture," he said, "that many of you have undoubtedly read but perhaps you have not understood." Elder Ballard said he believed "the Savior, in this parable, is teaching us how many times our Heavenly Father has tried to send His prophets among His people to establish His gospel and to bless the lives of His children."

Highlighting the history of servants (prophets) being sent into the vineyard, Elder Ballard suggested that many of the early Christian leaders and the medieval and early modern reformers of Christendom are among those the Lord has sent forth. "I want to talk to you about something we must never, ever, forget," Elder Ballard emphasized. "As we walk through this process of mortality as members of the Church, we must appreciate that there has been a terrible price paid for the privilege you and I have to be members of The Church of Jesus Christ of Latter-day Saints. I pray with all the power that I have, as an apostle of the Lord Jesus Christ, that there would not be one of you students that would ever take this privilege casually or lightly. I would pray that you would focus some of your study on what price has been paid, by those who have gone before us, to give us the privilege of walking in the light and knowledge of the gospel." He mentioned John Wycliffe and Jan Huss, William Tyndale, Martin Luther, Anne Askew, Hugh Latimer, and Nicholas Ridley. For most of us these are names little known if at all. And that was Elder Ballard's point. "You need to know," he said again and again, adding such imperatives as "you need to study," "we must never lose sight," and "we must never forget."

Elder Ballard's talk and the Spirit that inspired it have impressed many, including contributors to this volume, to study the men and women who labored largely in the dark in anticipation of the glorious Restoration. They helped make a world in which the Prophet Joseph Smith could function. If they did not see quite clearly, they may be excused, for they gave their all. What follows is offered in the spirit of contributing a small part toward realization of Elder Ballard's emphatic hope that we will become better acquainted with what "had to happen in order for the Lord in 1820 to take a boy in Palmyra into a grove of trees where he communicated with God the Father and his Beloved Son, the Lord Jesus Christ."

The 2004 Sidney B. Sperry Symposium Committee

Fred E. Woods
Steven C. Harper
Andrew H. Hedges
Patty A. Smith
Thomas R. Valletta

1

FORERUNNERS AND FOUNDATION STONES OF THE RESTORATION

Andrew C. Skinner

*I*n 1819 the Romantic poet Percy Bysshe Shelley wrote, in a flash of prophetic insight and historical analysis, that "the great writers of our own age are, we have reason to suppose, the *companions* and *forerunners* of some unimagined change in our social condition or the opinions which cement it. The cloud of mind is discharging its collected lightening, and the equilibrium between institutions and opinions is now *restoring,* or is about to be *restored.*"[1] Gordon K. Thomas, Brigham Young University English professor emeritus, has stated that "Shelley scholars have never known quite what to make of all this."[2] They are not aware of any historical events in the weeks or months following Shelley's declaration that fulfill his prophecy of "unimagined change" or "restoring."[3] Latter-day Saints know through the help of inspired interpreters, however, that Shelley's prescient rumblings presaged the monumental religious revolution of 1820 and that he was one of several other scholars, sages, and savants who anticipated and helped

Andrew C. Skinner is dean of Religious Education at Brigham Young University.

prepare the world for the restoration of all things that began with Joseph Smith's First Vision.

These other "forerunners," to use Shelley's own language, included such luminaries as John Wycliffe, Johannes Gutenberg, Martin Luther, John Calvin, William Tyndale, George Fox, Roger Williams, George Washington, Thomas Jefferson, William Words-worth, and many more. Among the women forerunners were Joan of Arc, Mary Washington, Charlotte Corday, Elizabeth Gurney, Anne Hutchinson, Hannah Moore, Abigail Adams, and others. These individuals, their good works and words, and the events they set in motion constitute what Elder Mark E. Petersen of the Quorum of the Twelve called a "significant *prelude* to the great events in which the Prophet Joseph Smith was the primary figure."[4] In other words, the planning for the restoration of the fulness of the gospel of Jesus Christ to the earth after an extended absence began long before Joseph walked into the Sacred Grove in 1820, even cen-turies before the earth-shaking revelations of the 1820s, '30s, and '40s brought the piercing light of revealed truth back to this earth. Beginning in the Middle Ages, the Lord "began to prepare those social, educational, religious, economic, and governmental condi-tions under which he could more easily restore the gospel for the last time among men."[5] Almost imperceptibly at times, God moved upon the minds of men and women, who in turn moved the world toward the Restoration.

THE CERTAINTY OF A PERIOD OF PREPARATION

Latter-day prophets and apostles have repeatedly affirmed that preparations for the latter-day restoration of God's ancient gospel took place in stages, throughout the long and varied periods of world history. Elder Petersen wrote, "The restoration of the gospel of the Lord Jesus Christ in these latter days, together with the advance preparation of conditions which made it possible, was indeed a divine drama which had many stages and many scenes, some of which were world shaking."[6]

The Restoration was not a surprise, nor was it a contingency plan of the Lord's. Before the foundations of this world, our Father in Heaven and His Beloved Son, Jehovah, knew of the Great Apostasy that would begin in the first century of the Christian era. More importantly, thousands of years before the Restoration occurred they foreordained the events and individuals that would be associated with the restoration of all things. President Brigham Young taught:

"We are a people whose rise and progress from the beginning, has been the work of God our Heavenly Father. . . . It was decreed in the counsels of eternity, long before the foundations of the earth were laid, that he, Joseph Smith, should be the man, in the last dispensation of this world, to bring forth the word of God to the people, and receive the fulness of the keys and power of the Priesthood of the Son of God. The Lord had his eyes upon him, and upon his father, and upon his father's father, and upon their progenitors clear back to Abraham, and from Abraham to the flood, from the flood to Enoch, and from Enoch to Adam. He has watched that family and that blood as it circulated from its fountain to the birth of that man. He was fore-ordained in eternity to preside over this last dispensation."[7]

The Lord began to teach His ancient covenant people about the future events of the latter-day Restoration even from the earliest dispensations of earth's temporal history. In the book of Moses, we read of Enoch's visions and conversations with God. The seer witnessed the future mortal ministry of Jesus Christ, His Crucifixion, Resurrection, and Ascension. Then Enoch asked about the Second Coming:

"And Enoch beheld the Son of Man ascend up unto the Father; and he called unto the Lord, saying: Wilt thou not come again upon the earth? Forasmuch as thou art God, and I know thee, and thou hast sworn unto me, and commanded me that I should ask in the name of thine Only Begotten; thou hast made me, and given unto me a right to thy throne, and not of myself, but through thine own grace; wherefore, I ask thee if thou wilt not come again on the earth.

"And the Lord said unto Enoch: As I live, even so will I come

in the last days, in the days of wickedness and vengeance, to fulfil
the oath which I have made unto you concerning the children of
Noah;

"And the day shall come that the earth shall rest, but before that
day the heavens shall be darkened, and a veil of darkness shall cover
the earth; and the heavens shall shake, and also the earth; and great
tribulations shall be among the children of men, but my people will
I preserve;

"And righteousness will I send down out of heaven; and truth
will I send forth out of the earth, to bear testimony of mine Only
Begotten; his resurrection from the dead; yea, and also the resurrection of all men; and righteousness and truth will I cause to sweep
the earth as with a flood, to gather out mine elect from the four
quarters of the earth, unto a place which I shall prepare, an Holy
City, that my people may gird up their loins, and be looking forth
for the time of my coming; for there shall be my tabernacle, and it
shall be called Zion, a New Jerusalem" (Moses 7:58–62).

Thousands of years before the actual events took place, Enoch
was taught that in the last days righteousness would come down out
of heaven and truth would be sent forth out of the earth prior to the
Second Coming. President Ezra Taft Benson declared, "We have
seen the marvelous fulfillment of that prophecy in our generation.
The Book of Mormon has come forth out of the earth, filled with
truth. . . . God has also sent down righteousness from heaven. The
Father Himself appeared with His Son to the Prophet Joseph
Smith. The angel Moroni, John the Baptist, Peter, James, and
numerous other angels were directed by heaven to restore the necessary powers to the kingdom."[8]

The point to be emphasized here is that the key events of the
Restoration were revealed by the Lord to His prophets many thousands of years before they happened. But it is also true that the
preparatory events leading up to the Restoration were revealed long
before they occurred. The prophet Nephi described some of the
significant preparatory events he saw for himself, which had also
been seen by his father, Lehi (1 Nephi 10:17 and 11:3). These
events include the voyage of Christopher Columbus across the

Atlantic Ocean (1 Nephi 13:10); the travails and travels of the Puritans and Pilgrims (1 Nephi 13:13); the colonization of America (1 Nephi 13:15–16); the American Revolutionary War involving Great Britain (1 Nephi 13:17); God's direct intervention in the affairs of the fledgling country of America (1 Nephi 13:18–19); the country's prosperity (1 Nephi 13:20); and the coming forth of the Book of Mormon (1 Nephi 13:35–40).

A careful study of Nephi's vision increases our own panoramic understanding of how the Lord orchestrated events in preparation for the Restoration of His gospel on the American continent. But we note with particular interest Nephi's comment, at the end of his sweeping vision, regarding others who saw the things he saw:

"But the things which thou shalt see hereafter thou shalt not write; for the Lord God hath ordained the apostle of the Lamb of God [John] that he should write them.

"And *also others who have been, to them hath he shown all things*, and they have written them; and they are sealed up to come forth in their purity, according to the truth which is in the Lamb, in the own due time of the Lord, unto the house of Israel" (1 Nephi 14:25–26; emphasis added).

Other prophets besides Nephi and Lehi saw all the preparatory events leading up to the Restoration of the fulness of the gospel of Jesus Christ. We have been told about some of these seers in scripture. For example, we know of Adam, who prophesied all things that would befall his posterity to the latest generation (D&C 107:56); the brother of Jared, who was shown all the inhabitants of the earth and all things pertaining to them (Ether 3:25–26); and Moses, who beheld every particle of the earth and every soul on the earth (Moses 1:27–29). Preparations for the latter-day Restoration were not planned nor carried out in a dark closet. Many were privileged to see the foreordained preparations as well as the foreordained forerunners. According to President Benson, "all of the great events that have transpired [in America], including the coming of Columbus and of the Pilgrim fathers, were foreseen by ancient prophets."[9]

President Joseph Fielding Smith, tenth President of The

Church of Jesus Christ of Latter-day Saints, interpreted part of the prophecy of the Old Testament seer Joel as a clear and sure prediction of events preparatory to the Restoration of the gospel as well as events that would accompany the rolling forth of the kingdom after the initial phases of its restoration. Joel declared the word of the Lord, saying: "And it shall come to pass afterward, that I will pour out my spirit upon all flesh; and your sons and your daughters shall prophesy, and your old men shall dream dreams, your young men shall see visions: and also upon the servants and upon the handmaids in those days will I pour out my spirit" (Joel 2:28–29). Of Joel's words, President Smith said:

"When Joel by inspiration stated that the Lord would pour out his spirit upon all flesh, he did not mean that this Spirit which should be poured in such abundance, was to be the Holy Ghost. That the Holy Ghost would be received by some is evident, but it was to be the Light of Christ that was to be so universally received. The many remarkable events, discoveries, and inventions of the later centuries, particularly since the restoration of the gospel, that have been poured out prove this thesis to be true. The time of preparation for the restoration of the gospel commenced several hundred years ago, when there was no one on the earth to perform legal baptisms or bestow the gift of the Holy Ghost. The inspiration given to the so-called reformers, the invention of printing and the making of books that could be placed in the hands of the multitude, the discovery of the western hemisphere and a thousand other things were the beginning of the fulfilment of the prophecy of Joel. These wonders have been coming rapidly since the beginning of the nineteenth century, and particularly since the organization of the Church. In bringing to pass these great discoveries, the Lord has used men who apparently and boastingly have no faith in him, yet because of their talents he has seen fit to use them."[10]

There is no doubt that the Lord's Spirit moved upon men and women from many backgrounds and countries. Forerunners of the Restoration included explorers, statesmen, poets, churchmen, and theologians. Sometimes their faith in God was strong, sometimes weak. But God used their talents for His purposes. In a remarkable general conference address in April 1972, Elder Ezra Taft Benson testified unequivocally: "God, the Father of us all, uses the men of the earth, especially good men, to accomplish His purposes. It has been true in the past, it is true today, it will be true in the future. . . . God is using [and has used] more than one people for the accomplishment of His great and marvelous work."[11]

RESTORATION PARALLELS

The restoration of the fulness of the gospel in the nineteenth century is not the first time the gospel of Jesus Christ has been restored to the earth after a long period of apostasy and spiritual decay. God's dealings with the human family display patterns and parallels. The meridian dispensation, the time of Jesus' mortal ministry, witnessed a great restoration of priesthood power, eternal principles, and sacred ordinances under the direction of the Savior Himself. In Joseph Smith's inspired revision of John's Gospel, Jesus Christ is designated as the Elias of restoration in the meridian dispensation:

"And this is the record of John, when the Jews sent priests and Levites from Jerusalem, to ask him; Who art thou?

"And he confessed, and denied not that he was Elias; but confessed, saying; I am not the Christ.

"And they asked him, saying; How then art thou Elias? And he said, I am not *that Elias who was to restore all things*. And they asked him, saying, Art thou that prophet? And he answered, No.

"Then said they unto him, Who art thou? that we may give an answer to them that sent us. What sayest thou of thyself?

"He said, I am the voice of one crying in the wilderness, Make straight the way of the Lord, as saith the prophet Esaias.

"And they who were sent were of the Pharisees.

"And they asked him, and said unto him; Why baptizest thou then, *if thou be not the Christ, nor Elias who was to restore all things, neither that prophet?*

"John answered them, saying; I baptize with water, but there standeth one among you, whom ye know not;

"He it is of whom I bear record. He is that prophet, even Elias, who, coming after me, is preferred before me, whose shoe's latchet I am not worthy to unloose" (Joseph Smith Translation, John 1:20–28; emphasis added).

These verses tell us that some of the Jewish leaders at the beginning of the Savior's mortal ministry were expecting a Messiah who would also function as the Elias of restoration and "restore all things" in their day (Joseph Smith Translation, John 1:22). They were expecting a restoration in their day, and God had planned and prepared for one. This profound insight helps us to comprehend that the latter-day restoration is truly in the likeness of a former-day restoration of all things during the meridian of time. Just as Jesus was the Elias of restoration in His day, so Joseph Smith was an Elias of restoration in his day. To repeat, we see patterns in God's dealings with the human family.

From the time of Adam to the days of the Abrahamic patriarchs, righteous men and women enjoyed the fulness of the gospel, including the Melchizedek Priesthood and temple ordinances. During the Egyptian captivity of Israel, there was a loss of sacred truths and spiritual power among the people generally. Moses took steps to restore that which had been lost or become dormant by trying to prepare Israel to be ushered into the literal, physical presence of the Lord (Exodus 19:10–11; D&C 84:23) and make them "a kingdom of priests, and an holy nation" (Exodus 19:6). But Israel rejected this opportunity and brought upon themselves and their posterity a long period of spiritual decay. From the time of Moses' last visits to Mount Sinai to the time of John the Baptist's mortal ministry, most of the house of Israel lived without the fulness of the gospel (though many prophets had it). The Lord revealed the plight of Israel's existence:

"And this greater priesthood administereth the gospel and holdeth the key of the mysteries of the kingdom, even the key of the knowledge of God.

"Therefore, in the ordinances thereof, the power of godliness is manifest.

"And without the ordinances thereof, and the authority of the priesthood, the power of godliness is not manifest unto men in the flesh;

"For without this no man can see the face of God, even the Father, and live.

"Now this Moses plainly taught to the children of Israel in the wilderness, and sought diligently to sanctify his people that they might behold the face of God;

"But they hardened their hearts and could not endure his presence; therefore, the Lord in his wrath, for his anger was kindled against them, swore that they should not enter into his rest while in the wilderness, which rest is the fulness of his glory.

"Therefore, he took Moses out of their midst, and the Holy Priesthood also;

"And the lesser priesthood continued, which priesthood holdeth the key of the ministering of angels and the preparatory gospel;

"Which gospel is the gospel of repentance and of baptism, and the remission of sins, and the law of carnal commandments, which the Lord in his wrath caused to continue with the house of Aaron among the children of Israel until John, whom God raised up, being filled with the Holy Ghost from his mother's womb" (D&C 84:19–27).

With the coming of Jesus Christ and His Apostles, the Melchizedek Priesthood, the ordinances of the temple, the higher covenants associated with the fulness of the gospel, and a personal knowledge of God the Father were restored and reinstituted among the membership of the new covenant community. The Apostles took the message of the restoration of their day to the world (Acts 1:8). They set the Church in order and administered the ordinances of the Melchizedek Priesthood until apostasy once again set in and the world had to wait for another restoration—the restoration of the latter days.

For our purposes it is important to note that the restoration of the meridian dispensation did not happen without significant preparations, just as the restoration of the latter days did not occur without significant preparation. One modern Church leader has said, "The [meridian] Apostles were not thrown into a world that was completely unprepared for their message. The Lord had made some very substantial preparations that permitted His Apostles to succeed in His commission to them."[12] In fact, three foundational preparations were in place so that the restoration of the gospel in the meridian dispensation could proceed:

1. A widely accepted translation of the Bible, in the dominant language and tied to the dominant culture of the period.

2. A stable political system to provide a base of operations from which the Restoration could go forward.

3. A culture and language which fostered the establishment of the gospel, including a spirit of restoration which anticipated a new dispensation.

These same three foundational preparations were also put in place for the restoration of the gospel in the latter days.

In the meridian dispensation, the Bible that served as the basis for the restoration of the first century was the Septuagint—the Greek translation of the Old Testament from the original Hebrew. It had been in place for more than two hundred years, was common to all, and was tied to the pervasive Greek culture of the period. In the nineteenth century, the Bible undergirding the Restoration was the King James Version—the latest iteration of English Bibles, made from the available Hebrew and Greek texts of the Old and New Testaments. It had been in place for two hundred years.

In the meridian dispensation, the political system that allowed for the gospel to be established in a stable environment (for its day) was the Roman Empire. It was largely the creation of one man, Octavian, called Caesar Augustus (31 B.C.–A.D. 14), who established it on the foundations of the Roman Republic. It was so well founded and provided such a period of peace and prosperity that it survived its founder for several hundred years (even with subsequent incompetent and wicked emperors at its helm) and left a legacy known as the Pax Romana (Roman Peace).

In preparation for the latter-day Restoration, the United States of America had been recently established. The system of government prepared by the Lord was grounded in the Constitution of the

United States, including the Bill of Rights, and the principles articulated in the Declaration of Independence.

In the meridian dispensation, the language and culture of the Mediterranean world that allowed for the restored gospel of Jesus Christ to take root and flourish for a season was Greek. In the nineteenth century, the English language and culture provided the seedbed for the flowering of the restored gospel. Both eras witnessed an expectation of restoration.

The Bible and the Latter-day Restoration

A key element in laying the foundation for the restoration of the gospel of Jesus Christ in the latter days was the bringing forth of the English Bible, especially the King James Version. Religious reformers of the Renaissance and Reformation periods played a vital role, as Elder Bruce R. McConkie testified: "The spirit of inspiration rested upon Wycliffe, Huss, Luther, Zwingli, Calvin, Knox, and others, causing them to rebel against the religious evils of the day and seek to make *the Bible* and other truth available to all who would receive such."[13] The Restoration owes much to the Protestant reformers. In addition to changing the theological landscape of Christendom, the reformers were instrumental in paving the way for the King James Bible and drawing attention to its doctrines and teachings—which were critical to the establishment of the Restoration. The English Bible was "in a sense . . . a Protestant book,"[14] and many of the reformers sacrificed much for it as well as the greater cause they believed in: giving the true word of God to the world. One modern prophet has described the reformers, in the main, as "honest men with yearning hearts, [who] at the peril of their very lives, attempted to establish points of reference, that they might find the true way. . . . The reformers were pioneers, blazing wilderness trails in a desperate search for those lost points of reference which, they felt, when found would lead mankind back to the truth Jesus taught. . . . Significant was the declaration of [William] Tyndale to his critics: 'I will cause a boy that driveth the plough shall know more of the scripture than thou doest.'"[15]

William Tyndale (1490–1536) is a superb example of one of the pivotal forerunners to the Restoration. He deserves much attention and credit for the quality of prose and clarity of expression found in early English Bibles. Tyndale's work is really the cornerstone of the King James Version. Scholars at Brigham Young University have compared the King James Version with Tyndale's English Bible and found that "nearly 84 per cent of the New Testament and close to 76 per cent of the portions of the Old Testament that Tyndale translated have been transmitted to the KJV [King James Version] just as he left them."[16] Tyndale was an intellectual and spiritual giant, "one of history's great heroes,"[17] who suffered martyrdom to put a readable Bible in the hands of lay people. Truly he exemplifies what is best about the Reformation's leaders and translators.

Thus, it is appropriate to laud the efforts of these early modern reformers and scholars in moving European Christianity toward the creation and use of a widely acceptable and reliable edition of the biblical text, culminating in the King James Version. However, it is also clear to me that almost from the onset of apostasy in the meridian dispensation, the Lord began laying the foundation for the Bible that would serve as the anchor for the Restoration. As early as the late fourth century, we see the Lord's Spirit working upon a man who has become known as one of history's most famous Bible translators—Eusebius Hieronymus Sophronius, better known as St. Jerome.

Jerome was born in northeast Italy in A.D. 345. By age twenty-nine he had become a disciplined scholar and Christian, living a life of contemplation and self-denial. But in a now well-known dream, a heavenly voice accused him of worshiping secular scholarship more than Jesus. "You are a follower of Cicero, not of Christ," he was told.[18] From that point on, he devoted his life to learning the original languages of the biblical texts. In 382 he became secretary to Pope Damasus and formulated a plan to produce a new, more trustworthy version of the Bible. This Bible would correct the problems existing in the Old Latin manuscripts of the biblical text that were in circulation. Whatever one thinks about Jerome—he was not without his faults—I believe Jerome's motives were honorable and that the Lord used his abilities to accomplish important purposes. I believe the spirit of restoration brooded over Jerome as a precursor to the development of the King James Version of 1611.

In a letter to Pope Damasus in 383, Jerome described the problem with the existing Latin manuscripts of just the New Testament. In language reminiscent of the Prophet Joseph Smith, Jerome said: "For if we are to pin our faith to the Latin texts, it is for our opponents to tell us *which;* for there are almost as many forms of texts as there are copies. If, on the other hand, we are to glean the truth from a comparison of many, why not go back to the original Greek and correct the mistakes introduced by inaccurate translators, and the blundering alterations of confident but ignorant critics, and further all that has been inserted or changed by copyists more asleep than awake?"[19]

Compare this statement with one by the Prophet Joseph Smith: "I believe the Bible as it read when it came from the pen of the original writers. Ignorant translators, careless transcribers, or designing and corrupt priests have committed many errors."[20] With the publication of Jerome's Vulgate, the Lord gave to the people of medieval Christendom that which they were ready to possess and which best served His purposes at the time. As Alma said, "The Lord doth grant unto all nations, of their own nation and tongue, to teach his word, yea, in wisdom, all that he seeth fit that they should have" (Alma 29:8).

The Vulgate was an early step in the preparation of a Bible ultimately suitable for the restoration of Christ's gospel on the English-speaking continent of America and for later missionary efforts in Great Britain from whence came much strength to the Latter-day Saint Church. The Vulgate was the direct precursor to the Wycliffe Bible, the first Bible translated completely into English from the Latin version. Wycliffe's Bible played a role in both the Reformation and the efforts to arrive at the King James Version.

John Wycliffe (1328–84) did not actually translate the Bible named after him; he inspired a group of his followers to render it into English.[21] Born in Yorkshire, England, and known to history as the "morning star of the reformation," Wycliffe was the harbinger of change, promoting doctrinal and practical reform of the Roman Catholic Church. The centerpiece of his theology was the Bible. Wycliffe lived at a time of great upheaval in the church. In particular, the Papal Schism of 1378 (when rival popes competed for the Holy See) caused him and others to see the church hierarchy as corrupt and far removed from the pattern established by the ancient Apostles. Wycliffe used the Bible as the yardstick by which to measure the morals and actions of church leadership and believed it should be the center of Christian thought and practice. Scriptural infallibility replaced papal infallibility. "To Wycliffe, Scripture was 'a divine exemplar conceived in the mind of God before creation, and before the material Scriptures were written down.'"[22]

Wycliffe's thinking influenced other reformers, including Jan Huss (1359–1415), and through Huss, the Moravians and Martin Luther (1483–1546). All of these reformers worked to release the people and their theology from the stranglehold of the Roman Church—a necessary step in preparing for the Restoration.

FOUNDING OF AMERICA

A second key event in preparing the world for the latter-day restoration of Christ's gospel was the founding of America. The Lord was intimately involved in its establishment. President Joseph F. Smith testified, "This great American nation the Almighty raised up by the power of his omnipotent hand, that it might be possible in the latter days for the kingdom of God to be established in the earth. If the Lord had not prepared the way by laying the foundations of this glorious nation, it would have been impossible (under the stringent laws and bigotry of the monarchical governments of the world) to have laid the foundations for the coming of his great kingdom. *The Lord has done this.*"[23]

America was discovered, colonized, and established by individuals and groups prepared, raised up, and inspired by God. Christopher Columbus is an example of one who believed and stated frankly that the Holy Ghost inspired him and that God gave him the faith and courage to undertake his great journey.[24] Scholars of the life of the great explorer recognize his profound belief in personal revelation and God's involvement in directing the affairs and future of humankind.

From the modern introduction to Columbus's own *Libro de las profecías* (*Book of the Prophecies*) we read:

"Christopher Columbus was a careful student of the Bible. He studied it systematically together with the opinions of learned scholars and commentators who were held in the highest regard in his day. The focus of the Discoverer's interest was the prophesied latter-day enlargement of the Christian Church which would take place through the discovery and evangelization of all the world's nations and tribes, with the consequent renewal and enrichment of Christendom. Although aided by the commentators, he interpreted the Holy Scriptures himself with confidence, claiming that he had the direct illumination of the Holy Spirit in his study of the sacred text. Columbus said and wrote that the divine guidance he received through the Bible not only generated the vision for all of his voyages to the New World but also supplied his motivating drive and sustained him through his trials and dangers. He professed to believe implicitly in his own special vocation as the 'Christ-bearer,' a missionary discoverer, divinely called and equipped for the task of announcing a new era of foreordained expansion and renewal for all Christendom. The *Libro de las profecías,* compiled by Christopher Columbus to substantiate each of these claims in minute detail, is surely the world's most unique notebook of an individual's personal Bible studies."[25]

Columbus, the Puritans, and later colonizers who came to the land of America were all brought here by the hand of the Lord. In fact, Father Lehi prophesied that "there shall none come into this land save they shall be brought by the hand of the Lord. Wherefore, this land is consecrated unto him whom he shall bring" (2 Nephi 1:6–7).

Many are the statements, both contemporary and historical, which attest to a belief in the inspiration and intervention of Deity on the side of the colonists and their struggle to establish independence in this land. George Washington, the very leader of the

American cause, was himself such a believer. In his farewell orders to the colonial army in 1783, he said:

"A contemplation of the complete attainment, at a period earlier than could be expected, of the objects for which we contended against so formidable a power, cannot but inspire us with astonishment and gratitude. The disadvantageous circumstances on our part under which the war was undertaken can never be forgotten. The singular interpositions of Providence in our feeble condition were such as could scarcely escape the attention of the most unobserving: while the unparalleled perseverance of the armies of the United States through almost every possible suffering and discouragement for the space of eight years was little short of a standing miracle."[26]

There can be no doubt that the creation of the United States Constitution was a giant step toward furthering the plan of salvation on this earth and setting the stage for the Restoration. The Lord Himself said that He caused the Constitution to be established to allow all men and women to act according to the eternal principle of moral agency: "And for this purpose have I established the Constitution of this land, by the hands of wise men whom I raised up unto this very purpose, and redeemed the land by the shedding of blood" (D&C 101:80).

It is significant that the Lord says that this land—the land prepared to host the Restoration—was redeemed by the shedding of blood. This redemption parallels and imitates the redemption of all of God's children through the shedding of the blood of Christ. When we examine the history of the Restoration, we realize that the restored gospel itself was redeemed, or purchased, by the shedding of the blood of Joseph Smith and his associates. What this means for me is that *my life* was redeemed and purchased by the blood of Christ; *my country,* my land of promise, was redeemed and purchased by the blood of patriots; *my religion* was redeemed and purchased by the blood of prophets. All of this was done for you and me. All of this was prepared for you and me. Preparation and redemption have come at a dear price.

CULTURE AND ENVIRONMENT

A third key element in laying the foundation necessary for the Restoration to succeed was a powerful and pervasive language and culture, which included a spirit of restoration and anticipation of a new dispensation. English was the culture and language of the British Empire, which circled the world in the nineteenth century. English culture and language functioned in much the same way as Hellenism (Greek culture and language) functioned in the first century to provide the intellectual and cultural infrastructure that allowed the gospel to spread and that formed the context of and linkage to the accepted Bible of the period (the Septuagint in the case of Hellenism, and the King James Version in the case of English culture).

Regarding the Restoration of the latter days, English was the language and culture of the nation that produced the freedom necessary to allow the gospel to be reestablished in the latter days and to flourish. English was the language and culture of the nation the Lord chose as His base of operations in the nineteenth century to take the gospel to the rest of the world—the world, not coincidentally, of the English-speaking British Empire and the King James Bible. (I once heard President Benson use the very words "Lord's base of operations" to describe the magnitude of the accomplishment of the Founding Fathers.[27])

The Constitution of the United States was adopted in 1789, but some states refused to ratify it without assurance and description of personal freedoms and guarantees (speech, religion, assembly, and so forth), which had not been delineated in the Constitution. James Madison led in the adoption of the ten amendments known as the Bill of Rights. By December 1791 enough states had ratified the Bill of Rights for it to become effective. It was no accident that these rights were concretely articulated in America. Many of the concepts written in the Bill of Rights came from various ideas in the Bible (by then found in the hands of a wider readership than during the Middle Ages, when it was controlled by the Roman Church), in the ancient Greek and Roman civilizations, and in the philosophies of such Englishmen as John Locke, John Milton, and John Stuart Mill. Significantly, these ideas were distilled by the Founding Fathers—early American leaders and thinkers such as James Madison, Thomas Jefferson, and Thomas Paine.

ANTICIPATION OF THE RESTORATION

All of these men and ideas were significant forerunners of the Restoration. President Wilford Woodruff testified that "those men who laid the foundation of this American government and signed the Declaration of Independence were the best spirits the God of Heaven could find on the face of the earth. They were choice spirits, . . . and all the men that labored for the purpose were inspired of the Lord."[28] Remarkably, as part of the preparation for the Restoration, and in addition to their work in founding the American republic, many of these same inspired men were moved upon by the Lord to voice a feeling of anticipation about a great restoration of original Christianity, or a revolution in religion. Two examples from among the men mentioned above will suffice: Thomas Jefferson and Thomas Paine.

In a letter to Jared Sparks dated November 4, 1820, just months after Joseph Smith's First Vision, Jefferson wrote: "I hold the precepts of Jesus, as delivered by himself, to be the most pure, benevolent, and sublime which have ever been preached to man. I adhere to the principles of the first age; and consider all subsequent innovations as corruptions of this religion, having no foundation in what came from him. . . . If the freedom of religion, guaranteed to us by law *in theory,* can ever rise *in practice* under the overbearing inquisition of public opinion, truth will prevail over fanaticism, and the genuine doctrines of Jesus, so long perverted by his pseudo-priests, will again be restored to their original purity. This reformation will advance with the other improvements of the human mind, but too late for me to witness it."[29]

In a letter to Benjamin Waterhouse dated June 26, 1822, Jefferson castigated the intrusion of Greek philosophy on primitive Christianity. And in a follow-up letter of July 22, 1822, he mused,

"Happy in the prospect of a *restoration of primitive Christianity,* I must leave to younger athletes to encounter and lop off the false branches which have been engrafted into it by the mythologists of the middle and modern ages."[30] Jefferson believed unequivocally in a restoration of primitive Christianity, even if he did not completely understand the nature of that restoration.

In 1794 Thomas Paine completed a book in Paris entitled *The Age of Reason.* He addressed it to "my fellow-citizens of the United States of America." In the following excerpt, he postulates a revolution in religion to accompany the recently completed revolution in American government: "Soon after I had published the pamphlet 'Common Sense,' in America, I saw the exceeding probability that a revolution in the system of government would be followed by a revolution in the system of religion. The adulterous connection of church and state, wherever it has taken place, whether Jewish, Christian or Turkish, had so effectually prohibited by pains and penalties every discussion upon established creeds, and upon first principles of religion, that until the system of government should be changed, those subjects could not be brought fairly and openly before the world; but that whenever this should be done, a revolution in the system of religion would follow."[31]

A great many other individuals from various fields of endeavor also anticipated the Restoration through their inspired ideas, though they were less explicit in stating their beliefs that a restoration was about to occur. Religious reformer Roger Williams, founder of both the Baptist Society of America and the colony of Rhode Island, is reported to have said at one point, "There is no regularly constituted church on earth, nor any person qualified to administer any church ordinances; nor can there be until new apostles are sent by the Great Head of the Church for whose coming I am seeking."[32] The English poet laureate William Wordsworth (1770–1850) has been called a poet who speaks "with a voice of divine authority" and "an inspired forerunner of the Gospel" largely because of his *Ode on Intimations of Immortality.*[33] Therein he waxes eloquent on the doctrine of preexistence, which was "an obscure idea for centuries between the time of the fall of the early church and the restoration of The Church of Jesus Christ of Latter-day Saints, which is the only Christian religion that still holds that belief as fundamental doctrine today."[34] Others of Wordsworth's writings are cited for their inspired concepts, including his autobiographical poem, *The Prelude,* which presents the idea that mankind can "move toward" godliness.[35]

CONCLUSION

Many more individuals, and the events in which they played a part, could be presented as examples of forerunners and foundation stones of the Restoration. They constitute the grand prelude that so many modern prophets have spoken about. A good place to start looking for the names of those who helped prepare conditions for the Restoration, or who believed in its eventuality, is the list of those for whom President Wilford Woodruff was baptized in the St. George Temple on August 21, 1877. In his journal for that date, he writes that he was baptized on behalf of one hundred notable individuals, that some of his associates served as proxies for still others, and that many of these people he served appeared to him in vision and requested the ordinances of the house of the Lord. The names listed included Columbus, Americus Vespucius, George Washington, Thomas Jefferson (in fact, all the signers of the Declaration of Independence except two), John Wesley, William Wordsworth, Lord Byron, Sir Walter Scott, Robert Burns, and Charles Louis Napoleon Bonaparte.[36]

President Woodruff also noted that "Sister Lucy Bigelow Young went forth into the font and was Baptized for Martha Washington and her famaly and seventy (70) of the Eminent women of the world."[37] These women also played a role in laying the foundation for the Restoration and the preaching of the gospel. This list includes Mary Ball Washington (1708–89), mother of George Washington; Charlotte Corday (1768–93), French patriot; Elizabeth Gurney of England (1780–1845), religious social reformer; Sarah Van Brugh Livingstone (1757–1802), wife of John Jay; Marie Antoinette of France (1755–93); Empress Maria Theresa of Austria (1717–80), mother of Marie Antoinette; Hannah Moore of England (1745–1833), religious author; Dorothy "Dolley" Madison (1772–1849), wife of President James Madison; and Abigail Smith Adams (1744–1818), wife of President John Adams.[38]

These names also serve to emphasize the amazing nature and power of the restored gospel (reaching beyond the grave), as well as how the Lord prepared the earth for it and who He used and inspired to bring it about. In the end, the convergence of ideas, institutions, and individuals that helped to bring about the restoration of the gospel of Jesus Christ is mind-boggling. Only God could have orchestrated it, using so many individuals over such a span of time. The latter-day Restoration of all things is too deep and complex and its preparations too vast and detailed, and yet so perfectly fitted together, for it to be attributed to anything but the plan of an infinite, all-knowing God. He prepared all things from the beginning to occur at the right time and the right place in world history in order to lay the foundation for the Restoration under the direction of the Prophet Joseph Smith, who is rightly called the capstone of all preparations.

The concept of a great prelude to the Restoration, of forerunners and foundation stones, of people and events preparing the earth for the restoration of all things, is a true principle. It is exciting to study this prelude. It is even better to demonstrate our appreciation for it by living the principles and keeping the covenants the Lord restored in this last dispensation.

NOTES

1. Percy Bysshe Shelley, as cited in Gordon K. Thomas, "'Companions and Forerunners': English Romantics and the Restoration," in *Mormon Identities in Transition,* ed. Douglas J. Davies (London: Cassell, 1996), 151; emphasis added.

2. Thomas, "'Companions and Forerunners,'" 151.

3. See Thomas, "'Companions and Forerunners,'" 151.

4. Mark E. Petersen, *The Great Prologue* (Salt Lake City: Deseret Book, 1975), 1; emphasis added.

5. Bruce R. McConkie, *Mormon Doctrine,* 2d ed. (Salt Lake City: Bookcraft, 1966), 717.

6. Petersen, *Great Prologue,* 2.

7. Brigham Young, *Discourses of Brigham Young*, comp. John A. Widtsoe (Salt Lake City: Deseret Book, 1971), 108.

8. Ezra Taft Benson, *A Witness and a Warning* (Salt Lake City: Deseret Book, 1988), 26.

9. Ezra Taft Benson, *The Teachings of Ezra Taft Benson* (Salt Lake City: Bookcraft, 1988), 575.

10. Joseph Fielding Smith, *Answers to Gospel Questions*, 5 vols. (Salt Lake City: Deseret Book, 1958), 2:155.

11. Ezra Taft Benson, "Civic Standards for the Faithful Saints," *Ensign*, July 1972, 59.

12. Dennis B. Neuenschwander, "The Voice of the Lord Is unto All Men" [Christmas Message to Quorum of the Seventy], December 18, 2003.

13. McConkie, *Mormon Doctrine*, 717; emphasis added.

14. Benson Bobrick, *Wide as the Waters* (New York: Simon and Schuster, 2001), 16.

15. Thomas S. Monson, in Conference Report, April 1997, 73–74.

16. John Nielsen and Royal Skousen, "How Much of the King James Bible Is William Tyndale's?" *Reformation* 3 (1998): 73.

17. Nielsen and Skousen, "How Much of the King James Bible," 74.

18. As cited in "The One Hundred Most Important Events in Church History: Jerome Completes the Vulgate," *Christian History* 9, no. 4 (1990): 14.

19. James Stevenson, ed., *Creeds, Councils and Controversies: Documents Illustrating the History of the Church A.D. 337–461* (London: SPCK, 1989), 183; emphasis in original.

20. Joseph Smith, *Teachings of the Prophet Joseph Smith*, sel. Joseph Fielding Smith (Salt Lake City: Deseret Book, 1972), 327.

21. See W. R. Cooper, ed., *The Wycliffe New Testament* (London: The British Library, 2002), v.

22. Cooper, *Wycliffe New Testament*, v.

23. Joseph F. Smith, *Gospel Doctrine* (Salt Lake City: Deseret Book, 1986), 409; emphasis in original.

24. See Petersen, *Great Prologue*, 26, 29.

25. Christopher Columbus, *Libro de las profecías*, trans. Delno C. West and August Kling (Gainesville: University of Florida Press, 1991), 3.

26. George Washington, as cited in Petersen, *Great Prologue*, 55–56.

27. See Benson, *Teachings of Ezra Taft Benson*, 571.

28. Wilford Woodruff, in Conference Report, April 1898, 89.

29. Thomas Jefferson, as cited in Norman Cousins, ed., *"In God We Trust"*—

The Religious Beliefs and Ideas of the American Founding Fathers (New York: Harper and Brothers, 1958), 156.

30. Thomas Jefferson, as cited in Cousins, *"In God We Trust,"* 162; emphasis added.

31. Thomas Paine, as cited in Cousins, *"In God We Trust,"* 396.

32. Roger Williams, as cited in *The Great Prologue: A Prophetic History and Destiny of America* (Salt Lake City: The Church of Jesus Christ of Latter-day Saints, 1976), 4.

33. Thomas, "'Companions and Forerunners,'" 153.

34. Gary Ellsworth, "'Trailing Clouds of Glory': Poets and Philosophers Examine the Preexistence," *Ensign,* October 1974, 49.

35. See Thomas, "'Companions and Forerunners,'" 153.

36. See Wilford Woodruff, *Wilford Woodruff's Journal, 1833–1898 Typescript,* ed. Scott G. Kenney (Midvale, Utah: 1985), 7:367–69.

37. Woodruff, *Wilford Woodruff's Journal,* 369; original spelling retained.

38. Vicki Jo Anderson, *The Other Eminent Men of Wilford Woodruff* (Cottonwood, Ariz.: Zichron Historical Research Institute, 1994), 411–18.

2

TRADITIONAL CHRISTIAN SACRAMENTS AND COVENANTS

Bryson L. Bachman and Noel B. Reynolds

Latter-day Saints associate ordinances with covenants. In Latter-day Saint theology, men and women establish a covenant relationship with the Lord by accepting covenants, receiving ordinances, and living up to the promises they have made.[1] Many Latter-day Saint ordinances correspond to the sacraments of traditional Christianity.[2] In the Roman Catholic tradition, the twelfth-century theologian Peter Lombard enumerated seven sacraments that were officially defined and accepted in the Council of Trent (1545–63).[3] The Orthodox tradition also holds seven sacraments, but the Reformation and subsequent Protestant tradition accepted only two: baptism and the Lord's Supper.

While emphasis on the importance of sacraments, or ordinances, is common among Christians, the pervasive connections made by Latter-day Saints between covenants and ordinances is unique. Whereas traditional Christian sacraments are generally considered

Bryson L. Bachman is a graduate student at Harvard Law School. Noel B. Reynolds is executive director of the Institute for the Study and Preservation of Ancient Religious Texts at Brigham Young University.

vehicles of Christ's unilaterally given grace, Latter-day Saints emphasize the bilateral nature of ordinances by focusing on the covenants that attach to them. Most ordinances entail covenants, by which the recipients make promises of obedience as required by conditional promises of blessings offered to them by the Lord. While the concept of covenant—absent in Christianity for many years—returned to prominence in the writings of some Reformation theologians, the full connection between covenants and ordinances would reappear only in the Restoration.

EARLY CHRISTIAN VIEWS

The scholarly commentary that exists regarding the Old Testament concept of covenant would fill a modest library.[4] God's covenants with the patriarchs and with Israel formed the basis of a special relationship, which entailed Israel's religion and laws. For Christians, however, Christ's advent not only initiated a new covenant, but Christ initiated a new form of covenant establishment and renewal that was to replace the rituals of the Mosaic law. Unfortunately, "little is known about the form of early Christian ritual except through late second-century sources."[5] Furthermore, while Old Testament rituals focused on the covenant concept, early Christian sources do not explicitly link sacraments to covenants.

To understand the development of sacramental theology, we must first review how the Christian tradition has defined sacraments as the means by which a priest mediates direct transmissions of grace from God to men. In their broadest sense, sacraments are outward and visible signs of inward and invisible grace. Sacraments accomplish the "transmission of spiritual power by material means."[6] More directly, sacraments are "actions or ceremonies believed to have been instituted by Christ as channels of divine grace."[7] One may also narrow the definition of sacrament to a phenomenological understanding and define it as "a ritual that enacts, focuses, and concentrates the distinctive beliefs, attitudes, and actions of any religious tradition."[8]

In the Catholic tradition, sacraments convey Christ's grace to the participant *ex opere operato,* meaning "on account of the work done" or "by virtue of the action." This doctrine emerged to negate the concern that unworthiness on the part of the priest or faithlessness on the part of the participant might nullify the effects of the sacraments. The Council of Trent concluded that in and of themselves the sacraments—blessed by the consecratory words of the priest—convey divine grace, the only exception being if the recipient places an obstacle against the sacrament's administration. Accordingly, the efficacy of the sacraments depends on Christ's virtue, not on human merit.[9] The concept of automatic conveyance of sacramental grace is antithetical to the covenant notion in that it deemphasizes human compliance as crucial to sacramental efficacy.

The word *sacrament* is derived from *sacramentum,* the Latin translation of the Greek *mustérion.* "The Greek *mustérion* is of uncertain etymology but is most probably associated with *muein,* meaning 'to close' (the mouth), and thus 'to keep secret.'"[10] The wide variety of Greek mysteries were secret initiation rituals that were often understood to ensure blessings to the initiates, particularly after death.[11]

The Latin term *sacramentum* was anciently employed in at least two ways. First, a *sacramentum* was "a sum of money laid in a sacred place by a litigant [in a case at law] which went to the gods if he lost the case. Thus it came to mean any consecratory act."[12] Second, a *sacramentum* was the military oath or vow of a soldier entering the Roman army. The soldiers swore an oath of allegiance and might even receive a brand on the arm to signify whose soldiers they were.[13] Jennings explains, "The initiatory function of this vow understood in relation to the vow of secrecy associated with [initiation into] the Greek mysteries made possible the appropriation of the term *sacramentum* for those activities (especially baptism) in which the Christian confession of faith (which, like the vow of soldiers, placed one in mortal danger) played an important role."[14]

An early and most interesting reference to sacraments in association with oaths or vows comes from a letter written in 112 by Pliny the Younger. Emperor Trajan sent Pliny to govern the Roman province of Bithynia, where Pliny heard a case concerning a band of rugged Christians accused of public disturbance. The fact that some of the tortured and interrogated Christians chose death rather than feigning allegiance to the Roman gods may evidence a prior allegiance or sacrament made with Christianity. Pliny's letter records that others in the interrogated group of Christians renounced Christianity so as to be released. Pliny wrote that these last Christians "declared that the sum total of their guilt or error amounted to no more than this: they had met regularly before dawn on a fixed day to chant verses alternately among themselves in honour of Christ as if to a god, and also to bind themselves by oath [*sacramento*], not for any criminal purpose, but to abstain from theft, robbery and adultery, to commit no breach of trust and not to deny a deposit when called upon to restore it. After this ceremony it had been their custom to disperse and reassemble later to take food of an ordinary, harmless kind; but they had in fact given up this practice since my edict, issued on your instructions, which banned all political societies."[15]

Other early Christian references to sacraments, however, rarely mention oaths or vows, let alone covenants. While Christians have always understood baptism as the means of initiation into the church (and the new covenant), early writers did not detail covenant obligations associated with the rite. Justin Martyr (ca. 100–165) gave the fullest descriptions of baptism and the Eucharist in the second century, but he focused more on the form of the rituals and on their centrality to Christian worship than on their possible covenant implications. He did describe baptismal candidates as "those who are persuaded and believe that the things we teach and say are true, and promise that they can live accordingly," but he made no direct mention of covenant in that context.[16] His mention of a promise might be a faint echo of an earlier covenant perspective. But while Justin Martyr wrote of baptism as a means of rebirth and forgiveness of sins and the Eucharist as a means of memorial and thanksgiving, he placed no explicit emphasis on a mutually formed covenant relationship.

Tertullian (ca. 160–225) is considered the first to designate the rites of the Christian church as sacraments, and in some of his writings the word *sacrament* describes oaths and sacred actions. But it appears that Tertullian never made any real connection between sacraments and covenants either. Tertullian's homily *On Baptism* (ca. 200), the earliest treatise dedicated solely to a single sacrament, speaks of baptism as a washing of sins in preparation for the Holy Ghost. Tertullian took baptism very seriously. In arguing against the baptism of children, he wrote, "All who understand what a burden baptism is will have more fear of obtaining it than of its postponement." He also instructed recently baptized Christians to "ask of your Lord, that special grants of grace and apportionments of spiritual gifts be yours," so as to be able to fend off the temptations that follow baptism.[17] Nonetheless, in *On Baptism* Tertullian did not make mention of any vow or covenant associated with baptism.

Cyprian of Carthage (ca. 200–258) likewise wrote extensively concerning baptism. In his epistles directed against heretics, Cyprian supported rebaptism of heretics and held a baptismal doctrine contrary to the later Catholic doctrine of *ex opere operato,* which had its beginnings in the fourth century with Augustine. Cyprian explained that the pronunciation of the Trinity and the ritual of baptism alone were not sufficient: "But who in the Church is perfect and wise who can either defend or believe this, that this bare invocation of names is sufficient to the remission of sins and the sanctification of baptism; since these things are only then of advantage, when both he who baptizes has the Holy Spirit, and the baptism itself also is not ordained without the Spirit?"[18] Nonetheless, Cyprian's epistles evidence no distinct covenant theology in relation to baptism.

Fluidity of Doctrine

During the first few centuries of Christianity, sacramental doctrine was apparently quite fluid, as practice determined the form of the rituals more than dogma. Early Eucharistic doctrines, for example, varied over time and among different church fathers. The *Didache,* which seems to have arisen in the first century as an oral tradition for training Christian converts, gives detailed instructions for both baptism and the Eucharist, including verbal formulas to be used for each. But the emphasis is on sacrifice, and covenants are not mentioned.[19] Ignatius (late first century) also used the term *Eucharist.* He condemned the heretics of his day for not considering the Eucharist to be the flesh of Jesus Christ.[20] Irenaeus (ca. 130–202) conceived of the Eucharist as an offering of bread and wine brought by Christians. Cyprian also considered the Eucharist an oblation; the Eucharist was seen as a sacrificial gift offered by the priest, who "imitates that which Christ did."[21] But while some patristic fathers appear to have understood the original Lord's Supper as the cup of the new covenant,[22] they did not attempt to formulate the Eucharist as a covenant meal for early Christians.

When early Christians do mention covenants, it is generally in reference to the Old Testament and its relation to the new Christian era. Of the thirty-three references to covenant in the New Testament, "almost half of these instances come in quotations from the Old Testament, and another five clearly look back to Old Testament statements."[23] Moreover, the Greek *diatheke* was used as the New Testament word for "covenant," even though its traditional meaning had been "last will and testament." This translation further mitigated the importance of covenant in the New Testament and created a semantic debate that continues today.[24]

In the writings of the Christian fathers, commentary on covenants came primarily in response to Marcion (85–160) and the Gnostics, who claimed that the old covenant and new covenant were antithetical. Indeed, Marcion claimed that the two testaments, or covenants, came from different gods. In answer to this heresy, Irenaeus argued that the commandment to love was the same in both covenants and hence "the Author of the Law and the Gospel is shown to be one and the same for the teachings of an absolutely perfect life, since they are the same in each covenant."[25] Tertullian conceded that the ancient covenant had run its course and that the new covenant was a "reformation, amplification, and progress." But despite the differences in the teachings and in the language of the covenants, Tertullian argued that "all this diversity is consistent with one and the same God."[26]

Clement of Alexandria (ca. 150–215) likewise believed the truth of the matter to be found in "the connection of the covenants."[27] In many of his writings, he emphasized the harmony of the two testaments, even referring to them as one "eternal covenant."[28] Clement reasoned that because there is only one God, there is only one church and one covenant, despite its different manifestations in different ages. Accordingly, while God was known by the Greeks, Hebrews, and Barbarians through different "covenants," the different arrangements were made with the same God. With Christ's advent, a new covenant was made with Christians, which covenant superseded all previous arrangements. But Clement made clear that the new covenant came from the same God and was consistent with the law previously given to the Hebrews.[29]

There can be little doubt that early Christians were aware of the covenant concept as expressed in the Old Testament. However, the oversimplified distinction between the old covenant as law and the new covenant as gospel may have made it difficult for early Christians to associate covenants with human obligations or promises. Hence, while Christians may have understood themselves as part of a new covenant community, little mention is made of specific vows, promises, or obligations that Christians would necessarily incur.

Given the Latter-day Saint perspective of associating sacraments and ordinances with covenants, this inconclusive evidence of covenants in early Christianity is interesting, if not puzzling. In *The Interpreter's Dictionary of the Bible*, George Mendenhall gives one plausible explanation for the surprising infrequency of references to covenants in both the New Testament itself and in the New Testament era: "The covenant for Judaism meant the Mosaic law, and for the Roman Empire a covenant meant an illegal secret society. This two-sided conflict made it nearly impossible for early Christianity to use the term meaningfully."[30] Christians obviously had good reason to avoid association with either the Jews or illegal secret societies. Emphasis on Christ's gospel as a testament or as a unilateral gift was one manner in which Christians could distinguish themselves from law-bound Jews and avoid the appearance of a community based on clandestine pacts.

Daniel Elazar offers another possible reason the covenant concept would not be prominent in the early Christian era. He argues that in establishing orthodoxy and unity, the concept of covenant may have "presented a number of practical and theological problems." According to Elazar, the church subsequently "deemphasized covenant, especially after it believed that it had successfully superseded the Mosaic covenant and transferred the authority of the Davidic covenant to Jesus. After Augustine (354–430), the Church paid little attention to covenant and, even though the Eucharist remained central to the Christian liturgy, it ceased to be a truly common meal and its covenantal dimension was overshadowed by other features and meanings attributed to the Last Supper."[31]

Yet despite the apparent lack of connection for early Christians between sacraments and covenants, there is late fourth-century evidence that baptism was sometimes associated with the formation of a contract with Christ. While some church fathers had certainly seen baptism as an initiation into the new covenant, St. John Chrysostom (347–407) went even further by specifying a contract with Christ that baptismal candidates made before entering the waters of baptism. In the rite of renunciation and profession, a deacon or priest anointed the candidates with oil, after which the candidates faced west and renounced Satan. The candidates then faced east and professed belief in the Father, Son, and Holy Ghost as well as in baptism. This rite dissolved one's covenant with hell and formulated a new contract, or covenant, with Christ. Hugh Riley explains that for Chrysostom, "the notion of a contract is the central vehicle whereby he interprets the act of renunciation and profession. . . . The term 'the contract [*suntheke*],' which occurs more than twenty times in the *Baptismal Instructions* of Chrysostom, is used to interpret several aspects of the rite of renunciation and profession. The verbal act by which the candidate expresses his turning away from Satan and turning toward Christ is called by Chrysostom his 'contract.'"[32]

REFORMATION VIEWS

Apart from Chysostom's reference to a Christian's "contract," it appears that the first theological work tying covenants to sacraments came in the Reformation. Sacramental doctrines during the Reformation were extremely divisive, just as they are today. One concept that divided the reformers was sacramentalism, which deals with how one connects the physical and spiritual realms of religion. Although it was Luther who raised the initial doubts concerning the medieval church's sacramental system, he soon found himself at odds with more radical reformers who denounced sacramentalism in a more extreme fashion. While Luther, and later Calvin, retained the belief that a degree of spiritual efficacy could result directly from physical symbols, Zwingli and Bullinger more strongly accented the humanist affirmation of "a metaphysical contrast between spirit and flesh."[33] The Platonistic belief that matter and spirit are fundamentally antithetical became antisacramental in its denial of the spiritual efficacy of the physical sacraments.

In redefining the sacraments, the reformers first reduced the number of sacraments to two: baptism and the Lord's Supper. The reformers considered these sacraments "signs" or "seals of the covenant." In their opposition to the baptismal doctrine of the Anabaptists, reformers such as Zwingli included Christians in the Abrahamic covenant and equated baptism with circumcision as a modern sign of the covenant. These reformers reasoned that if children in Old Testament times were circumcised into the covenant, Christian children should likewise be baptized into the covenant.

But differences arose among the reformers in defining exactly what was meant by covenant sign or covenant seal. "When Luther called the sacrament a covenantal seal, he meant that baptism visibly ratified and guaranteed God's promises, as a royal seal authenticated a government document on which it was inscribed. Only secondarily was baptism a pledge of obedience by men. For Zwingli, however, the sacrament was primarily 'a covenant sign which indicates that all those who receive it are willing to amend their lives and to follow Christ.'"[34]

Zwingli also referred back to the original use of *sacramentum* as a military oath or pledge to demonstrate how a Christian sacrament was also a pledge to hear and obey God.

Calvin picked up on at least part of Luther's sacramental theology. Calvin's covenant seals "graphically portray[ed] God's 'covenants' or promises" and were analogous to governmental seals of authentication. "For Calvin God's promise of salvation rather than man's pledge of obedience was the substance of baptism, and he criticized Zwingli for suggesting that the sacrament was 'nothing but a token and mark by which we confess our religion before men.'"[35]

Zwingli's successor in Zurich, Heinrich Bullinger, exchanged letters with Calvin on sacramental issues. Though the two reached some consensus, as in the case of the Zurich Consensus Formula of 1549, their doctrines ultimately differed. Bullinger, like Zwingli, held a subjective doctrine of the sacraments, which he saw as badges of human commitment. Bullinger also associated baptism with *sacramentum* and its ancient function as a military oath, and he saw the Lord's Supper primarily in terms of remembrance of Christ. Calvin opposed these ideals with his more objective doctrine of sacraments, which he saw as increasing and nourishing faith. Holifield explains that for Calvin the Lord's Supper contained an "objective sacramental reality, a spiritual presence of Christ that could not be overthrown by human faithlessness."[36]

Heinrich Bullinger's reformed covenant theology is also unique for its emphasis on the bilateral or mutual nature of covenants—the idea that covenants are conditional upon human behavior. For Bullinger, "baptism is nothing other than an initial sign of the people of God, which binds us to Christ and to an irreproachable life. Secondly, its effect is to keep us for Christ in the covenant or in a life pleasing to God."[37] Baker explains that Bullinger's baptism "reminded the Christian of his covenant obligation to live a holy life. . . . The individual was obligated to love and trust God through faith in Christ and to love and serve his neighbor."[38] Bullinger's discussion of the conditional nature of God's covenant brought into focus a debate over whether God's covenants are conditional or unconditional that the Puritans would continue in the centuries that followed. While the precise origins of reformed covenant theology are uncertain, Zwingli and Bullinger's treatment of covenant ideas was crucial to the reintroduction of covenant ideas to the forefront of religious thought.[39]

Bullinger also picked up on and extended a covenant idea used by some of the early church fathers in their debate with those challenging the applicability of the Old Testament to Christianity.[40] Bullinger featured the unity of the testament, or unity of the covenant, as his central theological concept. According to Bullinger, God had made only one covenant with humanity throughout history. The covenant began with Adam, "For first He [Christ] was promised to Adam, then the promise was renewed with Noah, and now with Abraham. And all this is but one promise, one Savior and one faith. . . . The covenant conditions were the same for Abraham as they had been for Noah and Adam. They were simply, faith and love."[41]

Bullinger saw the patriarchal tradition as pristine. God revealed the covenant and its conditions directly to Adam and later to Abraham. With Abraham came circumcision, which was a sacrament of the covenant. The covenant continued through the patriarchs until the time of Moses and the law, which law was simply an interregnum between the patriarchs and Christ. When Christ came He restored the covenant and reexpressed its conditions in their less explicit form, as they were known before the law. Christ brought an end to the ceremonial law (the nonessential practices of law) and instituted new sacraments, but the covenant and its original conditions remained unchanged.

Bullinger discussed various reforms of the covenant, such as those initiated by Hezekiah and Josiah. Bullinger even saw a similarity between these ancient reforms and the reform and purification of the one covenant being carried out by his Zurich church.

Less than three centuries after Bullinger, Joseph Smith would initiate a complete reformation of the covenant not only by restoring precious covenant doctrines but also by restoring the authority by which individuals can participate in the ordinances that act as essential witnesses to covenants.

Though Bullinger's theology was not the most influential, it may indeed have come the closest to the understandings that would be restored through the Book of Mormon and Joseph Smith's other revelations. The Protestant Reformation generally had pushed the idea of covenant back onto center stage after many centuries of absence from that light. Zwingli and Bullinger recognized that the covenant was an important step for each Christian and, like Nephi and Alma, saw baptism as an external sign or witness of an internal covenant that one makes with God when one repents by promising to obey His commandments henceforth. The Book of Mormon clarifies the proper relationship between ordinances such as baptism and covenants. "Now I say unto you, if this be the desire of your hearts, what have you against being baptized in the name of the Lord, as a witness before him that ye have entered into a covenant with him, that ye will serve him and keep his commandments . . . ?" (Mosiah 18:10; see also 1 Nephi 13:26; 2 Nephi 30:2; 31:12–14; Mosiah 18:10–13; Alma 7:15). The Reformation also reemphasized the continuity of the gospel. Bullinger recognized that the new covenant was the same as the ancient covenant given to Adam, Noah, Abraham, and Moses.[42] Of all the Reformation thinkers, Bullinger's views were the most advanced in this respect. His treatment of the covenant foreshadowed the thoroughly covenantal approach to the ordinances of salvation that would be established in the Restoration through Joseph Smith.

NOTES

1. See Jorge A. Rojas, "Covenants and Ordinances," *Ensign*, November 1991, 44.

2. For example, of the seven Catholic sacraments, only penance (confession) is not directly represented in Latter-day Saint ordinances: Baptism=*baptism*, Confirmation=*confirmation (gift of the Holy Ghost)*, Holy Eucharist=*the*

sacrament, Extreme Unction=*priesthood blessings,* Orders=*priesthood ordination,* Matrimony=*temple marriage.*

3. "The Council of Trent solemnly defined that there are seven sacraments of the New Law, truly and properly so called, viz., Baptism, Confirmation, Holy Eucharist, Penance, Extreme Unction, Orders, and Matrimony" (D. J. Kennedy, *The Catholic Encyclopedia,* ed. Charles G. Herbermann [New York: Robert Appleton, 1912], 13:299; see also New Advent, *The Catholic Encyclopedia,* sacraments, www.newadvent.org [accessed February 27, 2004]).

4. A few of the more influential works on the Old Testament include Julius Wellhausen, *Prolegomena to the History of Israel* (Edinburgh: n.p., 1885); Walther Eichrodt, *Theology of the Old Testament,* trans. J. A. Baker, 4 vols. (Philadelphia: Westminster, 1961), vol. 1; George E. Mendenhall, *Law and Covenant in Israel and the Ancient Near East* (Pittsburgh: Biblical Colloquium, 1955); Dennis J. McCarthy, *Old Testament Covenant: A Survey of Current Opinions* (Richmond, Va.: John Knox, 1972); Delbert R. Hillers, *Covenant: The History of a Biblical Idea* (Baltimore: Johns Hopkins University Press, 1969); Ernest W. Nicholson, *God and His People* (New York: Oxford University Press, 1986).

5. Monika K. Hellwig, "Christian Sacraments," *The Encyclopedia of Religion,* ed. Mircea Eliade (New York: Macmillan, 1993), 12:505–8.

6. J. W. C. Wand, *The Development of Sacramentalism* (London: Methuen & Co., 1928), 2–3.

7. Thomas M. Finn, "Sacraments," *Encyclopedia of Early Christianity,* ed. Everett Ferguson, 2d ed. (New York: Garland, 1997), 1011.

8. Theodore W. Jennings Jr., "Sacrament: An Overview," *Encyclopedia of Religion,* 12:504.

9. See Kennedy, *Catholic Encyclopedia,* 302–4; see also New Advent, *Catholic Encyclopedia,* sacraments, www.newadvent.org (accessed February 27, 2004).

10. Jennings, "Sacrament," 501.

11. See Walter Burkert, *Greek Religion* (Cambridge, Mass.: Harvard University Press, 1985), 276–77. In light of the Greek origins of *sacramentum,* some scholars have searched for connections between early Christian sacramental ideas and Greek mystery religions by finding parallels between ancient mystery rites and Christian sacraments (Wand, *Development of Sacramentalism;* Oliver Chase Quick, *The Christian Sacraments* [Milwaukee: Morehouse, 1927]).

12. Jerald C. Brauer, ed., *The Westminster Dictionary of Church History* (Philadelphia: Westminster, 1971), 734.

13. See Ann Loades, "Sacrament," *The Oxford Companion to Christian Thought,* ed. Adrian Hastings, Alistair Mason, and Hugh Pyper (New York: Oxford University Press, 2000), 634–35.

14. Jennings, "Sacrament," 501.

15. Pliny, *Letters and Panegyricus*, ed. E. H. Warmington and Betty Radice (Cambridge, Mass.: Harvard University Press, 1969), 288–89.

16. L. W. Barnard, *Justin Martyr: His Life and Thought* (New York: Cambridge University Press, 1967), 136. The passage cited was originally translated by C. C. Richardson.

17. Tertullian, *Homily on Baptism*, trans. Ernest Evans (London: SPCK, 1964), 39–43.

18. Cyprian, *Epistle LXXIV*, found in "The Fathers of the Church" database at New Advent, link Church Fathers—Epistles of Cyprian, www.newadvent.org/fathers/0506.htm (accessed February 27, 2004).

19. See Aaron Milavec, *The Didache: Text, Translation, Analysis, and Commentary* (Collegeville, Minn.: Liturgical Press, 2003), 19–25, 35.

20. See Ignatius, *The Epistle of Ignatius to the Smyraeans*, found in "The Fathers of the Church" database at New Advent, link Church Fathers—Epistle to the Smyraeans, www.newadvent.org/fathers/0109.htm (accessed February 27, 2004).

21. Bernhard Lohse, *A Short History of Christian Doctrine*, trans. F. Ernest Stoeffler (Philadelphia: Fortress, 1966), 133–35.

22. See *Ancient Christian Commentary on Scripture, vol. 7:1–2 Corinthians*, ed. Gerald Bray (Downers Grove, Ill.: InterVarsity, 1999), 112–13.

23. J. Guhrt, "Covenant," *The New International Dictionary of New Testament Theology*, ed. Colin Brown (Grand Rapids, Mich.: Zondervan, 1975), 369. In contrast to the meager thirty-three instances of covenant in the New Testament, "covenant is found almost 300 times in the OT" (369).

24. The first Greek translation of the Old Testament, the Septuagint (ca. 250 B.C.), translated the Hebrew word for covenant (*berit*) with the Greek *diatheke* instead of *suntheke*. While *suntheke* generally signified a covenant or agreement between two people in Greek society, *diatheke* generally signified a will as in "last will and testament" (William Barclay, *New Testament Words* [Philadelphia: Westminster Press, 1974], 64–66; *The New Testament: God's Word to the Nations (GWN)* [Cleveland: Biblion Publishing, 1988], 531–40).

25. Irenaeus, *Against Heresies*, in *Ante-Nicene Fathers*, ed. Alexander Roberts and James Donaldson (Peabody, Mass.: Hendrickson, 1995), 1:429; cited in David W. Bercot, *A Dictionary of Early Christian Beliefs* (Peabody, Mass.: Hendrickson, 1998), 179.

26. Tertullian, in *Ante-Nicene Fathers*, 3:345–46, 361; cited in Bercot, *Dictionary of Early Christian Beliefs*, 179.

27. Clement of Alexandria, in *Ante-Nicene Fathers*, 2:552–53; cited in Bercot, *Dictionary of Early Christian Beliefs*, 179.

28. Douglas Andrew Stoute, "The Origins and Early Development of the Reformed Idea of the Covenant" (Ph.D. diss., King's College, Cambridge, 1979), 22.

29. See Stoute, "Origins and Early Development," 19–22.

30. George E. Mendenhall, "Covenant," in *The Interpreter's Dictionary of the Bible* (New York: Abingdon Press, 1962), 722.

31. Daniel J. Elazar, *Covenant and Commonwealth: From Christian Separation through the Protestant Reformation*, The Covenant Tradition in Politics (New Brunswick, N.J.: Transaction, 1996), chapter 1, "Covenant Traditions in the West," Jerusalem Center for Public Affairs—Daniel Elazar Papers Index, www.jcpa.org/dje/books/ct-v012-ch1.htm (accessed February 27, 2004). Elsewhere in the same chapter Elazar writes: "In the days of the early church, *sacramentum* was a secular term referring primarily to the soldiers' oath of loyalty to the emperor—whose formula goes back to the time of the Hittites—the early church used it to refer to the Last Supper as the central covenant enactment of Christianity. Those who were parties to the reenactment of this *sacramentum* became the *ekklesia*, the assembly, or the Greek equivalent of the *edah*. It was the post-Apostolic church which transformed those two terms and gave them their present meaning of sacrament and church."

32. Hugh M. Riley, *Christian Initiation*, The Catholic University of America Studies in Christian Antiquity 17, ed. Johannes Quasten (Washington, D.C.: Catholic University of America Press, 1974), 92.

33. E. Brooks Holifield, *The Covenant Sealed: The Development of Puritan Sacramental Theology in Old and New England, 1570–1720* (New Haven, Conn.: Yale University Press, 1974), 2.

34. Holifield, *Covenant Sealed*, 6.

35. Holifield, *Covenant Sealed*, 14–15.

36. Holifield, *Covenant Sealed*, 24.

37. J. Wayne Baker, *Heinrich Bullinger and the Covenant: The Other Reformed Tradition* (Athens, Ohio: Ohio University Press, 1980), 7.

38. Baker, *Henrich Bullinger*, 52.

39. See Stoute, "Origins and Early Development."

40. See Stoute, "Origins and Early Development," 12–32.

41. Baker, *Henrich Bullinger*, 58–59. Bullinger's quotation comes from *Der alt gloub* (see Baker for index of Bullinger's works).

42. Through modern revelations we learn that not only was the covenant the same in Old Testament times but the same ordinances of the covenant were

present as well. "Adam cried unto the Lord, and he was caught away by the Spirit of the Lord, and was carried down into the water, and was laid under the water and was brought forth out of the water. And thus he was baptized" (Moses 6:64–65; see also 7:11; 8:23–24).

3

THE RISING OF THE HOLY BIBLE TO THE RESTORATION

Richard E. Bennett

In his well-known autobiography, Parley P. Pratt describes an important missionary event in Church history. While in Toronto, Upper Canada, in 1835, he tells of a meeting in which John Taylor's conversion hung delicately in the balance: "In a large apartment, well furnished," Pratt recalls, "was soon convened a solemn, well dressed, and, apparently, serious and humble people, nearly filling the room. Each held a bible, while Mr. Patrick presided in their midst, with a bible in his hand and several more lying on the table before him. With one of these I was soon furnished, as was any other person present who might lack this, apparently, necessary article. In this manner these people had assembled twice each week for about two years, for the professed purpose of seeking truth."[1] Pratt was invited to speak for two to three hours, in which time he taught John Taylor and others how Daniel's prophecies of a "stone . . . cut out of the mountain without hands" (Daniel 2:45) was now being fulfilled in a latter-day restoration of priesthood authority and

---

Richard E. Bennett is a professor of Church history and doctrine at Brigham Young University.

gospel truths. That meeting profoundly affected the history of the Church.

Latter-day Saints would do well to pause and reflect on the debt we owe to the Holy Bible, what President Heber J. Grant called that "Book of books." It was, after all, the Holy Bible that inspired the boy prophet, Joseph Smith, in the spring of 1820. It was from the Holy Bible that Moroni, a Book of Mormon prophet, quoted so liberally during his nocturnal visits in the fall of 1823 (Joseph Smith–History 1:36–42). And it was from Joseph Smith's inspired version of the Bible that so many important revelations were received, including the divine discourse on Christ's infinite atonement in Doctrine and Covenants 76, the eternal nature of marriage and the family in section 132, and the doctrines of creation and man's purpose and destiny as found in the book of Moses.

Likewise it was from the pages of the Bible that most early missionaries preached the gospel, whether Daniel 2, Acts 3, or Revelation 14, to a public who had already come to know the Bible. It was from the pages of the Bible that early missionaries taught the Restoration, and it was in comparison to the Bible that so many early converts found their way to accept the message of Cumorah.[2] Again from the Book of Mormon: "For behold, this [the Book of Mormon] is written for the intent that ye may believe that [the Bible]; and if ye believe that ye will believe this also; and if ye believe this ye will know concerning your fathers" (Mormon 7:9). In the years immediately leading up to the organization of The Church of Jesus Christ of Latter-day Saints, something quite remarkable occurred that promoted the "biblicization" of the Western world, that went far to create a Bible culture, an awareness and widespread popular ownership of the Bible that had not existed before.

Although the Bible had been printed and in circulation for centuries before, only in the late eighteenth and early nineteenth centuries did it finally begin to be printed in vast quantities and distributed worldwide into the hands of millions who before that time had never owned their own personal copy of scripture. Between the years 1780 and 1830, the popular availability of the Bible to the common person multiplied many times over. Commentators of

the late eighteenth century in England and in America speak of a
dearth, a famine of owning the word of God. Yet by 1831, at least
here in America, Alexis de Tocqueville reported that "there is hardly
a pioneer's hut that does not contain a few odd volumes of
Shakespeare" and that book dealers peddled "an enormous quantity of religious works, Bibles, [and] sermons."[3] What had happened
to change this equation in those intervening years? What initiated
this change? Certainly the formation, rise, and phenomenal achievements of the Bible dissemination movement of the early nineteenth
century are at least partially responsible. Who was instrumental in
beginning this movement? And what factors explain its remarkable
success?

THE BRITISH AND FOREIGN BIBLE SOCIETY

The year 2004 marks the bicentennial celebration of the founding of the venerable British and Foreign Bible Society in London,
England, on March 7, 1804. What started inauspiciously quickly
exceeded every expectation of its founders. Speaking in the spring
of 1820, the Right Honourable Lord Teignmouth, former governor
general of the British East India Company and president of the
British and Foreign Bible Society, took justifiable pride in the society's spectacular accomplishments:

"Never has the benign spirit of our holy religion appeared with
a brighter or a more attractive lustre, since the Apostolic times, than
in the zeal and efforts displayed, during the last sixteen years, for
disseminating the records of divine truth and knowledge. The bene-
fit of these exertions has already extended to millions; and, when we
contemplate the vast machinery now in action for the unlimited dif-
fusion of the Holy Scriptures, the energy which impels its movements, and the accession of power which it is constantly receiving,
we cannot but indulge the exhilarating hope, 'that the Angel, having the everlasting Gospel to preach to them that are upon the
earth' has commenced his auspicious career. Even now, the light of
divine revelation has dawned in the horizon of regions which it
never before illuminated, and is again becoming visible in others in

which it had suffered a disastrous eclipse. . . . By his special favour the Bible Institution has proved a blessing to mankind, and with the continuance of it . . . it will be hailed by future generations as one of the greatest blessings, next to that of divine Revelation itself, ever conferred on the human race."[4]

If the Bible had been the custody of the monastery for so many centuries, it became the veritable anthem of the Reformation. In 1384 John Wycliffe, at the peril of his life, was the first to produce a handwritten manuscript copy of the Bible in English. With Gutenberg's invention of the printing press in 1455, the first printed book was the Bible in Latin. In 1522 Martin Luther printed his German New Testament, and four years later William Tyndale printed the first English New Testament. Then in 1611 appeared the magisterial King James Version of the Bible, soon accepted as the authorized version for the realm. The Bible became the discourse of sinner and saint, puritan and pilgrim. With the passage of time, the Church of England found itself on the defense against the rise of radical religious Nonconformists in the early eighteenth century whose interpretations of the Bible varied widely from those of the established church.

It was the rise of John Wesley, especially, and his brand of Methodism, beginning in the mid-eighteenth century, that would revolutionize Christianity and bring the Bible to the fore. Wesley traveled twenty-five thousand miles and preached 52,400 times between 1738 and his death in 1791. Due, in part, to his skill of skirting the niceties of theological debate, his doctrines of justification by faith while rejecting the complementary Calvinistic doctrine of predestination, his genius at organization, and his capacity to inspire and recruit legions of itinerant preachers ("illiterate enthusiasts," as their detractors derided them), Wesley would eventually count his followers in the millions. Trumpeting the authority and the inerrancy of scripture, he taught out of the Bible that all men and women needed to be saved and that "before God all souls were of equal value,"[5] a message that resonated with the masses of poor among the lower classes of British society.[6]

In the process, Wesley and his popular brand of revivalism

helped to defuse and deflect the seething unrest of the working classes away from anarchy and revolution and towards morality and Christian conversion. As one leading historian noted, "The elite of the working class, the hard-working and capable bourgeois, had been imbued by the Evangelical movement with a spirit from which the established order had nothing to fear."[7]

His gospel message equipped his followers to reject the anti-Christian doctrines of the French Revolution, the deism of Thomas Paine and his widely read *Rights of Man,* and the agnosticism of the Utilitarian school of Jeremy Bentham and James Mill. By the end of the eighteenth century, more Englishmen may have counted themselves Methodist than they did Anglican, even though Wesleyan Methodism had ever so carefully sought to reform the established church, not dethrone it.[8] Little wonder that with Methodism's soaring rise to popularity, Parliament passed the New Toleration Act of 1812, which essentially provided legal recognition of the Nonconformist movement and granted religious freedom.

It would be erroneous, however, to conclude that the Evangelicals alone loved and promoted the Bible. Besides some within the Church of England itself, many intellectually gifted, deeply spiritual Christians other than the more rigid Evangelicals had long been advocating free and independent study of the Bible. Samuel W. Coleridge and those who followed him in the so-called Coleridge Movement of the early nineteenth century shunned the excesses of evangelical enthusiasm and stressed more the broader harmony of reason with religion in the deepest spiritual sense, that "it is the spirit of the Bible, and not the detached words and sentences, that is infallible and absolute."[9] Coleridge's views would later be echoed by such Scottish luminaries as Thomas Erskine, Thomas Carlyle, and Macleod Campbell.[10]

After Wesley's death in 1791, the Evangelical movement centered at Cambridge University where it was nurtured by reverend-scholars Isaac Milner and Charles Simeon, and at London, where it was advanced by the so-called Clapham Group. This progressive society was led by such men as Lord Teignmouth, Zachary Macaulay, James Stephen, Sir Richard Hill, the well-known abolitionist M. P. William Wilberforce, and Hannah More. Referred to as that "Bishop in Petticoats," More was a "novelist, theologian, reformer of morals, evangelist of the poor, founder of schools, and a woman who was treated on an equal footing with bishops."[11] Above all, the Clapham Group sought to imbue the Church of England with Wesley's spiritual fervency.

Wesley's immensely popular revivals did much to instill a renewed British interest in the Bible, an interest that was soon channeled in other ways. The rise of the Sunday School movement, · as started by Robert Raikes (d. 1811) in 1782 and promoted by John Wesley, Sarah Trimmer, Sydney Smith, and Hannah More, also played a contributing role.[12] Ever suspected by conservative Anglicans as a hotbed for Methodist propaganda, the Sunday School movement and its eventual success were ever underestimated by the established church. Though the British population was increasing, school attendance and literary rates in the late 1700s were declining, particularly in northern and western regions of England, because of rapid industrialization, redistribution of population, parents abandoning their children to work in new-age factories, and the need for more and younger workers, both male and female. As the established church offered little in the way of educating children and youth, the Sunday School movement, with its emphasis on learning how to read, experienced almost instantaneous popularity.[13] Sunday Schools became "the best and most widely known 'agencies · of working class education,'" where children were also taught cleanliness, decency, honesty, and moral obedience.[14] From out of Hannah More's Chedder schools, for instance, came many of her famous morality tracts and didactic writings, such as her famous "The Shepherd of Salisbury Plain."[15] Her popular book, *Coelebs in Search of a Wife,* sold in the millions of copies and was as well read as anything by Sir Walter Scott or Jane Austen. The cumulative number of those learning to read and write and worship by 1820 · reached at least six million![16] And at the core of the Sunday School movement was the Holy Bible, to be read, studied, and committed · to memory. Yet the truth was that very few students and not many teachers could afford their own personal copy of scripture. In the

year 1800 a Bible "would have cost the equivalent of a day's wage
for a labouring man, and half a day's wage for a New Testament."[17]

Simultaneous with the Sunday School movement was the rise
in Protestant foreign missionary societies and missionary tract societies, which greatly contributed to the need for Bibles. Indeed, missionaries could do little without them. The appeals of William Carey
in England had led to the establishment of the Baptist Missionary
Society in 1792. Three years later the London Missionary Society
was formed "with the aim of evangelising those South Sea Islands
described to the world by Captain Cook."[18] The Church Missionary
Society, with an eye on reaching Africa, followed in 1798. By 1817
there were at least 117 such missionary societies in Great Britain
and its colonies, all seeking to proclaim the word of God.[19] Their
purpose was to spread the gospel "in every quarter of the globe and
in the distant islands of the Sea." By 1822 missionary stations had
been formed in Africa, Russia, India, Ceylon, the Sandwich Islands,
the West and the East Indies, Labrador, New Zealand, and
Greenland, and among the Delaware, Chippewa, Cherokee,
Arkansas, and Osage Indians.[20]

In the wake of these missionary endeavors, the demand for the
Bible—and unique methods of payment—followed, as this 1818
report from Tahiti indicates: "Reading is becoming general among
this people, and they are diligently engaged in teaching each other:
3000 copies of Luke have been printed and sold for 3 gallons of
cocoa-nut oil each copy. Many thousands are sadly disappointed that
there are no more. We believe ten thousand might have been sold
in ten days."[21]

With the rise of domestic and foreign missionary societies came
the concomitant development of Missionary Tract Societies, beginning with the London Religious Tract Society in 1799. While most
were British, scores of tract societies also sprang up in America in
the first two decades of the nineteenth century.[22]

Thus, the Sunday School movement, the rise of missionary societies, and the emphasis on distributing Christian tracts were all con-
tributive to increasing Bible awareness. However, the spark that
ignited the Bible movement was the desperate lack of Bibles in

northern Wales most poignantly felt by a "sweet Welsh maiden." Since 1791 Wales had been experiencing a religious awakening, and among the converts was one Mary Jones, then a girl of about ten years of age. She walked two miles every Saturday to a relative's home to read from the nearest Bible. Over the next several years, she saved enough money to finally purchase her own. At age seventeen, she walked twenty-eight miles barefoot to buy her first Bible from the good Reverend Thomas Charles. As the popular story goes, "he reached her a copy, she paid him the money, and there [they] stood, their hearts too full for utterance, and their tears streaming from their eyes."[23]

Inspired by the young girl's devotion, Thomas Charles traveled to London in 1802 in quest of ten thousand Welsh Bibles from the almost moribund Society for Promoting Christian Knowledge (SPCK), an Anglican Bible society that had begun in 1698.[24] Its representatives questioned, doubted, and declined his request. He then approached the London Missionary Society and Religious Tract Society. It was the Reverend Joseph Hughes of the latter society who wondered why no such vibrant Bible society existed. Subsequently he, along with Rev. C. Steinkopf of the German Lutherans; Rev. John Owen, chaplain to the Anglican Bishop of London; Mr. Samuel Mills; Zachary Macauley; William Wilberforce; Granville Sharp; and some three hundred others set about organizing the founding meeting of the "Society for Promoting a More Extensive Circulation of the Scriptures at Home and Abroad" on March 7, 1804, at 123 Bishopsgate Street in London.

Quickly renamed "The British and Foreign Bible Society" (BFBS), the fledgling organization immediately garnered interdenominational, "pan-evangelical" support with its first three secretaries acting as a triumvirate: John Owen, Anglican; Joseph Hughes, Evangelist or Nonconformist; and Carl F. Steinkopf, Foreign. The respected John Shore, Lord Teignmouth, was appointed president, an office he would hold for thirty years. Its purpose: "To encourage a wider dispersion of the Holy Scriptures . . . through the British dominions, and . . . to other countries, whether Christian, Mahomedan, or Pagan."[25] Thus was born "a society for furnishing the means of religion, but not a religious society."[26] The new institution in short order not only would print 20,000 Welsh Bibles but would in the space of only three years print and distribute 1,816,000 Bibles, Testaments, and portions thereof in sixty-six different languages![27]

"ALL SCRIPTURE IS GIVEN BY INSPIRATION OF GOD"

What accounts for this remarkable success? Most scholars rightly point to the British and Foreign Bible Society's multi-denominational organization and support as a critical positive factor. While some Anglican prelates in particular bemoaned the absence of the Book of Common Prayer, and later arguments erupted over whether or not to include the Apocrypha, virtually everyone rallied around the society's constitution, the seminal first article of which mandated that its Bibles (then only the King James Version) be distributed "without note or comment." Prefaces, explanatory notes, and particular creeds and theologies "were explicitly forbidden."[28] The conviction reigned that the power of the word was sufficient enough to inspire, reprove, correct, and instruct "in righteousness" (2 Timothy 3:16).

While the original leadership was deeply religious, they were also tough-minded business people, innovators, and risk takers with a global perspective. Soon after the society's formation and in the wake of Napoleon's recent Moscow defeat in 1812, Secretary Steinkopf, a Dr. Pinkerton, the Rev. R. W. Sibthorp, John Owen, and others embarked upon incredibly ambitious tours of Prussia, Denmark, Russia, Sweden, Finland, and even the Middle East. Unforeseen by these founders was the remarkable and immediate popularity of what rapidly became a thriving business and vast international grassroots movement. The rapid multiplication of auxiliaries and associations, in chain-reaction style, in virtually every county in the United Kingdom, throughout Europe (including France), in Russia, in North America, and even in parts of the Orient was a critical element of the society's success.[29] Its phenomenal expansion was clear evidence of the popular need for Bibles at home and abroad.[30]

Local leaders of various Christian faiths, including Roman Catholic priests in several areas, with independent boards soon took ownership, promoting subscriptions, appointing agents, and receiving and filling orders for scriptures. This capillary action, right down to the hosts of volunteer "home visitors" and colporteurs (traveling salesmen) who went from house to house, skirted the traditional bookseller method of distribution. And at this level, women served by the thousands, often appointing their own auxiliaries with their own presidents, officers, and appointments. The ladies' associations were "enormously more successful and widespread than those of gentlemen."[31] By 1819 the British and Foreign Bible Society counted 629 such auxiliaries, and in 1820 women home visitors in Liverpool alone made 20,800 Bible visits.[32]

The great barrier, however, to popular ownership of the Bible in the United Kingdom and elsewhere was not so much ignorance, illiteracy, indifference, or even Catholic resistance but poverty—abject and universal poverty. As late as 1812, British bishops estimated that at least half the population of the United Kingdom was destitute of Bibles.[33] In Ireland and other more impoverished countries, the percentage was steeply higher.

But thanks to significant contributions of hundreds of wealthy philanthropists and of thousands of small donations from supporters everywhere, the British and Foreign Bible Society vigorously financed ways to reduce the costs of production. By former royal decree, Cambridge University, Oxford Press, and the King's Printer owned the charters for printing the Authorized King James Version of the Bible, if for no other reason than to ensure accuracy and dependability. But by ordering vast quantities, utilizing such new advances as steam-power presses and stereotype printing ("a process by which pages of type were cast as permanent metal plates and stored for reprinting"[34]), using cheaper paper and binding, and printing in smaller, quarto-size volumes, the society continued to reduce the costs of its Bibles. A Bible that once would cost a day's wages to buy now sold for twenty-five shillings, within reach of most family incomes.

Nor was the proliferation in Bibles just a matter of reduced cost. The society early on vigorously sought to translate the scriptures into foreign languages, beginning with the Mohawk Indian language for those in Upper Canada. Other early translations soon followed, including Italian (1807), Portuguese (1809), Dutch (1809), Danish (1809), French (1811), and Greek (1814). As one contemporary put it: "The most extraordinary dispensation of the whole, however, is the remarkable exertions in translating the Bible into so many different languages—into seventeen languages in the Russian empire alone. . . . This is an extraordinary event. The like, in all circumstances, has never taken place in the world before."[35]

Yet even this winning combination of affordability, sound leadership, excellent organization, spirited volunteers, and a distribution system that sailed the world on board the Royal Navy does not fully explain the phenomenon. The fact is, in this prescientific epoch before the negativism and agnosticism of the mid-nineteenth century, the time was right for this new "Holy War." Many interpreted the successful termination of the Napoleonic Wars as a victory of Christian thought against the godless secularism of the French Revolution, a divine approbation of the expanding British Empire. It was a new "Age of Light" of blessed opportunities, a "New Morality."[36] "Since the glorious period of the reformation," wrote one American observer in 1818, "no age has been distinguished with such remarkable and important changes."[37]

And what were the results? By 1834 the British and Foreign Bible Society had distributed 8,549,000 volumes in 157 different languages.[38] By 1900 that figure had grown to 229,000,000 volumes in 418 languages. And by 1965 the society had printed 723,000,000 volumes in 829 languages![39]

"ERRAND OF MERCY"—THE AMERICAN BIBLE SOCIETY

On this side of the Atlantic, the need for copies of the Bible was no less real and immediate. Until 1780 almost all Bibles in America

had been printed in Great Britain. The Puritans had brought with •
them the Geneva Bible, first published in 1560, with its notes and •
teachings by John Calvin. Other immigrants brought the Bishop's•
Bible, published by the Church of England in 1568.[40] But with the •
suspension of British imports during the Revolutionary War, there •
developed a "famine of Bibles," which was one of the many ills •
which "a distracted Congress was called upon promptly to rem- •
edy."[41] Scottish-born Robert Aitken, at the direction of Congress,
became America's first Bible publisher in 1781. Isaiah Thomas
printed the first folio Bible from an American press ten years later. •
The Quaker Isaac Collins began printing his Bibles, known for their
accuracy, that same year. The Irish-American Matthew Carey
became the best-known Bible printer in early America, publishing
more than sixty different editions in the early 1800s.[42] Propelled in
part by the Second Great Awakening, the formation of Bible societies, and the aim of evangelizing the West,[43] between 1777 and •
1820 four hundred new American editions of Bibles and New •
Testaments had been issued. By 1830 that number had climbed to •
seven hundred.[44]

Yet production could not keep up with population. Between
1790 and 1830, America's population skyrocketed from 3.9 to 9.6
million, with a very large number not owning their own Bibles. For
instance, an 1824 Bible society report from Rochester, New York,
noted that in Monroe County alone, some 2,300 families were without Bibles.[45] An 1825 report stated at least 20 percent of Ohio families were without, and out of thirty-six counties in Alabama, half did
not own scriptures. In that same year, a reported ten thousand
people in Maine were without Bibles and similarly, in North
Carolina there "cannot be less than 10,000 families . . . without the
Bible." Even large metropolitan areas such as New York and
Philadelphia were reported as seriously lacking.[46]

Such lack had been the reason for the organization of the
Philadelphia Bible Society in 1808, the Connecticut and
Massachusetts Bible Societies in 1809, and the New York Bible
Society in that same year. Scores of others followed throughout New
England and in the South. Yet even with these, many feared a

famine in the land, not of food but of hearing the word of God. Among these was the intrepid Reverend Samuel J. Mills, who viewed the Louisiana Purchase and the opening of a vast new western frontier as a potential new "Valley of the Shadow of Death" in a future America unschooled in the Bible. In a series of tours and travels throughout the Ohio and Mississippi Valleys, Mills spread his message of Christian revivalism. More than any other person, Mills was the inspiration for the establishment of the American Bible Society.[47]

Seeing the need for cheaper American Bibles, at a convention of Bible societies in New York, Samuel Mills, Lyman Beecher, Thomas Biggs, Jedediah Morse, John E. Caldwell, William Jay and several others presided over the formation of the American Bible Society in May 1816. Elias Boudinot, a former New Jersey delegate to the Continental Congress, presided over the society in its infant years. Soon forty-two other smaller state and regional societies merged under its expanding banner.[48]

Like its British parent and model, the American Bible Society had as its "sole object" "to encourage a wider circulation of the Holy Scriptures, without note or comment"[49] and to "supply all the destitute families in the United States with the Holy Scriptures, that may be willing to purchase or receive them."[50] Initially headquartered on Nassau Street in New York City, the American Bible Society constantly enlarged its facilities to keep up with demand and with advances in technology. Stereotype plates facilitated the printing process, auxiliaries soon spread to most American cities (301 by 1821), and every effort was made to put copies of the scriptures in every home. Among the society's many early translations were French, Spanish, and some Native American languages, the first of which was Delaware. After just four years in operation, the American Bible Society had printed and distributed 231,552 Bibles and New Testaments.[51] By 1830 the numbers stood at 1,084,000.[52] By 1848 that figure would reach 5,860,000. And by 1916, after its first century, the corresponding figure stood at 115,000,000 volumes of scripture in 164 different languages.[53]

CONCLUSION

What, then, are we to make of the rise of the Bible as precursor to the Restoration? We return to that room full of copies of the Bible and Pratt's preaching from the scriptures. Due to many people, from John Wesley to Mary Jones, and to many factors, including Sunday Schools, missionary and tract societies, and the rise of Bible societies in far reaches of the globe, and to indefinable currents in world history, there occurred in the years just before the Restoration a mighty movement to print and distribute the holy scriptures on a scale never before seen. Joseph Smith credits the Bible for inspiring him to go the grove that spring morning in 1820. His successor, Brigham Young, once said: "I never asked for any book when I was preaching to the world, but the Old and New Testaments to establish everything I preached, and to prove all that was then necessary."[54] And John Taylor accepted the teachings of Parley P. Pratt only after he was convinced that they conformed to biblical teachings.[55] This establishing culture of the Bible prepared the way for the message of Cumorah.

NOTES

1. Parley P. Pratt, *Autobiography of Parley Parker Pratt*, ed. Parley P. Pratt Jr. (Salt Lake City: Deseret Book, 1980), 140.

2. For a thorough discussion of this point, see Terryl L. Givens, *By the Hand of Mormon: The American Scripture That Launched a New World Religion* (Oxford: Oxford University Press, 2002), 184–208. See also David J. Whitaker, "The Book of Daniel in Early Mormon Thought," in *By Study and Also by Faith: Essays in Honor of Hugh Nibley on His 80th Birthday,* ed. John M. Lundquist and Stephen D. Ricks (Salt Lake City and Provo, Utah: Deseret Book and FARMS, 1990), 1:155–99.

3. Alexis de Tocqueville, *Democracy in America,* ed. Phillips Bradley (New York: Vintage Books, 1990), 2:55.

4. From a speech by the Right Hon. Lord Teignmouth, President, at the Sixteenth Anniversary of the Society, May 3, 1820. *The Sixteenth Report of the British and Foreign Bible Society* (London: Benjamin Bensley, 1820), 223, 225.

5. Asa Briggs, *The Age of Improvement, 1783–1867* (New York: David McKay, 1959), 68.

6. John Wesley's enormous success was, in some part, "due to [his] recognition of the new individualistic sense of the person, which was different from the old corporateness that continuous close social life in a village or small town had produced. It was not just a call to attendance at church, or daily prayer, it was a call to a new kind and quality of life brought about by conversion" (Philip B. Cliff, *The Rise and Development of the Sunday School Movement in England, 1780–1980* [Nutfield, Redhill, Surrey, England: National Christian Education Council, 1986], 77).

7. Elie Halevy, *History of the English People* (New York: Ark Paperbacks, 1987), 371.

8. See Halevy, *History of the English People*, 374.

9. Samuel W. Coleridge, *Aids to Reflection and the Confessions of an Inquiring Spirit* (London: G. Bell and Sons, 1913), 298.

10. See John Tulloch, *Movements of Religious Thought in Britain during the Nineteenth Century* (New York: Leicester University Press, 1971), 30.

11. Halevy, *History of the English People*, 381.

12. See *Guardian* (New Haven, Conn.), January 1819, 22–26; see also "Robert Raikes: Founder of the Sunday Schools," *Juvenile Instructor*, April 1922, 177–80.

13. The conviction was that if one cannot read, he or she cannot read the Bible. The British Sunday School Union was committed to teaching students how to read; see its 1816 report in which it reported ordering 436,297 spelling books, 87,092 Testaments, and 8,177 Bibles (Cliff, *Rise and Development of the Sunday School Movement*, 10–19).

14. Cliff, *Rise and Development of the Sunday School Movement*, 72.

15. Mary Alden Hopkins, *Hannah More and Her Circle* (New York: Longmans, Green and Company, 1947), 217.

16. "At a quarterly meeting of the Liverpool Sunday School Union [in 1819] Mr. Charles Dudley stated that the number of children under Sunday School instruction in the United Kingdom, was computed to be about 670,000, and of teachers about 52,000, and that the whole number who had been taught in Sunday Schools was supposed to be about six millions." (*Evangelical Recorder*, 25 December 1819, 80).

17. Cliff, *Rise and Development of the Sunday School Movement*, 116. By 1816 the Sunday School movement had also spread to America. In America the New York Sunday School Society was established in 1816 and within three years was sponsoring 36 schools, 400 teachers, and 3,700 children and adults "receiving literary and religious instruction" (proceedings of the First Quarterly Meeting of the New York Sunday School Union Society, Seymour Printer, 1816; see also *Christian Herald*, May 15, 1819, 87). And from another report: "A few years ago, and the name of a Sunday School was scarcely known in our land. Missionary, Bible, and

Tract Societies, have multiplied, but the exertions of these have been materially accelerated since the establishment of Sunday Schools" (*Christian Herald*, May 15, 1819), 93. Soon afterward the American Sunday School Union was organized.

18. Henry Otis Dwight, *The Centennial History of the American Bible Society* (New York: Macmillan, 1916), 7.

19. Appearing in the *Evangelical Guardian Review* (New York) in May 1817 was an alphabetical list of 118 Protestant missionary stations throughout the world as sponsored by the London Missionary Society, the Baptist Missionary Society, the Church [Anglican] Missionary Society, the Edinburgh Missionary Society, the Wesleyan Methodists, the American Board of Missions, the United Brethren, the Christian Knowledge Society, and the Royal Danish Mission College.

20. *Evangelical Monitor* (Woodstock, Vermont), April 14, 1821, 2.

21. *Evangelical Recorder,* October 23, 1819, 59.

22. These included the Massachusetts Missionary Society (1800), the Massachusetts Society for the Promotion of Christian Knowledge Among the Indians (1803), the Connecticut Tract Society (1807), New York Religious Tract Society, and many more, all of which by 1820 had distributed many millions of tracts in America.

Topics covered in such tracts ranged broadly but most often centered on Christian morality themes, including Sabbath-day observance, sobriety, repentance, prayer, prohibition of card playing, and much more. As one report put it: "These tracts must be simple, serious, practical. They must be intelligible to the way-faring man, and the tenant of the cottage" (*6th Annual Report of the Executive Committee of the New England Tract Society,* May 1820, 4).

23. William Canton, *History of the British and Foreign Bible Society* (London: John Murray, 1904), 1:466; see also John Owen, *The History of the Origin and First Ten Years of the British and Foreign Bible Society* (New York: James Eastburn, 1817), 15. The above famous account was first published in the January 1867 issue of the Bible Society's *Monthly Reporter.*

24. The Society for Promoting Christian Knowledge had distributed some copies of the Bible in England, Wales, India, and Arabia. In 1701 the Society for the Propagation of the Gospel in Foreign Parts commenced, with special emphasis on the American colonies. The year 1750 saw the startup of the Scottish Society for Propagating Christian Knowledge Among the Poor, and in 1780 the Naval and Military Bible Society began; see www.newadvent.org/cathen.

25. George Browne, *The History of the British and Foreign Bible Society, From Its Institution in 1804, to the Close of Its Jubilee in 1854* (London: Bagster and Sons, 1859), 1:10.

26. Leslie Howsam, *Cheap Bibles: Nineteenth-Century Publishing and the*

British and Foreign Bible Society (Cambridge: Cambridge University Press, 1991), 7.

27. See Canton, *History of the British and Foreign Bible Society,* 1:318.

28. Howsam, *Cheap Bibles,* 6.

29. Within fourteen years of the establishment of the British and Foreign Bible Society, the following societies had been organized in imitation of the BFBS: the Basel Bible Society (Nuremberg, 1804), the Prussian Bible Society (1895), the Revel Bible Society (1807), the Swedish Evangelical Society (1808), the Dorpat British Society (1811), the Riga Bible Society (1812), the Finnish Bible Society (1812), the Hungarian Bible Institution (1812), the Russian Bible Society (1812), the Swedish Bible Society (1814), the Danish Bible Society (1814), the Saxon Bible Society (1814), the Hanover Bible Society (1814), the Netherlands Bible Society (1814), the American Bible Society (1816), and the Norwegian Bible Society (1817). By 1817 these societies had printed 436,000 copies of the scriptures (Bibles and Testaments) and had received from the parent British and Foreign Bible Society gifts of 62,000 volumes; see www.encyclopedia.org/Bible Societies.htm.

30. In the very first publication of the American Bible Society in 1816, it was reported that 550,000,000 people on earth "had never heard of Christ, compared with a population of 213,000,000 in nominally Christian lands. Even in the latter territories . . . only one in five persons in Denmark owned a Bible, one in a thousand in Ireland." Creighton Lacy, *The Word-Carrying Giant: The Growth of the American Bible Society (1816–1966)* (South Pasadena, Calif.: William Carey Library, 1977), 33.

31. Howsam, *Cheap Bibles,* 53, On the positive influence of women, a Rev. Steudel of the University of Tuebingen wrote the following in January 1820: "No gentleman could be found, who would undertake the task of going from house to house, to receive the subscriptions, and to make the necessary inquiries into the actual want of Bibles; but . . . [the ladies] immediately set to work with cheerfulness and courage, not minding the cold and even unfriendly reception which they met with here and there. . . . On entering a room whence an old woman was about to dismiss them with repulsive language, a poor girl, who had earnestly listened to their representations, rose from her spinning wheel, saying, in a cheerful tone, 'I believe I have a few halfpence in my box; most gladly will I give them for so blessed a design.' She fetched them, and they were her little all. Her conduct softened the old woman, and she likewise came forward with a few pence" (*16th Report of the British and Foreign Bible Society 1820* [London: Benjamin Beasley, 1820], 102). Whenever possible, the societies sought to sell their Bibles rather than merely give them away.

32. See Browne, *History of the British and Foreign Bible Society,* 1:76.

33. As one bishop lamented, "Half the population of the labouring classes in the metropolis of the British empire were destitute of the Holy Scriptures" (Browne, *History of the British and Foreign Bible Society,* 1:60).

34. Howsam, *Cheap Bibles,* 79.

35. *Remembrancer,* January 22, 1820, 88. Serious consideration was early on given to translating into the languages of India; however, the East India Company was for many years resistant to missionary work and Bible distribution, for fear of possible revolt (see Browne, *History of the British and Foreign Bible Society,* 1:34).

36. As Briggs put it: "The wars against France reinforced the movements for the reformation of manners and the enforcement of a strict morality; in many ways, indeed, they widened the 'moral gap' between Britain and the Continent as much as they widened the economic gap. . . . Only moral standards, supported by 'vital religion,' were guarantees of social order, national greatness, and individual salvation" (*Age of Improvement,* 172).

37. *Evangelical Recorder,* January 31, 1818, 1. And from another missionary, writing in February 1820: "We are labouring in a pacified world! The sword is beaten into the plough-share, and the spear into the pruning hook. . . . The spirit of enterprize, nurtured in a protracted contest, is bursting forth in the discovery of new nations. The relations of Commerce, broken by war, are renewed; and are extending themselves on all sides. Every shore of the world is accessible to our Christian efforts. The Civil and the Military Servants of the Crown throughout its Foreign Possessions . . . are freely offering their labour and their influence to aid the benevolent designs of Christians. . . . Let us offer, then, as we have never yet offered. Let us meet the openings of Divine Providence" (from "Extract from the 19th Report of the Church Missionary Society," *Remembrancer,* February 12, 1820, 99).

38. See Browne, *History of the British and Foreign Bible Society,* 1:155.

39. See Library of British and Foreign Bible Society, Cambridge University Library Web Page: www.mundus.ac.uk/cats.

40. See Kent P. Jackson, "Joseph Smith's Cooperstown Bible: The Historical Context of the Bible Used in the Joseph Smith Translation" (*BYU Studies* 40, no. 1 [2001], 41). For an excellent study of the history of the Bible in America, see Paul C. Gutjahr, *An American Bible: A History of the Good Book in the United States, 1777–1880* (Stanford: University of Stanford Press, 1999).

41. Henry Otis Dwight, *The Centennial History of the American Bible Society* (New York: Macmillan, 1916), 3.

42. See David Daniell, *The Bible in English—Its History and Influence* (New Haven, Conn.: Yale University Press, 2003), 594–96, 598–99, 627–29.

43. For a comprehensive and detailed study of the various American Bible

editions, see Margaret T. Hills, ed., *The English Bible in America: A Bibliography of Editions of the Bible and the New Testament Published in America, 1777–1957* (New York: American Bible Society, 1962).

44. See Daniell, *Bible in English*, 639.

45. See Dwight, *Centennial History*, 85. Dwight finds it "worth noting that the Bible which fed the soul of Abraham Lincoln in the Kentucky log cabin of his boyhood, was one of those cheap little Bibles imported from London" (*Centennial History*, 3).

46. Lacy, *Word-Carrying Giant*, 50; see also Dwight, *Centennial History*, 84; see also *A Brief Analysis of the System of the American Bible Society* (New York: Daniel Fanshaw, 1830), 45.

The following report was from an agent in Long Island, New York: "I am confident no region will be found in a Christian land where Bibles are more needed. There are here multitudes of people but just able to live, and who live and die almost as ignorant of the gospel as the Heathen. Many who observe no Sabbaths, enjoy no religious ordinances, and have no religion, and they value them not, for they have no Bibles" (Lacy, *Word-Carrying Giant*, 41).

47. See Lacy, *Word-Carrying Giant*, 49.

48. See *Evangelical Guardian Review* (New York), July 1817, 137.

49. Strickland, *History of the American Bible Society*, 31.

50. Lacy, *Word-Carrying Giant*, 51.

51. See *Methodist Magazine*, August 1821, 312.

52. See *Brief Analysis of the System of the American Bible Society*, 33.

53. See Dwight, *Centennial History*, 521.

54. Brigham Young, *Journal of Discourses*, 26 vols. (London: Latter-day Saints' Book Depot, 1854–86), 8:129–30.

55. As he himself said before his conversion: "We rejected every man's word or writing, and took the Word of God alone . . . [and] made it a rule to receive no doctrine until we could bring no scriptural testimony against it" (*The Gospel Kingdom*, ed. G. Homer Durham [Salt Lake City: Bookcraft, 1964], 367).

4

THOMAS MÜNTZER AND THE RADICAL REFORMATION

Steven C. Harper

$\mathcal{M}$any scholars find no transcendent meaning in the religious history of early modern Europe, a world Latter-day Saints tend to see as a precursor to the Restoration. Looking backward from the vantage of the Restoration, however, one discerns commitment to Christ, willingness to sacrifice, and spirituality in the lives of those who defended saving principles at the cost of their lives. Admirable, meaningful examples of such individuals may be found among all three major divisions of Christianity in the early modern era (1500–1800): Catholics, Protestants, and Anabaptists. Radical reformer Thomas Müntzer was one of them. An early modern martyr, he foreshadowed the Restoration by teaching the radical notion that ongoing revelation was absolutely necessary for Christians. Some of Müntzer's ideas continue to be evident in the Restoration.

Steven C. Harper is an assistant professor of Church history and doctrine at Brigham Young University.

EARLY MODERN MARTYRS

A Jesuit priest who embarked on an underground ministry in Elizabethan England, William Weston wrote in 1586 that "at no hour are we certain to survive, but as we make no account of living, the expectation of death only puts an edge on our zeal."[1] Weston was executed for his unflinching Catholic faith after spending nearly two decades in prisons on the Continent and in England, including five years (1598–1603) in London's legendary Tower, during a self-sacrificing ministry. Weston was not alone. Scholars suggest that from 20 to 25 percent of the seminary priests who worked in the English underground were executed by officials of Queen Elizabeth I.[2]

Studying Weston's life introduced me to a generation of scholarship that is skeptical of the motives of early modern martyrs. Weston's opponents included Marian exiles (Protestants who fled England for the Continent during the reign of Elizabeth's Catholic sister, Mary, before returning to England under Elizabeth's reign). Because Catholics and Protestants persecuted each other and both persecuted Anabaptists and all were remarkably certain of their respective causes, many scholars have given up on finding anything objectively admirable among the violent, dogmatic world of William Weston, Martin Luther, and Thomas Müntzer. But I suggest a perspective recently made credible by scholar Brad Gregory, namely, that the early modern martyrs shared much in common, and much of that they shared with the primitive Church. I found William Weston to be truthful and sincere to the point of self-sacrifice. I began to understand, as Brad Gregory has recently written, that "the underlying problem is less early modern invention and credulity than modern or postmodern skepticism and cynicism."[3]

Gregory's resurrection of the lives and testimonies of the Catholic, Protestant, and Anabaptist martyrs of the early modern period convincingly shows believers that the martyrs, not their critics, more nearly understood things as they actually were and will be. Of the Dutch Anabaptist martyr Hans van Overdam, it was said, "Hans, dear, faithful Hans, from God you understood better what was to come than many of us understand about what is present."[4]

The martyrs understood that this world is not to be coveted. They understood the irrationality of setting one's heart on this world. Early modern martyrs knew with certainty that the only rewards worth pursuing are in heaven and that Jesus, their exemplar, marked the path and led the way. From prison in 1561, the Anabaptist Jacques de Lo wrote: "'It is given to us by Christ not only to believe in him, but also to suffer and endure for him' [Philemon 1:29]. I am now experiencing the whole, for the four or five days that I am in prison . . . from day to day and from hour to hour I wait to be stretched on the rack like a parchment; I expect in the end a harsh and rigorous sentence, to be burned alive. These are frightful things to the flesh, and nevertheless my God has made it so that there is only jubilation and joy in me; when I think on the promises of Christ, when I meditate on this excellent saying of St. Peter [1 Peter 4:13–14], who said that in speaking about the afflictions of Christ, we must rejoice and are blessed, for the spirit of God rests on us—I have a consolation that outstrips all anxieties."[5]

Brad Gregory, a most thorough scholar of early modern martyrs, writes: "When pushed to the edge, devout Christians could see more clearly the staggering power of God's word: a practical hermeneutics of the prison fused the relevant biblical passages into the only sensible framework within which to understand their experience. No matter how excruciating the temporal pain of torture and execution, God's promise of eternal joy had relativized it absolutely."[6]

The early modern martyrs may not have understood doctrine the Restoration has clarified, but there would have been no Restoration without them. Moreover, the Restoration provides them posthumously the redemptive doctrine and ordinances they sought unsuccessfully in mortality. In 1834 the Prophet Joseph Smith borrowed a copy of *Foxe's Book of the Martyrs* from the Stevensons in Michigan. According to Edward Stevenson, when Joseph returned the book he said, "I have, by the aid of the Urim and Thumim, seen those martyrs, and they were honest, devoted followers of Christ, according to the light they possessed, and they will be saved."[7]

Thomas Müntzer: Radical Reformer

Though not included in Foxe's book, Thomas Müntzer gave his life for the most important principle of the Restoration. Müntzer died for the idea that "all true parsons must have revelations, so that they are certain of their cause."[8] Latter-day Saints refer regularly to what scholars term the magisterial reformation as an antecedent to the Restoration. By "magisterial," scholars mean the work of Luther, Calvin, and other reformers who were content to work within the political structures of their time and places and who did not advocate sweeping political change as part of their reforms. Comparatively little has been said about the significant role of the Radical Reformation, including reformers like Thomas Müntzer. Like *Dark Ages* or *Enlightenment,* the term *radical* prejudices all that follows it for good or evil, depending on one's preconceived notions. By *radical* in this context, scholars refer to the idea that society needed a complete restructuring in anticipation of the impending Millennium, and that required new revelation. Though carnal security militates against it, this belief should resonate with Latter-day Saints.

Born in the country town of Stolberg in the Harz, Thuringia (now central Germany), about 1489, Müntzer was a toddler when Columbus landed in the Americas. Little is known of his early years. He attended university, probably at Leipzig and Frankfurt, becoming master of arts and bachelor of holy scripture, and he was ordained a priest before 1514.[9] Between then and Luther's controversial critique of the Catholic sale of indulgences in 1517, Müntzer too became part of a popular reform movement. His views were shaped by widespread frustration with the Catholic Church hierarchy. As Goertz explained, "The reproach was heard everywhere, that the shepherds had abandoned the sheep, had led them astray or had crept in like thieves in the night into Christ's sheep pen and had harried the frightened flock. They were flaying and fleecing the sheep, it was said; they did not serve, but ruled. Christ himself did not rule, he served. . . . And so an anticlerical climate developed, in which sermon, propaganda and agitation worked for a renewal of

Christianity and in which Luther's slogan of the 'priesthood of all believers' ignited like the veritable spark in the powder keg. It initiated the social dissolution of the clerical estate in countless towns and territories."[10] Müntzer shared the Lutheran laity's distaste for priestly privilege and abuse of power.

His chief critique of the clergy came of the hypocrisy inherent in their lip service to the written word of God and yet denial of what Müntzer called the "living word of God."[11] Speaking in Prague in 1521, Müntzer criticized clergy who would not confess the need for continuing revelation. "These villainous and treacherous parsons are of no use to the church in even the slightest matter," Müntzer wrote, "for they deny the voice of the bridegroom, which is a truly certain sign that they are a pack of devils. How could they then be God's servants, bearers of his word, which they shamelessly deny with their whore's brazenness? For all true parsons must have revelations, so that they are certain of their cause."[12] This seemed the logical extension of Luther's critiques, but as Müntzer became more outspoken Luther retreated from the implications of his own conversion experience, however it may have come, and "did not share Müntzer's belief that the Holy Spirit gave new revelations in the present."[13]

Müntzer wrote admiringly to Luther in 1523, assuming a shared sense of mission and explaining a guarded but certain faith in continuing revelations. Luther used a term that translates to *fanatic* to describe such faith, though, as his biographer Richard Marius notes, "In many respects the *Schwärmer* [fanatics] were much more akin to the disciples of the New Testament church than Luther's carefully regulated institution in Wittenberg."[14] As Müntzer went from one pastorate to another, gaining popular support but upsetting the political status quo wherever he went, "the conviction grew in him that God still spoke directly through his chosen prophets."[15]

In 1523 Müntzer received a temporary post at St. John's Church in Allstedt, where "his preaching pleased the people but frightened the local count, Ernest of Mansfield, who reported his concern to the Elector," Frederick the Wise.[16] In Allstedt, Müntzer married, banned infant baptism, and taught that the wine and bread of the

Eucharist were not the real presence of Christ but emblems of His sacrifice. In March 1524 Müntzer's followers destroyed the nearby Mallerbach Chapel and its icons, including an image of the Virgin reputed to have healing powers. The miners of Allstedt loved Müntzer in proportion to the fear he instilled in the politically powerful. Frederick the Wise and his brother Duke John Frederick, crown prince of Saxony, saw the political implications of Müntzer's testimony. As Michael Baylor wrote, revelations pose "a special threat to the existing authorities, and, conversely, the political use of dreams [revelations] had an obvious affinity for oppositional or revolutionary politics. This was simply because revelatory dreams represented an alternative authority, one that was by its very nature unchallengeable. Neither human traditions nor traditional interpretations of Scripture could counter the mandate of direct and personal divine revelations."[17] Political authorities rarely appreciate revelators since prophetic authority rests solely on revelation and revelation trumps all other authority. So it is no surprise that even as Müntzer's views were received well by ordinary people, authorities objected. Saxon crown prince John Frederick "and members of his court came to a castle near Allstedt and ordered Müntzer to appear and preach before them" in July 1524.[18] He chose as his text an exposition of the second chapter of Daniel.

With no subtlety Müntzer declared that the kingdoms of this world crumble as nothing and predicted that the fate Daniel foresaw for Nebuchadnezzar awaited his hearers unless they heeded the living word of God. "In such momentous and dangerous matters as those which true preachers, dukes, and princes have to deal with," he said, "it would never be possible to guard themselves securely against error on all sides, and to act blamelessly, if they did not rely on revelations from God."[19] Müntzer implied strongly that he was a new Daniel, positioned to reveal God's mind to Saxony's political elite. When Müntzer had the sermon printed, Luther came out in opposition, leveling the same criticisms that had earlier been directed toward himself. Violence followed as Müntzer's supporters were killed and threats of retribution were sounded by the outspoken Luther. When support dwindled, however, Müntzer left

Allstedt for Mulhausen, a free imperial city in central Germany in a politically precarious position, which Müntzer exploited, along with other radicals, in order to "institute the rule of God on earth: 'the people will go free and God alone will be their Lord,'" he wrote. He wanted a theocracy that would "resolve the duality between secular rule and spiritual power and burst open the walls of an Imperial city."[20]

He and others led popular uprisings against political and spiritual oppression. Hessian and Saxon soldiers brutally put down the rebellion, however, and delivered Müntzer to the princes. Under torture he confessed to sedition and recanted his most revolutionary ideas. Finally, though, he wrote, "I, too, am heartily content that God has ordained things in this way." He lamented only that the people were not yet ready for the kingdom and that the princes must continue to rule.[21] Müntzer was beheaded on May 27, 1525, outside Mulhausen, where his impaled head and body were displayed as a warning to agitators who might trumpet the idea that all true parsons must have revelations or who dared to act courageously on the best light available in a darkened world.

SETTING THE STAGE FOR THE RESTORATION

In Thomas Müntzer one finds remarkable foreshadowing of the ministry of the Prophet Joseph Smith. Revelation was fundamental to both, and both suffered for that testimony. The "world"—using that term as it is used in Joseph's revelations to mean *the fallen earth* (D&C 1:16; 2)—cannot tolerate the Spirit of God, Müntzer taught. Joseph was called to gather the elect, a mission Müntzer felt called to as well. "But who were the Elect? In Müntzer's view they were those who had received the Holy Spirit or, as he usually called it, 'the living Christ.'"[22] "In brief," said Müntzer, "each person must receive the holy spirit . . . otherwise he neither hears nor understands the living God."[23] So both Müntzer and Joseph equated election with hearing the voice of Christ (D&C 29:7). Joseph received revelation affirming that the Church was both true and living, a reference to ongoing revelation as opposed to denying the power of godliness, a point Müntzer would no doubt appreciate. Müntzer spoke often of the "living word of God," God's "living finger," and His "living voice."[24] He resonated with the words of another revelator, Daniel, and focused on chapter 2 especially. In verse 44 he thought he saw a mirror of his own time: "And in the days of these kings shall the God of heaven set up a kingdom, which shall never be destroyed: and the kingdom shall not be left to other people, but it shall break in pieces and consume all these kingdoms, and it shall stand for ever." Daniel 2:44 was a favorite text of Joseph Smith, who was no less revolutionary than Thomas Müntzer and suffered no less for it.

A "Court of Inquisition," as Parley Pratt called it, "inquired diligently into our belief of the seventh chapter of Daniel concerning the kingdom of God, which should subdue all other kingdoms and stand forever." The judge presiding over the Richmond, Missouri, hearing in November 1838, Austin A. King, regarded literal belief in Daniel's prophecy as "a strong point for treason."[25] Joseph did not escape the next charge of treason. He was being held for treason in June 1844 when a vicious lynch mob butchered him as violently as Müntzer had been. That was a few weeks after Joseph began to organize the kingdom Daniel foresaw and promised it would revolutionize the whole world.[26]

Daniel's prophecy of the kingdom was a favorite text for leaders of the Church in nineteenth-century Utah and continued to be among the most popular themes in twentieth-century conference addresses.[27] Introducing the October 2003 general conference, President Gordon B. Hinckley evoked this text again, leaving little doubt that Joseph Smith began what Müntzer longed for and that ongoing revelation to living prophets continues to establish a kingdom that will "stand forever" in contrast to all other short-lived kingdoms. Said President Hinckley: "It was said that at one time the sun never set on the British Empire. That empire has now been diminished. But it is true that the sun never sets on this work of the Lord as it is touching the lives of people across the earth.

"And this is only the beginning. We have scarcely scratched the surface. We are engaged in a work for the souls of men and women everywhere. Our work knows no boundaries. Under the providence of the Lord it will continue. Those nations now closed to us will someday be open. That is my faith. That is my belief. That is my testimony.

"The little stone which was cut out of the mountain without hands is rolling forth to fill the earth (Daniel 2:31–45; D&C 65:2)."[28]

This prophetic declaration echoes and confirms Joseph Smith's 1842 testimony that "the truth of God will go forth boldly, nobly, and independent, till it has penetrated every continent, visited every clime, swept every country, and sounded in every ear."[29] From Joseph Smith to Gordon B. Hinckley, that work has been presided over on earth by living prophets who receive the living word for which Thomas Müntzer sacrificed so much. Müntzer would have appreciated both the tone and the content of a revelation Joseph received in October 1831: "Hearken, and lo, a voice as of one sent down from on high, who is mighty and powerful, whose going forth is unto the ends of the earth, yea, whose voice is unto men— Prepare ye the way of the Lord, make his paths straight.

"The keys of the kingdom of God are committed unto man on the earth, and from thence shall the gospel roll forth unto the ends of the earth, as the stone which is cut out of the mountain without hands shall roll forth, until it has filled the whole earth.

"Yea, a voice crying—Prepare ye the way of the Lord, prepare ye the supper of the Lamb, make ready for the Bridegroom.

"Pray unto the Lord, call upon his holy name, make known his wonderful works among the people.

"Call upon the Lord, that his kingdom may go forth upon the earth, that the inhabitants thereof may receive it, and be prepared for the days to come, in the which the Son of Man shall come down in heaven, clothed in the brightness of his glory, to meet the kingdom of God which is set up on the earth.

"Wherefore, may the kingdom of God go forth, that the kingdom of heaven may come, that thou, O God, mayest be glorified in heaven so on earth, that thine enemies may be subdued; for thine is the honor, power and glory, forever and ever. Amen" (D&C 65).

Both Joseph Smith and Thomas Müntzer died for the ideas

contained in those verses. They, along with many other martyrs, envisioned a better world, one governed by revelation dictated in the voice of the Lord Jesus Christ. They looked for a classless society of the elect presided over by the living God. They both died before their radical, apocalyptic visions were realized. Perhaps the price they paid will spur us to deeper commitment to the living word and the revealed commands to be one (D&C 38:26–27) and to gather the elect (D&C 29:7). Meanwhile, under the direction of the Prophet Joseph Smith and his successors in the presidency of The Church of Jesus Christ of Latter-day Saints, the "stone which is cut out of the mountain without hands shall roll forth, until it has filled the whole earth" (D&C 65:2). "May the kingdom of God go forth, that the kingdom of heaven may come" (D&C 65:6), that He whose right it is may reign as King of kings (Revelation 17:14), and that those who were "beheaded for the witness of Jesus, and for the word of God" may reign "with Christ a thousand years" (Revelation 20:4). Therefore, "come, Lord Jesus" (Revelation 22:20).

NOTES

1. Philip Caraman, ed., *William Weston: The Autobiography of an Elizabethan* (New York: Longmans, 1955), 55.

2. Patrick McGrath estimated that one-fourth of the seminary priests to work in the English underground were executed. Christopher Haigh's estimate of one-fifth is probably more accurate, but only a little less grim for William Weston (Patrick McGrath, "Elizabethan Catholicism: A Reconsideration," *Journal of Ecclesiastical History* 35 [July 1984]: 425; and Christopher Haigh, "Revisionism, the Reformation and the History of English Catholicism," *Journal of Ecclesiastical History* 36 [July 1985]: 401–2).

3. Brad S. Gregory, *Salvation at Stake: Christian Martyrdom in Early Modern Europe* (Cambridge, Mass.: Harvard University Press, 1999), 21.

4. Cited in Gregory, *Salvation at Stake*, 125.

5. Cited in Gregory, *Salvation at Stake*, 128.

6. Gregory, *Salvation at Stake*, 129.

7. Cited in Edward Stevenson, *Reminiscences of Joseph the Prophet and the Coming Forth of the Book of Mormon* (Salt Lake City: n.p., 1893), 6.

8. Thomas Müntzer, "The Prague Protest," in *Revelation and Revolution:*

Basic Writings of Thomas Müntzer, trans. and ed. Michael G. Baylor (Bethlehem, Pa.: Lehigh University Press, 1993), 55.

9. Hans-Jurgen Goertz, *Thomas Müntzer: Apocalyptic Mystic and Revolutionary* (Edinburgh: T&T Clark, 1993), 35.

10. Goertz, *Thomas Müntzer,* 25–26.

11. Müntzer, "The Prague Protest," 55.

12. Müntzer, "The Prague Protest," 54–55.

13. Richard Marius, *Martin Luther: The Christian between God and Death* (Cambridge, Mass.: Harvard University Press, 1999), 406.

14. Marius, *Martin Luther,* 397.

15. Marius, *Martin Luther,* 398.

16. Marius, *Martin Luther,* 398–99.

17. Michael G. Baylor, "Dreams and Politics in the Sixteenth Century: Thomas Müntzer's Theory of Dream Interpretation," unpublished paper, 12.

18. Marius, *Martin Luther,* 400.

19. Cited in Baylor, "Dreams and Politics," 11.

20. Goertz, *Thomas Müntzer,* 173.

21. Cited in Goertz, *Thomas Müntzer,* 188–90.

22. Norman Cohn, *The Pursuit of the Millennium,* 2d ed. (New York: Harper & Brothers, 1961), 253.

23. Müntzer, "The Prague Protest," 53.

24. Müntzer, "The Prague Protest," 55.

25. Parley P. Pratt, *Autobiography of Parley P. Pratt,* comp. Parley P. Pratt Jr., 4th ed. (Salt Lake City: Deseret Book, 1950), 211–12.

26. Andrew F. Ehat, "'It Seems like Heaven Began on Earth': Joseph Smith and the Constitution of the Kingdom of God," *BYU Studies* 20, no. 3 (Spring 1980): 253–79.

27. Richard C. Galbraith, "Scriptural Index to the Journal of Discourses," published privately by the author, 21; used courtesy of Richard C. Galbraith. Richard C. Galbraith, "Scriptural Index to *Ensign* General Conference Reports April 1971–October 2000," published privately by the author, 8; used courtesy of Richard C. Galbraith.

28. Gordon B. Hinckley, "The State of the Church," *Ensign,* November 2003, 4–5.

29. Joseph Smith, *History of the Church of Jesus Christ of Latter-day Saints,* ed. B. H. Roberts, 2d ed. rev., 7 vols. (Salt Lake City: The Church of Jesus Christ of Latter-day Saints, 1932–51), 4:540.

5

DEFENDERS OF THE DOCTRINE OF DEIFICATION

J. B. Haws

*I*n the Holy Scriptures, where God himself speaks, we read of a unique call directed to us. God speaks to us human beings clearly and directly: 'I said, "You are gods, sons of the Most High—all of you"' (Ps. 82:6; John 10:34). Do we hear that voice? Do we understand the meaning of this calling? . . . In other words, we are each destined to become a god, to be like God himself, to be united with him. . . . This is the purpose of life: that we be participants, sharers in the nature of God . . . to become just like God, true Gods."[1]

This striking passage is not from one of the Prophet Joseph Smith's Nauvoo sermons, although it seems to ring with that type of familiarity. Neither is the passage taken from the discourses of, say, Brigham Young or Lorenzo Snow, although it also seems to resonate with their writings. No, this passage comes from a book written in 1976 by Christoforos Stavropoulos, a Greek Orthodox scholar and ordained priest. And Professor Stavropoulos is by no means some theological maverick. His straightforward call for theosis—human

J. B. Haws is principal at South Ogden Junior Seminary.

deification—matches the prominence given to that doctrine in all of Eastern Orthodox thought.

This belief in humanity's potential to become gods has recently been called Orthodoxy's "ruling principle or mode of understanding salvation in Christ since at least the late 2nd [century]."[2] It is a theme that was dominant in St. Irenaeus's classic formula— "The Word of God, our Lord Jesus Christ, who did, through His transcendent love, become what we are, that He might bring us to be even what He is Himself"[3]—as well as in Vladimir Lossky's twentieth-century paraphrase—"God made Himself man, that man might become God";[4] in the writings of St. Athanasius—"The Word of God Himself . . . assumed humanity that we might become God";[5]—as well as in those of Timothy (Bishop Kallistos of Diokleia) Ware, a British convert to Orthodoxy—"God became human that we might be made god."[6] For Eastern Orthodox Christians, this emphasis on theosis is "like a continuous golden thread running throughout the centuries of Orthodoxy's ancient theological tapestry."[7] Another twentieth-century writer concluded that the "chief idea of . . . all of Eastern theology, [was] the idea of deification."[8]

For centuries, Orthodox theologians have faithfully defended this tenet again and again. Yet their defense has largely gone unnoticed and unheralded, perhaps because the Eastern Orthodox Church itself is often overlooked or misunderstood.[9] But when the topic of deification *does* draw attention from outside observers, many Christians are taken aback.[10] Daniel Clendenin, an evangelical Protestant scholar who has been a visiting professor at several Eastern European universities, could not help but concede that the doctrine of deification "sounds very strange indeed to [the] ears" of most Western Christians.[11] To Latter-day Saint ears, however, Orthodoxy's approach to human deification sounds refreshingly familiar. Like Eastern Orthodox Christians, Latter-day Saints equate human salvation, in its fullest sense, with human deification—that is, we also believe that humans can become gods. Often, because of that belief, Latter-day Saint doctrine has been portrayed as unique, baffling, and even blasphemous by some observers. Such portrayals should make the equally straightforward assertions of the Eastern

Orthodox Church about humans becoming gods especially intriguing for Latter-day Saints. While Eastern Orthodox Christians and Latter-day Saints amenably part company at several critical theological junctures, there is often a strong and remarkable correspondence.

The potential for doctrinal parallels that these verbal affinities suggest has caused several Latter-day Saint writers to take an appreciative notice of Eastern Orthodoxy's position on theosis.[12] Those Latter-day Saint authors who have cited references to theosis in the works of early Christian Fathers or Eastern Orthodox theologians seem to have done so with a common purpose in mind, and that is to demonstrate that other Christians—and especially some very prominent Christians—have spoken and do speak very plainly about humans becoming gods.[13] However, such comparisons have drawn criticism from some outside observers who question the appropriateness of suggesting a Latter-day Saint and Eastern Christian correspondence on this topic.[14] Stephen Robinson's experience seems representative: "When I read Clement or Irenaeus or C. S. Lewis and say, 'There! That's *exactly* what I believe,'" a typical response has been "'No, that's not what you believe at all'" because, he has frequently been told, "these authors used the term *gods* differently from the way the LDS do."[15] It is my belief that modern Eastern Orthodox thinkers essentially do *not* use the term *gods* differently from the way that Latter-day Saints do.

And yet Eastern Orthodox Christians do understand the nature of *God* differently from the way Latter-day Saints understand it— Eastern Orthodox Christians believe in the creedal formulations of God the Trinity[16]—and that difference must not be minimized. But the Latter-day Saint understanding of the nature of *gods*—deified humans—shares a basic commonality with the Orthodox understanding of gods. Those observers who differentiate between Latter-day Saint and Orthodox views on theosis should therefore focus on the contrasting positions concerning the nature of God and not the nature of deified humanity, since on that topic there is often a real agreement.

The position of The Church of Jesus Christ of Latter-day Saints concerning humans becoming gods may sound strange to many Christians, but it should sound no stranger than the Eastern Orthodox position, because Latter-day Saints essentially do not say anything more about the topic than Eastern Christians do. True, Latter-day Saints are more explicit in their beliefs about the perpetuity of marriage relationships as well as humanity's premortal existence.[17] But with those basic exceptions in mind, contemporary Eastern Orthodox Christians seem to be as bold and straightforward in their explanations of human deification as are the Latter-day Saints. Both traditions speak of deified humanity's enjoyment of divine life, of their future eternality, and of their progressive attainment of the fulness of divine attributes and power. Therefore, the discovery that another major, worldwide Christian denomination teaches many of the same things that Latter-day Saints teach about human deification speaks to the criticism that the Latter-day Saint plan of salvation is not authentically Christian, especially considering what Eastern Christians believe their church to be and what they believe their church has faithfully defended for nearly two thousand years.

THE EASTERN ORTHODOX POSITION—"THE ONE, HOLY, CATHOLIC, APOSTOLIC CHURCH"

Eastern Orthodoxy has been called both the "forgotten family" of Christianity and the "great unknown among American religious denominations," even though the Eastern Orthodox Church—that is, the communion of over a dozen regional or national, autocephalous (self-governing) sister churches linked together by loyalty to Eastern Orthodox doctrine and ritual practice—has a worldwide membership of some 200 to 250 million adherents.[18] Thanks to the foundation laid by early immigrants (especially Greek and Russian) and their descendants, Orthodox Christians in the United States alone number in the millions.[19] This sizable church membership notwithstanding, many people in the West have mistakenly equated Eastern Orthodoxy with Roman Catholicism because of a sense of their shared sacramental and priestly rites.[20] The outward similarities that these two traditions share point to their common origins in the early Christian church of the Roman Empire. In reality, however, Orthodoxy's unique history and beliefs come into focus only when viewed against the backdrop of the Eastern Church's medieval split with Roman Catholicism, a division that deepened over the course of several centuries, mainly on the questions of papal supremacy and the doctrine of the Holy Ghost. Bishop Ware has observed that Western Christians usually see the Roman Catholic and Protestant positions as representing the two general, opposing approaches to Christianity. Eastern Orthodox Christians, however, consider Roman Catholics and Protestants to be "two sides of the same coin."[21] The Orthodox see themselves as wholly distinct—distinct in their history and distinct in their theology.

The importance of this self-understood distinctiveness cannot be overstated. The East-West division (which most historians date to the fateful, mutual Rome-Constantinople excommunications of the year 1054) started the Eastern Orthodox and Roman Catholic Churches on divergent paths a millennium ago.[22] Eastern Orthodox Christians contend that the path they have followed—and the path from which Western Christianity has deviated—is the path marked by the original Apostles.[23] As one convert to Orthodoxy succinctly wrote, "The Orthodox Church in all humility believes itself to be the 'one, holy, Catholic, and Apostolic Church,' of which the Creed speaks."[24] Eastern Christians also believe that the Orthodox Church is the exclusive path to salvation.[25] In Orthodoxy, church members find what they believe is the faith of the original Apostles, a faith that has been entrusted to the guardianship of the Eastern Orthodox Church.

It is true that other religious institutions consider themselves to be the "guardians" or "custodians" of true Christianity, or at least the possessors of a more perfect understanding of some aspect of Christianity; it is this very belief that gives life to each diverse tradition. However, both Orthodox and non-Orthodox observers[26] concur with the following assertion made by Daniel Clendenin: "To an extent matched by no other Christian communion, Orthodoxy claims that it alone has maintained an unbroken continuity with the apostolic faith of the New Testament, that it alone is the true visible church, and that salvation outside of the Orthodox church is a questionable assumption."[27]

Latter-day Saints take careful notice of statements such as these, because Latter-day Saints make similar-sounding claims. In that same vein, the importance of dispelling Orthodoxy's anonymity takes on something of a greater urgency for Latter-day Saints when we hear Eastern Orthodox Christians speak of carefully guarding and fiercely defending the apostolic faith, and then we find that the doctrine of deification is so dominant in that very defense.[28] Latter-day Saints cannot help but ask these questions: To what extent do Eastern Christians mean what they say when they talk about humans becoming gods? Does the Eastern Orthodox doctrine of deification correspond with the Latter-day Saint doctrine of exaltation?

Those observers who insist that the respective doctrines of the two traditions do *not* correspond define the distinction by pointing to the tenet in Eastern Orthodoxy that explains that a deified human participates in the divine *energies,* but not the divine *essence.* This paper proposes that a correct understanding of what Eastern Orthodox Christians mean by technical theological terms like *divine energies* and *divine essence* and *person* reveals that the doctrinal distinction between deification and exaltation is not as pronounced as has been suggested. In fact, the doctrinal agreement is often striking. Perhaps the best way to define those terms and to highlight that agreement is to trace the defense of the doctrine of deification through three defining moments in the history of the Eastern Orthodox Church: the *filioque* controversy that hastened the Eastern Orthodox break with Roman Catholicism, the iconoclast controversy of the eighth and ninth centuries, and the hesychast controversy of the thirteenth and fourteenth centuries.

The *Filioque* Controversy

In strict chronological terms, the *filioque* controversy did not come to its dramatic head until after the iconoclast controversy. But because Eastern Orthodox Christians feel that the *filioque* doctrine challenged the very definition of God as set forth by the earliest Ecumenical Council of Nicaea, and because it dealt with the most fundamental issues of the nature of the Trinity involved in later deification discussions, it seems appropriate to begin there.

The Latin word *filioque* ("from the Son") was added to the Nicene Creed in the sixth century, probably by church leaders in Spain.[29] Other Latin Western churches gradually adopted this modified creed, so that by the year 1014 the church in Rome accepted the *filioque* phrase as part of the formulaic discussion of the procession of the Holy Ghost. Whereas the original fourth-century Creed had stated that the Spirit proceeded only from the Father,[30] the Roman Catholic Church began to teach, by inserting *filioque*, that the Spirit also proceeded "from the Son." Eastern Orthodox theologians fiercely opposed the *filioque* addition as early as 850. This doctrinal disagreement became inflammatory to the point that it significantly precipitated the Great Schism between the Roman Catholic and Eastern Orthodox Churches.

Orthodox Christians have resisted the *filioque* for centuries because, for them, the so-called "double procession of the Holy Ghost" doctrine confuses the important diversity-in-unity of the Trinity. Like Roman Catholics and most Protestants, Eastern Orthodox Christians align themselves with the creeds that emerged from the ecumenical councils of the fourth and fifth centuries, affirming that the Father and the Son and the Holy Ghost are "one in essence" or "consubstantial." Yet the Orthodox also confess—with an emphasis that seems stronger than that of Roman Catholics or Protestants[31]—that the Father and the Son and the Holy Ghost are Three Persons. Their faith is that "there is in God genuine diversity as well as true unity. The Christian God is not just a unit but a union, not just unity but community."[32] Because, in the Orthodox mind, the *filioque* doctrine blurs that crucial distinctiveness, the three-in-one nature of the Trinity is compromised.

This description of "three persons in one essence" creates a feeling of paradox that even Orthodox theologians admit, and the mystery of the Trinity is not easily verbalized.[33] Roughly, it seems possible to associate "essence" (*ousia* in Greek) with that quality of being that makes a species uniquely what it is, its ultimate otherness of nature. At the same time, this crude analogy must be qualified by acknowledging that God, in Orthodoxy, is not merely some other "species," but rather an incomparable "Other"—meaning that there will always be an "ontological gap"—a gap of "being" between Creator and creature—because of the differences in their respective natures or essences.[34] In turn, each individual of the "species" brings to life the shared "essence" by becoming a unique "person" or *hypostasis*.

Bishop Ware cites what he calls "a favourite analogy for the Trinity . . . that of three torches burning with a single flame."[35] Christos Yannaras proposes that "schematically: God is a Nature and three Persons; man is a nature and 'innumerable' persons. God is consubstantial and in three hypostases, man is consubstantial and in innumerable hypostases."[36] Essence could thus be characterized as that nature which, for the Trinity, is divinity, and that nature which, for humans, is humanity.[37]

And so, in the *filioque* controversy, the "Orthodox suspect that . . . Western Trinitarian thinking . . . overstressed the unity of the divine essence at the expense of the diversity of the persons."[38] If the Holy Ghost proceeded from both the Father and the Son, they ask, in what ways are the Father and the Son distinct? Orthodox fear that the *filioque* phrase suggests that the Father and the Son are really one Person (who acts alternately as Father or Son) from whom the Spirit proceeds. For Eastern Christians then and now, it is only by maintaining that the Father is the unique source of the Holy Ghost that the diversity of the Three Persons can be safeguarded.[39]

Both diversity and unity were thus reaffirmed by rejecting the *filioque*. Importantly, the Trinity also becomes for the Orthodox a model for theosis: Humans can be united with divinity without being absorbed into the divine essence or losing their individual natures—their diversity. As prominent Romanian theologian

Dumitru Staniloae wrote, "man's deification" means the "greatest possible union with God wherein the *fullness of God* is stamped upon man yet without man thereby being *dissolved* into God."[40]

THE ICONOCLAST CONTROVERSY

Diversity in Personhood, yet unity in essence, is also critical for an understanding of the intensity of the iconoclast struggle. While the *filioque* question demanded an Orthodox response in defense of their understanding of the nature of God the Trinity, iconoclasm called into question specifically the Person of the Son. What did it mean for Jesus Christ to assume humanity? And what does it mean for humans to be created in the image of God?

For much of the eighth and ninth centuries, various ecclesiastical leaders questioned—and even attacked—the practice of using sacred paintings or icons (Greek for "images") in worship.[41] The principal accusation was that the icons contributed to idolatry. Led by some persuasive defenders, especially St. John of Damascus, the iconodules (the "venerators of icons") preserved victory over the iconoclasts ("destroyers of icons") when icons received the final approbation of Empress Theodora in 843. Her decree, now celebrated in the Orthodox Church as the "Triumph of Orthodoxy," safeguarded the icons' place of prominence in communal and personal worship, a prominence that has become one of the distinguishing features of Eastern Christianity.[42]

Yet this victory meant so much more than securing the right to display paintings; it was the victory of two central, related doctrines of Orthodox Christianity: first, that humans are divine icons, as Genesis 1:26–27 teaches; and second, that Jesus Christ is *the* Divine Icon.[43] By denying the propriety of icons in the churches, the iconoclasts seemed to repudiate the full implications of these two doctrines by striking at the possibility that the holy and the divine could be portrayed through, and *connected with,* material images. This apparent disparaging of the material, physical elements pointedly threatened the Orthodox understanding of the Incarnation of the Lord Jesus Christ, as well as their understanding of what it means for men and women to be created in the image of God, since Orthodox Christians believe that the divine image is in both the spirit *and* body of humans.[44]

That belief concerning the divine image in both spirit and body deserves some qualification. Orthodox Christians do not believe in a corporeal God the Father in the way that Latter-day Saints do, but they do say some remarkable things about the *image* of God as it relates to physical form—especially the human form of Jesus Christ. They also believe that because of the Incarnation, "deification is something that involves the body."[45] This was central to John of Damascus's defense of icons. After affirming that God "made man after His own image and likeness," John turned to the witness of the Old Testament prophets: "Jacob saw and struggled with God, for it is evident that God *appeared* to him as a man. Moses saw, as it were, the back of a man; Isaiah saw Him as a man sitting upon a throne." Then, returning to the important Orthodox tenet that God in His *essence* is eternally different from—and incomprehensible to—humans, John emphasized that "no one saw the divine *nature*, but the image and figure of *what was yet to come.* For the invisible Son and Word of God was to become truly man."[46] This connection between Old Testament anthropomorphisms and the foreshadowed Incarnation highlights the Orthodox belief that because of Jesus' assumption of a human, material body, "all men are created according to the image of God," or, most precisely, "according to the image of the Logos," Jesus Christ.[47] John went on to say that "the invisible Son and Word of God was to become truly man, that He might be united to our nature, and be seen on earth." This unifying of the heavenly and the earthly was the ultimate meaning behind the icons: "God . . . became a man by nature and in truth."[48] Thus, "a bridge is formed between God and humanity" because Jesus Christ is "both fully God and fully human."[49]

This idea of a "bridge" also underlies Orthodoxy's designation of Jesus Christ as "*the* Divine Icon." He becomes the Archetype, the Way. Orthodox Christians believe that the divine image in all humans endows them with the potential to progress incrementally

from that seminal *image* toward an increasing *likeness* with God.[50]
The model for this full likeness is Jesus Christ, and thus the Apostle
John's charge to strive so that "we shall be like him" (1 John 3:2)
takes on added meaning.[51] For Orthodox Christians, the doctrines
behind the use of icons speak to the reality of the Incarnation, to
the importance of the physical bodies of humans, and to the potential for divine likeness—all three of these beliefs meet in the
Resurrection. The Orthodox are adamant that Jesus, *the* Divine
Icon, resurrected with His glorified, physical body, a body which He
deified, in that He united that body with divinity.[52] It follows in their
doctrinal system that because the image of God in humans involves
the whole person, soul and body, and because every human can follow the archetypal image of God, Jesus Christ, in growing toward
full likeness, which is deification, humans can also receive glorified
bodies that are "the kind that the body of our Master Christ was
after the Resurrection."[53] As John of Damascus wrote, "He has deified our *flesh* forever, and has sanctified us."[54]

To the iconodules, if there were no hope that material, physical
images could be connected with divinity and consequently sanctified—which Orthodox Christians insist was the fallacy of the
iconoclasts—then there would be no hope for the sanctification/
deification of the material, physical bodies of humans, who are
themselves divine icons because they are created in the image of
God.[55] For that reason, the defeat of the iconoclasts is celebrated as
nothing less than the "Triumph of Orthodoxy." It reminds Eastern
Orthodox Christians that because the Son fully entered humanity,
He opened the way for humans to fully enter divinity. "It is the possibility of every Christian to *imitate* Jesus in his entrance to the
heavenly," so that in theosis, humans become "as much a real god
as Christ became a real man."[56]

THE HESYCHAST CONTROVERSY

If the *filioque* controversy centered on Eastern Orthodoxy's
view of Deity, and the inconoclast controversy on their view of

humanity, the hesychast controversy focused on Eastern Orthodox beliefs about the possibilities for union between the two.

In the fourteenth century, a debate raged among Eastern Orthodox theologians over hesychasm—the ritual practice, especially by monks, of pursuing a mystical communion with the divine, often through repeated prayers. A hesychast is someone who pursues "inward stillness" and "continual prayer."[57] These medieval mystics maintained that Christians who conformed their lives to the influence of the Spirit and who sought for continual communion with God could approach divine likeness to such a degree that they could literally experience the same radiance of heavenly light that Peter, James, and John experienced on the Mount of Transfiguration. That radiance became the goal of their Christian living.

The hesychasts' claims were disputed, principally by an Italian named Barlaam, who saw in hesychasm a blasphemous reduction of God's transcendence. Hesychasm was defended by St. Gregory Palamas in the 1300s, and his eloquent defense, upheld by two councils at Constantinople, has become an integral part of Orthodox theology.[58]

Palamas centered his explanation of divine light on the distinction between God's essence and His energies. Following Palamas's reasoning, Eastern Orthodox theologians today qualify their statements about human deification by consistently repeating that humans become gods by *grace*—divine energies—and not by *nature*—divine essence.[59] In Eastern Orthodox Christianity, Creator and creature will always be infinitely different in nature. That is the first tenet of faith when the Eastern Orthodox approach discussions of deification. When humans become gods, they do not become *ontologically*—by nature—what God is. God, in His essence, is eternally unknowable, incomparably other. Because humans are *created* beings, they never lose their humanity, nor do they take on the divine *ousia* or "inner being," the essence of God's uncreatedness and self-existence.[60] Theosis does not imply for Eastern Orthodox Christians the dissolution of this natural uncreated/created distinction between God and humans.

However, deified humans participate in every way in the divine *energies*. The full import of "divine energies" is difficult to verbalize. They are alternately equated with God's grace, with His knowable "activities," and with His "operations or acts of power."[61] But the significance of the energies runs even deeper than this. Divine energies are more than divine attributes: "they are God Himself," uncreated as He is uncreated, the manifestations by which humans experience and know Him.[62] Therefore, in the energies are combined the *totality* of His attributes, minus His essence. And those humans who experience theosis will enjoy full communion and share in those same realities and attributes of divine energy—activities, acts of power, "divinity, goodness, grace, light, and others."[63]

This real possibility for illumination through the "light" of the divine energies was central to Gregory Palamas's defense of hesychasm—and deification. "How then do we know this light is also deification?" he asked. "Listen to [the Eastern Father, Maximus]. Having explained as far as possible the way in which deified men are united to God—a union akin to that of the soul and the body, so that the whole man should be entirely deified, divinised by the grace of the incarnate God—he concludes: 'He remains entirely man by nature in his soul and body, and becomes entirely God in his soul and body through grace, and through the divine radiance of the blessed glory with which he is made entirely resplendent.'" After quoting Maximus, Palamas asked another, concluding question: "Do you note that this light is the radiance of God?"[64]

By validating the hesychasts' strivings for an experience with this radiance, Gregory Palamas also forcefully advocated this tenet of Orthodoxy: Deified humans unite with and participate *fully* in the divine energies because their human energies have been changed to perfectly conform to divinity. The "participant is transformed into the nature of that which it participates in," so that "the participant (man) becomes what God is," according to a contemporary Orthodox scholar.[65] By this, Orthodox Christians do not mean to say that humans become what God is *in essence*—that is, humans will always be created beings; they will always be *humans*. But, through grace, humans *can* become gods, and share in *all* of the divine attributes and energies. Or, as Georgios Mantzaridis recently wrote in summarizing Palamas's works, "The deified man is made *god in all things,* but he neither is identified with the divine essence nor shares it."[66] Deification through Christ is, and for two millennia has been, the glorious message of the Eastern Orthodox Church.

LATTER-DAY SAINT REFLECTIONS

Elder B. H. Roberts felt that "perhaps no passage in the Prophet's [King Follett] discourse has given more offense than [this] one": "You have got to learn how to be Gods . . . by going from one small degree to another, and from a small capacity to a great one; from grace to grace."[67] While this striking statement might surprise some readers because of what seems to them to be the strange talk of humans becoming gods, it is a call that corresponds well with what has been labeled the "central concept and emblem of Greek [Orthodox] Christian theology," the doctrine of human deification.[68] With something of the same spirit of the Prophet Joseph Smith's invitation, Bishop Ware issued this challenge: "If someone asks, 'How can I become god?' the answer is very simple: go to church, receive the sacraments regularly, pray to God 'in spirit and in truth,' read the Gospels, follow the commandments. The last of these items—'follow the commandments'—must never be forgotten. Orthodoxy, no less than Western Christianity, firmly rejects the kind of mysticism that seeks to dispense with moral rules."[69]

The consistency and clarity of these kinds of Orthodox teachings seem to speak to the very criticism of Latter-day Saint doctrine that Elder Roberts was describing. True, questions about "iconoclasm," or the "double procession of the Holy Ghost," or "mystical communion with divine energies" are foreign to the Latter-day Saint experience. But the underlying doctrine at issue in those medieval controversies—the issue of whether or not humans can really become gods through the saving grace of Jesus Christ—is the very fabric of faith for Latter-day Saints. It is also true that Latter-day Saints do not make the technical distinctions between divine essence and person and energies that Orthodox Christians make, since the Latter-day Saint understanding of the nature of God is that God the Father is an exalted Man with a glorified, perfect, radiant body of flesh and bones. The Prophet Joseph Smith taught: "God himself was once as we are now, and is an exalted man. . . . If the veil were rent today, . . . if you were to see him today, you would see him like a man in form—like yourselves in all the person, image and very form as a man."[70] But Latter-day Saints are careful to emphasize that we believe, with Eastern Orthodox Christians, that God is all-powerful, all-knowing, and perfect in every attribute, and that our scriptures repeatedly teach the same (2 Nephi 9:20; Mosiah 4:9; Alma 26:35; Doctrine and Covenants 88:41). We also maintain that neither God's past nor His corporeal form limit His divinity in any way.[71] Latter-day Saint writers have noted that the Incarnation—and especially the Resurrection—of Jesus Christ guides the Latter-day Saint belief that *corporeal* and *infinite* need not be mutually exclusive descriptions of Deity,[72] a belief that resonates with the twentieth-century Eastern Orthodox writer Vladimir Lossky's estimation of Christ's mutual corporeality and infinity: "After the Resurrection, *the very body of Christ mocks spatial limitations.*"[73]

Still, because of the unique Latter-day Saint doctrine that God is now an exalted Man and that all humans are His spirit children, Latter-day Saints differ from Eastern Orthodox Christians in that we believe that humans are presently and significantly different in degree from God's perfect nature, but not radically different in kind.[74] There is no corresponding Latter-day Saint doctrine of divine "otherness" of essence because we believe that humans and the Father are of the same species, such that Latter-day Saints see no theological need to qualify "all that the Father hath" with the Orthodox exception concerning the divine essence of self-existence and uncreatedness.[75] Yet because of this "same species" belief, Latter-day Saints are very comfortable with the Orthodox contention that deified humans never lose their human nature or essence. We too believe that deified humans—gods—will be just that: human.

Likewise, Latter-day Saints stand with Orthodox Christians in asserting that deification/exaltation never implies a replacing or usurping of God. The presiding councils of The Church of Jesus Christ of Latter-day Saints have stated officially that "though [exalted humans] be gods, they are still subject to Jesus Christ as their Father in this exalted relationship."[76] They then cited Doctrine and Covenants 76:59 as scriptural support for this aspect of the doctrine of exaltation: "They [exalted humans] are Christ's, and Christ is God's." And even more recently President Gordon B. Hinckley has explained that "this lofty concept in no way diminishes God the Eternal Father. He is the Almighty. He is the Creator and Governor of the universe. He is the greatest of all *and will always be so.* But just as any earthly father wishes for his sons and daughters every success in life, so I believe our Father in Heaven wishes for his children that they might approach him in stature and stand beside him resplendent in godly strength and wisdom."[77]

The Eastern Orthodox Church claims derivation from, and continuity with, the most ancient of Christian traditions; Latter-day Saints claim modern restoration of ancient truths and authority. While we base our beliefs about deification/exaltation on the foundation of the revelatory experiences of the Prophet Joseph Smith and the scriptural witness of several passages in the Doctrine and Covenants, the remarkable survival of the doctrine of deification in Orthodoxy and its persistence as a central tenet of Orthodox theology bolster our assertion that this is both an ancient and an authentic Christian teaching, as well as one reasonable interpretation of pertinent biblical texts.

In spite of this apparent doctrinal connection, Richard and Joan Ostling have recently written that "support for the Mormon doctrines of a corporeal and limited God, eternal progress, and deification cannot be found in Eastern Orthodoxy."[78] But their interpretation of cited sources suggests a misunderstanding of the canonical Latter-day Saint doctrine of human deification.[79] The assertion that Eastern Orthodox Christians do not believe in a corporeal God *the Father* seems fair (we would take exception with the Ostlings' characterization of God as "limited" in Latter-day Saint theology). However, the Ostlings' conclusions concerning Orthodoxy's beliefs concerning eternal progression and human deification seem more precarious,[80] for while the respective views of Latter-day Saints and Eastern Orthodox Christians regarding the nature of God differ, their views about the potential deification of humanity consistently correspond. Even those Orthodox scholars quoted by the Ostlings repeatedly cited the "otherness" of God, not the status of godhood for sanctified humans, as the fundamental difference between Eastern Christian theosis and Latter-day Saint exaltation.[81] That is where the deification contrasts should center.

Eastern Orthodox Christians believe that because of Christ's victory, deified humans will receive their physical bodies in a glorious resurrection; Latter-day Saints believe the same. Eastern Orthodox Christians believe that they will "participate in the grace, power, and glory of God"[82]; Latter-day Saints believe the same. Eastern Orthodox Christians believe that humans enter the realm of infinity, "becoming eternal like God," without losing their humanity[83]; Latter-day Saints believe the same. Eastern Orthodox Christians believe that even though they may become "gods," they will never cease to worship God, nor somehow replace Him as their God, because they will be gods by grace; Latter-day Saints believe the same.[84] As cited earlier, Eastern Orthodox Christians use terms like "fullness" and "all things" and "becoming what God is" when speaking of deification; Latter-day Saints use that same language (see D&C 76:55, 58, 94; 84:38). Eastern Orthodox Christians see the Son of God as the perfect model for understanding human deification: as Jesus Christ became like "us, in all ways except sin, . . . he will also fulfill the mystical act of man's theosis by making man like himself *in all ways* except the divine essence" of eternal uncreatedness.[85] And Eastern Orthodox Christians believe that "if the saints are heirs of God and co-heirs with Christ, they will also share in the divine *glory* and *dominion*"[86]; Latter-day Saints believe the same, in that they also see in Paul's teachings concerning "joint-heirs with Christ" (Romans 8:17) the promise of deification.[87] The revered Eastern writers Macarius and John Chrysostom spoke of the *full* participation in the divine life that deification represents when they compared theosis to a marriage relationship, and their words make for a wonderful summation: "Just as two people are joined together in one flesh yet all the while maintain the integrity of their separate identities, just as they share a single existence and *hold all things in common,* so the believer is joined to God in an 'ineffable communion' (see 1 Corinthians 6:15–17)."[88]

With all this, it seems difficult to argue that Eastern Orthodox Christians do not mean what they repeatedly say or to argue that Latter-day Saints and Eastern Orthodox Christians do not *believe* similar things about deification when they frequently *profess* similar ideas about deification. It does not seem at all unreasonable, then, to suggest that "support" (in the sense that parallel doctrines are taught by another worldwide Christian church) "for the Mormon [doctrine] of . . . deification" *is* found in Eastern Orthodoxy.[89]

Those who defend theosis, whether Latter-day Saints in Moscow, Idaho, or Eastern Orthodox Christians in Moscow, Russia, see in this doctrine the real possibility which the saving work of Jesus Christ opens to all humans; it is the opportunity that humans have inherited because they have been created in God's own image—created with the potential to "be like Him" (1 John 3:2; Moroni 7:48). With Christoforos Stavropoulos, we ask, "Do we understand the meaning of this calling?"[90]

NOTES

1. Christoforos Stavropoulos, "Partakers of Divine Nature," in *Eastern Orthodox Theology: A Contemporary Reader,* ed. Daniel B. Clenendin (Grand Rapids, Mich.: Baker Books, 1995), 184.

2. Michael Prokurat, Alexander Golitzin, and Michael D. Peterson, *Historical Dictionary of the Orthodox Church* (Lanham, Md.: Scarecrow, 1996), s.v. "theosis."

3. Irenaeus, *Against Heresies* V, preface, as cited in *The Apostolic Fathers— Justin Martyr—Irenaeus,* vol. 1 of Alexander Roberts and James Donaldson, eds., *The Ante-Nicene Fathers: Translations of the Writings of the Fathers down to* A.D. *325,* comp. A. Cleveland Coxe (New York: Charles Scribner's Sons, 1899), 526. Irenaeus lived between 130 and 200. For the dates of his life, as well as for the dates of the other church fathers cited here, I am relying on Timothy (Bishop Kallistos of Diokleia) Ware, *The Orthodox Way* (Crestwood, N.Y.: St. Vladimir's Seminary, 1980), in his section "Authors and Sources," 186–94.

4. Vladimir Lossky, *In the Image and Likeness of God,* ed. John H. Erickson and Thomas E. Bird (Crestwood, N.Y.: St. Vladimir's Seminary, 1974), 97. See also Sister Marta Ryk, "The Holy Spirit's Role in the Deification of Man According to Contemporary Orthodox Theology," *Diakonia* 10, nos. 1–2 (1975): 119.

5. Athanasius, *On the Incarnation: The Treatise De Incarnatione Verbi Dei,* trans. A Religious of C.S.M.V., with an introduction by C. S. Lewis (Crestwood, N.Y.: St. Vladimir's Orthodox Theological Seminary, 1953; reprint, 1982), 93.

6. Timothy (Bishop Kallistos of Diokleia) Ware, *The Orthodox Church,* new and rev. ed. (London and New York: Penguin Books, 1997), 21. Here Bishop Ware is quoting Athanasius.

7. Daniel B. Clendenin, *Eastern Orthodox Christianity: A Western Perspective* (Grand Rapids, Mich.: Baker Books, 1994), 120.

8. S. L. Epinanovic, as cited in Jaroslav Pelikan, *The Spirit of Eastern Christendom (600–1700),* vol. 2 of *The Christian Tradition* (Chicago: University of Chicago Press, 1974), 10.

9. Daniel Clendenin argues for this point, that Orthodoxy is frequently overlooked and misunderstood. See his *Eastern Orthodox Christianity,* 17–18, as well as 14, where Clendenin notes that the "Pelican History of the Church series, for example, contains no volume on Eastern Christianity." Clendenin also argues that not only does "the West [lack] any developed notion of theosis," but Western theologians have also "given only scant attention to the central importance of theosis in Orthodox thought" (*Eastern Orthodox Christianity,* 125, 121). Orthodox theologians worry that this "scant attention" comes at the expense of a fundamental—and ancient—Christian tenet that was consistently taught by early church fathers. Craig Blomberg, another Protestant scholar, agrees: "The early church, like Eastern Orthodoxy throughout its history, felt much freer than Protestantism or Catholicism has felt to speak of believers' deification, divinization or even of their becoming gods or godlike" (Craig J. Blomberg and Stephen E. Robinson, *How Wide the Divide? A Mormon and an Evangelical in Conversation* [Downers Grove, Ill.: InterVarsity, 1997], 100).

10. See F. L. Cross and E. A. Livingstone, eds., *Oxford Dictionary of the Christian Church,* 3d ed. (New York: Oxford University Press, 1997), s.v. "deification": "In the W[est] such language [Athanasius, Irenaeus, etc.] became less popular. It was retained in the E[ast]." See also Richard P. McBrien, ed., *The HarperCollins Encyclopedia of Catholicism* (New York: HarperCollins, 1995), s.v. "deification."

11. Clendenin, *Eastern Orthodox Christianity,* 119. Consistent with most literature that deals with the Eastern Orthodox Church, the designations "the West" and "Western Christians" refer here to those Christians whose traditions reflect an inheritance of either Roman Catholicism or Protestantism. The designations

"the East" and "Eastern Christians" will be used in referring to those Christians who belong to the Eastern Orthodox Church. See Ware, *Orthodox Church,* 3–7, for a discussion of these terms. It should be noted that other Christian denominations—primarily the Syrian Church, the Coptic Church, and the Ethiopian Church—often use some form of the titles "Eastern" and "Orthodox" in describing their churches. However, these churches rejected the fifth-century Council of Chalcedon and are therefore grouped together as "non-Chalcedonian Orthodox Churches." This study will focus on the much larger *Chalcedonian* Eastern Orthodox Church, the churches "in communion with Constantinople" (John Binns, *An Introduction to the Christian Orthodox Churches* [Cambridge: Cambridge University Press, 2002], vii–viii; see also Ware, *Orthodox Church,* 7).

12. See, for example, Daniel C. Peterson and Stephen D. Ricks, "Comparing LDS Beliefs with First-Century Christianity," *Ensign,* March 1988, 6–11; Robert L. Millet and Noel B. Reynolds, eds., *Latter-day Christianity: Ten Basic Issues* (Provo, Utah: FARMS, 1998), 26–28; Keith E. Norman, "Deification, Early Christian," in *Encyclopedia of Mormonism,* ed. Daniel H. Ludlow (New York: Macmillan, 1992), 369–70; Stephen E. Robinson, *Are Mormons Christians?* (Salt Lake City: Bookcraft, 1991), 60–65; Blomberg and Robinson, *How Wide the Divide?* 80–81; Keith E. Norman, "Divinization: The Forgotten Teaching of Early Christianity," *Sunstone* 1 (Winter 1975): 15–19; Philip L. Barlow, "Unorthodox Orthodoxy: The Idea of Deification in Christian History," *Sunstone* 8, no. 5 (September–October 1983): 13–18.

13. See Millet and Reynolds, *Latter-day Christianity,* 26–28: "The doctrine of deification of man is not an exclusive teaching of the restored Church of Jesus Christ. Rather, it can be found in early Christian history. . . . All five of the above writers [who spoke of human deification] were not just orthodox Christians, but also in time became revered as saints. . . . This doctrine was a part of historical Christianity until relatively recent times, and it is still an important doctrine in some Eastern Orthodox churches." See also Blomberg and Robinson, *How Wide the Divide?* 209 n. 16.

14. See Richard N. Ostling and Joan K. Ostling, *Mormon America: The Power and the Promise* (New York and San Francisco: HarperCollins, 1999), 309–10: "[Mormon] writers . . . often express a kinship to Eastern Orthodoxy in that branch of Christendom's use of the term 'deification.' . . . The embrace, however, is one way." See also Blomberg and Robinson, *How Wide the Divide?* 100–102, 212 n. 18.

15. Blomberg and Robinson, *How Wide the Divide?* 209 n. 16.

16. See Ware, *Orthodox Church,* 210.

17. Latter-day Saints seem to be unique in their strong beliefs about eternal marriages (and thus eternal families) and human premortal existence. Because there are occasional references to both doctrines in modern Eastern Orthodoxy,

however, even on these points it does not seem that the Latter-day Saint and Eastern Orthodox positions wholly diverge.

On marriage: Latter-day Saints directly tie human deification to marriage—exaltation is only possible for those who are faithful in an eternal marriage covenant (D&C 131:1–4; 132:19–20). This direct doctrinal tie between marriage and deification is not found in Orthodoxy, but, interestingly, the idea that marriages might be perpetuated in the life to come does find expression in Orthodox thought. See Father John Meyendorff, *Byzantine Theology: Historical Trends and Doctrinal Themes* (New York: Fordham University Press, 1979), 197, where he writes that because marriage is a church sacrament, it must be "an eternal bond, which death itself does not destroy. In its sacramental nature, marriage transfigures and transcends both fleshly union and contractual legal association: human love is being projected into the eternal Kingdom of God." Meyendorff's position on marriage as an "eternal bond" resonates with the Latter-day Saint doctrine of eternal marriage, but see Christos Yannaras, *Elements of Faith: An Introduction to Orthodox Theology* (Edinburgh: T&T Clark, 1991), 74, for an apparently opposing view concerning the perpetuation of marital vows in the next life: "The resurrection which abolishes the marital relationship, as it also abolishes death, is a resurrection 'from the dead.'" Yannaras also suggests that those who entered the celibate monastic orders were thus making a preparatory "leap" toward the type of sociality which would exist in the future kingdom of God. Because in Orthodoxy there are contradictory opinions about either the future indissolubility or future abolition of the marital relationship, there seems to be no definitive Orthodox doctrine about the eternality of marriages. In this sense, the Latter-day Saint understanding of exaltation is distinct in that it is more definitive and explicit.

On premortal existence: Orthodox Christians are uncomfortable with suggestions about the preexistence of humanity insofar as they see those suggestions limiting the transcendence of God as Creator. Still, Orthodox theologians do give qualified suggestions of some form of human preexistence. The main Orthodox emphasis seems to be that all humans, because of the inherent divine image, possess some connection with God's preexistence, as well as some uncreated and eternal component of the soul. See Ware, *Orthodox Church*, 243, where he is quoting nineteenth-century Russian theologian Alexis Khomiakov: "Those who are alive on earth, those who have finished their earthly course, those who, like the angels, were not created for a life on earth, *those in future generations who have not yet begun their earthly course*, are all united together in one Church, in one and the same grace of God" (emphasis added). See also Panagiotes Chrestou, *Partakers of God* (Brookline, Mass.: Holy Cross Orthodox Press, 1984), 18–19: "The world was created according to an eternal plan that included the 'substantive reasoning' of beings. . . . Since the will of God is completely uncreated, the reason of human beings is also uncreated. . . . Every created being has been made according to a corresponding reason which defines both its origin and essence. Consequently, it has had a connection with the uncreated ever since its creation. And if all beings partake of divinity in proportion to their creation, this is much more true of rational beings and, especially, of man, who is part of God because of this: 'Because of his reason, preexistence in God, man is called and is a part of God.' On the basis of his reason, preexistence in God, the making of man constitutes the first foundation of his potentiality of being raised above his natural state and gives him a pledge of eternity ever since his genesis." Therefore, even though Latter-day Saints differ from Orthodox Christians in their beliefs about the eternality of the elements (and thus their rejection of "ex nihilo" creation), they agree with Orthodox Christians that there is something uncreated about the soul and that God is rightfully worshipped as the Creator in that He organized the eternal elements and thus gave life to all humans.

18. Clendenin, *Eastern Orthodox Christianity*, 29; Thomas Doulis, ed., *Journeys to Orthodoxy: A Collection of Essays by Converts to Orthodox Christianity* (Minneapolis: Light and Life, 1986), 7, as cited in Clendenin, *Eastern Orthodox Christianity*, 14. These statistics on Orthodox Christians—200 to 250 million worldwide, and 4 million in North America—are admittedly debatable, and are taken from Prokurat, Golitzin, and Peterson, *Historical Dictionary of the Orthodox Church*, 8. See also Clendenin, *Eastern Orthodox Christianity*, 17–18, where he gives an estimate of 185 million Orthodox Christians worldwide and 6 million in the United States. For an overview of the current makeup of the Orthodox Church, see Ware, *Orthodox Church*, 3–7. See also Binns, *Introduction to the Christian Orthodox Churches*, 10–26. On the bonds that keep the Orthodox churches together, see Ware, *Orthodox Church*, 7: "The Orthodox Church is . . . held together, not by a centralized organization, not by a single prelate wielding absolute power over the whole body, but by the double bond of unity in the faith and communion in the sacraments. Each Church, while independent, is in full agreement with the rest on all matters of doctrine, and between them all there is full sacramental communion." It is important to note that while the patriarch of Constantinople is called the "ecumenical patriarch," all Orthodox commentators stress that the patriarch's position of "first among equals" in no way designates authoritative supremacy, unlike the pope for Roman Catholics, since each church is self-governing. See Binns, *Introduction to the Christian Orthodox Churches*, 13–14, for a description of the powers of the ecumenical patriarch.

19. For a history of Orthodoxy in the United States, see Father John Meyendorff, *The Orthodox Church: Its Past and Its Role in the World Today*, 4th ed., rev. (Crestwood, N.Y.: St. Vladimir's Seminary, 1996), 167–69, 227–31; see also Ware, *Orthodox Church*, 178–87. Both Meyendorff and Ware note the Russian Orthodox Church's eighteenth-century presence in Alaska as Orthodoxy's first entrance into what is now the United States.

20. See Clendenin, *Eastern Orthodox Christianity*, 15; Ware, *Orthodox Church*, 2.

21. Ware, *Orthodox Church*, 2.

22. For an excellent overview of the factors contributing to this "Great Schism," see Timothy (Bishop Kallistos of Diokleia) Ware, "Eastern Christendom," in *The Oxford History of Christianity*, ed. John McManners (Oxford and New York: Oxford University Press, 1993), 151–54.

23. See Ware, *Orthodox Church*, 1–2 and 314–21 for a discussion of Orthodoxy's distinctiveness from Western Christianity as well as the Orthodox proposal that Christian unification depends largely on Roman Catholicism's and Anglicanism's return to doctrinal Orthodoxy.

24. Ware, *Orthodox Church*, 307.

25. See Sergius Bulgakov, *The Orthodox Church*, trans. Lydia Kesich (Crestwood, N.Y.: St. Vladimir's Seminary, 1988), 1: "Orthodoxy is the Church of Christ on earth"; see also Ware, *Orthodox Church*, 247: "Orthodoxy also teaches that outside the Church there is no salvation."

26. Besides those whose observations have already been cited—Ware, Bulgakov, Meyendorff, and Clendenin—see Pelikan, *Spirit of Eastern Christendom*, 3, 8–9; see also the entry for "Orthodoxy" in Prokurat, Golitzin, and Peterson's *Historical Dictionary of the Orthodox Church*, 248, as well as their introduction, 1, 3–4. Especially interesting is Clendenin's inclusion of the account of Peter Gillquist and his formerly Protestant followers who converted to Orthodoxy precisely because they "longed for 'a twentieth century expression of the first century church'" (Clendenin, *Eastern Orthodox Christianity*, 29–30).

27. Clendenin, *Eastern Orthodox Christianity*, 30.

28. See H. A. Hodges, *Anglicanism and Orthodoxy* (London: n.p., 1955), 46–47, as cited in Ware, *Orthodox Church*, 321. See also Aidan Nichols, *Light from the East: Authors and Themes in Orthodox Theology* (London: Sheed & Ward, 1995), 1–2.

29. See Ware, *Orthodox Church*, 50–57, for a summary of the history behind the *filioque*. On page 50 he points out that the *filioque* was added by the local "third Council of Toledo (589), if not before."

30. While the creed which emerged from the first ecumenical council at Nicaea in 325 (the "Nicene Creed") has served as the basis for all subsequent Orthodox creeds, Bishop Ware explains that the creed that actually explains the Orthodox doctrine of the procession of the Holy Ghost was the modified Nicene Creed that emerged from the second ecumenical council at Constantinople in 381 (see Ware, *Orthodox Church*, 22–23).

31. See Meyendorff, *Byzantine Theology*, 184. Bishop Ware senses this same distinction in East-West philosophical approaches in the Latin addition of the

filioque to the creeds: "This . . . has the effect of depersonalizing the Latin doctrine of the deity. God is conceived not so much in concrete and personal terms
but as an essence in which various relations are distinguished" (*Orthodox Church*,
214–15). See Lossky, *In the Image and Likeness*, 71–96, for a more detailed discussion of the East-West divergence. Lossky sees in Western thought "the general
character of this triadology [that] may be described as a pre-eminence of natural
unity over personal trinity, as an ontological primacy of the essence over the
hypostases" (*In the Image and Likeness*, 77). See also Yannaras, *Elements of Faith*,
23, for a similar characterization of the "Roman" approach.

32. Timothy (Bishop Kallistos of Diokleia) Ware, *Orthodox Way* (Crestwood,
N.Y.: St. Vladimir's Orthodox Theological Seminary, 1979), 33; see also Yannaras,
Elements of Faith, 20; Meyendorff, *Byzantine Theology*, 182–83.

33. See Ware, *Orthodox Way*, 39; see also 37: "God the Trinity is thus to be
described as 'three persons in one essence.' There is eternally one true unity, combined with genuinely personal differentiation: the term 'essence,' 'substance' or
'being' (*ousia*) indicates the unity, and the term 'person' (*hypostasis, prosopon*)
indicates the differentiation."

34. "Ontological gap" is the term used by Bishop Ware, as cited in Ostling and
Ostling, *Mormon America*, 311.

35. Ware, *Orthodox Way*, 35.

36. Yannaras, *Elements of Faith*, 59.

37. See Yannaras, *Elements of Faith*, 27.

38. Ware, "Eastern Christendom," 153.

39. Meyendorff, *Byzantine Theology*, 91–92.

40. Dumitru Staniloae, "Image, Likeness, and Deification in the Human
Person," trans. Ioan Ionita and Robert Barringer, *Communio* 13, no. 1 (Spring
1986): 73; emphasis added.

41. For summaries of this debate, as well as definitions of terms like *iconodules*, see Ware, "Eastern Christendom," in *The Orthodox History of Christianity*,
148–51; Bruce L. Shelley, *Church History in Plain Language*, 2d ed. (Dallas:
Word Publishing, 1995), 148–49. See also Aurel Jivi, "The Relevance of the
Seventh Ecumenical Synod," *The Greek Orthodox Theological Review* 38, nos.
1–4 (1993): 291.

42. See Clendenin, *Eastern Orthodox Christianity*, 157: "The centrality of
icons [is] quite foreign to Protestant theology."

43. These two doctrines are repeated over and over in Orthodox treatises.
Representative of these are Chrestou, *Partakers of God*, 17; Georgios I.
Mantzaridis, *The Deification of Man: St. Gregory Palamas and the Orthodox
Tradition*, trans. Liadain Sherrard (Crestwood, N,Y.: St. Vladimir's Seminary,
1984), 15–17; Ernst Benz, *The Eastern Orthodox Church: Its Thought and Life*,

trans. Richard and Clara Winston (Garden City, N. Y.: Doubleday, 1963), 18–19. See especially Matti Sidoroff, "Man as the Icon of God," *The Greek Orthodox Theological Review* 38, nos. 1–4 (1993): 24: "In our worship [icons] have a central place. We have a direct and close relation to them. They are dear to us Orthodox. But the icon is not just an object, external to us. It is that, too, but we should remember that we ourselves are called to be icons of God, because God created us in his own image and likeness."

44. See, for example, Mantzaridis, *Deification of Man,* 19; see also Ware, *Orthodox Church,* 220.

45. Ware, *Orthodox Church,* 232.

46. St. John of Damascus, *On the Divine Images: Three Apologies against Those Who Attack the Divine Images,* trans. David Anderson (Crestwood, N.Y.: St. Vladimir's Seminary, 1980), 80–81; emphasis added.

47. Meyendorff, *Byzantine Theology,* 159. See also Nichols, *Light from the East,* 172–73, 177, for a discussion of God's foreknowledge and humanity's creation in the image of the Son, even though at the time of the Creation the Incarnation was still a future event.

48. St. John of Damascus, *On the Divine Images,* 80–81.

49. Ware, *Orthodox Church,* 21.

50. See, for example, Ware, *Orthodox Church,* 219: "And if we make proper use of this faculty for communion with God, then we will become 'like' God, we will acquire the divine likeness; in the words of John Damascene, we will be 'assimilated to God through virtue.' To acquire the likeness is to deified."

51. See Meyendorff, *Byzantine Theology,* 159.

52. See St. John of Damascus, *On the Divine Images,* 29–30: "He rose by the excellence of His power, keeping the immortal flesh by which He had saved us from corruption"; see also Ware, *Orthodox Way,* 111: "It is not sufficient to explain away the Resurrection by saying that Christ's 'spirit' somehow lived on among his disciples. . . . We Orthodox believe that there was a genuine resurrection from the dead, in the sense that Christ's human body was reunited to his human soul, and that the tomb was found to be empty." See also Prokurat, Golitzin, and Peterson, *Historical Dictionary of the Orthodox Church,* s.v. "Pascha—the Resurrection of Christ."

53. St. Symeon the New Theologian, as cited in Constantine Cavarnos, *The Future Life According to Orthodox Teaching,* trans. Hieromonk Auxentios and Archimandrite Chrysostomos (Etna, Calif.: Center for Traditionalist Orthodox Studies, 1986), 42. See also Ware, *Orthodox Church,* 225: "In His own person Christ showed what the true 'likeness of God' is, and through His redeeming and victorious sacrifice He set that likeness once again within our reach."

54. St. John of Damascus, *On the Divine Images,* 29; emphasis added.

55. See Ware, *Orthodox Church*, 33–35, for this connection between the victory for icons, the Resurrection, and the sanctification of the physical bodies of humans.

56. Prokurat, Golitzin, and Peterson, *Historical Dictionary of the Orthodox Church*, s.v. "Pascha—the Resurrection of Christ"; Chrestou, *Partakers of God*, 51.

57. Mantzaridis, *Deification of Man*, 135.

58. For a summary of the hesychast controversy, as well as Gregory Palamas's defense, see Ware, *Orthodox Church*, 65–70; Mantzaridis, *Deification of Man*, 122–29.

59. See Ware, *Orthodox Church*, 232; see also Meyendorff, *Byzantine Theology*, 164; Vladimir Lossky, *Orthodox Theology: An Introduction* (Crestwood, N.Y.: St. Vladimir's Seminary, 1978), 130.

60. See Ware, *Orthodox Way*, 27.

61. Thomas Fitzgerald, "Orthodox Tradition," in *Dictionary of Christianity in America*, ed. Daniel G. Reid (Downers Grove, Ill.: InterVarsity, 1990), 850; Ware, *Orthodox Way*, 27.

62. See Ware, *Orthodox Church*, 68: "These energies are not something that exists apart from God, not a gift which God confers upon men: they are God Himself in His action and revelation to the world." See also Chrestou, *Partakers of God*, 62.

63. Chrestou, *Partakers of God*, 62.

64. St. Gregory Palamas, *The Triads*, ed. John Meyendorff, trans. Nicholas Gendle (New York: Paulist Press, 1983), III.iii.13 (pages 109–10).

65. Chrestou, *Partakers of God*, 62, based on the writings of Gregory of Nyssa; see also Fitzgerald, "Orthodox Tradition," 850–51.

66. Mantzaridis, *Deification of Man*, 122; emphasis added.

67. Joseph Smith, *Teachings of the Prophet Joseph Smith*, sel. Joseph Fielding Smith (Salt Lake City: Deseret Book, 1976), 346–47. Elder B. H. Roberts's comment is found on page 346, note 3.

68. Chrestou, *Partakers of God*, 35.

69. Ware, *Orthodox Church*, 236.

70. Smith, *Teachings*, 345. For additional commentary on Lorenzo Snow's and Joseph Smith's teachings, see also Stephen E. Robinson, "God the Father: Overview," in *Encyclopedia of Mormonism*, ed. Daniel H. Ludlow (New York: Macmillan, 1992), 2:549; Blomberg and Robinson, *How Wide the Divide?* 86.

71. For a concise explanation and reconciliation of Latter-day Saint beliefs about the Father's mortal past and "the fact that he now has all power and all

knowledge and possesses every virtue, grace, and godly attribute," see Millet and Reynolds, eds., *Latter-day Christianity,* 32; see also 31–33.

72. See David L. Paulsen, "The Doctrine of Divine Embodiment: Restoration, Judeo-Christian, and Philosophical Perspectives," *BYU Studies* 35 (1996): 84–94. See also Blomberg and Robinson, *How Wide the Divide?* 89, for Stephen Robinson's view: "I would argue that if the full divinity of Christ was not impaired or limited by his incarnation, then . . . God *can* have a physical body and still be God, infinite and eternal. The incarnation of the Son proves this." See also Robert L. Millet, "What We Believe," *Brigham Young University 1997–98 Speeches* (Provo, Utah: Brigham Young University Publications and Graphics, 1998), 157.

73. Lossky, *Orthodox Theology,* 75; emphasis added. See also Prokurat, Golitzin, and Peterson, *Historical Dictionary of the Orthodox Church,* s.v. "Pascha—the Resurrection of Christ."

74. See, for example, this recent summation by President Gordon B. Hinckley: "Two beings of substance were before [Joseph Smith]. He saw them. They were in form like men, *only much more glorious in their appearance.* . . . They were beings of flesh and bone whose nature was reaffirmed in later revelations which came to the Prophet" ("What Are People Asking about Us?" *Ensign,* November 1998, 71; emphasis added).

75. For an excellent summary of the doctrinal basis for exaltation in Latter-day Saint theology, especially that theology surrounding the idea of humans and God being of the same species, see Elder Boyd K. Packer, "The Pattern of Our Parentage," *Ensign,* November 1984, 66–69. Because there is no Latter-day Saint belief about the "Otherness" of the divine *ousia,* there also is no corresponding Latter-day Saint doctrine regarding the "two natures in one person" in Christ. See Stephen E. Robinson, "LDS Doctrine Compared with Other Christian Doctrines," in *Encyclopedia of Mormonism,* ed. Daniel H. Ludlow (New York: Macmillan, 1992), 401: "Latter-day Saints are monophysite in their christology; that is, they believe Christ has only one nature, which is simultaneously both human and divine. This is possible because the human and the divine are not mutually exclusive categories in LDS thought, as in the duophysite christology of much orthodoxy."

76. "The Father and the Son: A Doctrinal Exposition by The First Presidency and The Twelve," in James E. Talmage, *Articles of Faith* (Salt Lake City: Deseret Book, 1984), 424.

77. Gordon B. Hinckley, "Don't Drop the Ball," *Ensign,* November 1994, 48; emphasis added. I am indebted to Professor Roger Keller for bringing this reference to my attention.

78. Ostling and Ostling, *Mormon America,* 313.

79. Stephen Robinson makes this same argument about the misrepresentation

of the official Latter-day Saint doctrine of exaltation, and he calls for increased attention to canonical sources (Blomberg and Robinson, *How Wide the Divide?* 86–94).

80. While Orthodox theologians are never explicit in their description of the activities in which deified humans will engage (after all, participation in the divine life is a mystery for mortals precisely because the divine life is presently a mystery), they affirm that such participation will be, in Bishop Ware's words, of "an inexhaustible variety" and never "monotonous"; Bishop Ware also calls it an "unending progress" and a "neverceasing advance," because "never, in all eternity, shall we reach a point where we have accomplished all that there is to do, or discovered all that there is to know" (Ware, *Orthodox Way,* 184–85). See also Chrestou, *Partakers of God,* 64, under the subheading "Infinite Progress": "Gregory of Nyssa had earlier indicated that he recognized only one limitation in perfection, that it has no limit." For additional statements on the Orthodox view of eternal progress, see Cavarnos, *Future Life According to Orthodox Thought,* 45–46: "St. John Klimakos, having in mind the righteous who have attained to spiritual love (the highest of virtues), says: 'We shall never cease to advance in love, either in the present or in the future life, continually adding light to light . . . they will ever receive more and more glory, more and more knowledge.' . . . The same thing is expressed by another great mystic of the Church, St. Gregory of Sinai, who writes: 'It is said that in the future life the Angels and the Saints will never cease to progress in the increase of divine gifts.'"

81. See Ostling and Ostling, *Mormon America,* 310–13. See especially the comments by Bishop Ware on page 311, Jaroslav Pelikan on 312, and Thomas Hopko on 313. For a similar argument about Orthodox and Latter-day Saint deification parallels, see Robinson, "LDS Doctrine Compared with Other Christian Doctrines," 401.

82. Ware, cited in Ostling and Ostling, *Mormon America,* 311.

83. Chrestou, *Partakers of God,* 62.

84. See Elder Boyd K. Packer, "The Pattern of Our Parentage," 69, for this straightforward expression of faith: "The Father *is* the one true God. *This* thing is certain: no one will ever ascend above Him; no one will ever replace Him. Nor will anything ever change the relationship that we, His literal offspring, have with Him. He is Eloheim, the Father. He is God. Of Him there is only one. We revere our Father and our God; we *worship* Him."

85. Chrestou, *Partakers of God,* 53; emphasis added.

86. St. John of Damascus, *On the Divine Images,* 28; emphasis added.

87. See, for example, Millet and Reynolds, *Latter-day Christianity,* 25–26.

88. Macarius and Chrysostom, as cited in Clendenin, *Eastern Orthodox Christianity,* 131; emphasis added.

89. See Millet and Reynolds, *Latter-day Christianity*, 29, for this excellent summary: "Since the scriptures teach that those who gain eternal life will look like God, receive the inheritance of God, receive the glory of God, be one with God, sit upon the throne of God, and exercise the power and rule of God, then surely it cannot be un-Christian to conclude with C. S. Lewis and others that such beings as these can be *called* gods, as long as we remember that this use of the term *gods* does not in any way reduce or limit the sovereignty of God our Father. That is how the early Christians used the term; it is how C. S. Lewis used the term; and it is how Latter-day Saints use the term and understand the doctrine."

90. Stavropoulos, "Partakers of Divine Nature," in *Eastern Orthodox Theology*, ed. Daniel B. Clenendin, 184.

6

"THE LIGHT SHALL BEGIN TO BREAK FORTH"

PROTESTANT MISSIONS TO THE INDIANS IN COLONIAL AMERICA

Andrew H. Hedges

The restoration of the knowledge of the gospel to the Lamanites is a recurring prophecy in the Book of Mormon, occupying the attention of prophets from Lehi to Moroni and constituting one of the book's central themes. Today, with thousands of missionaries preaching the gospel to the descendants of Book of Mormon peoples, and with several million of these descendants claiming membership in the Church, we can see how literally this prophecy is being fulfilled. It is important to remember, however, that Latter-day Saint efforts and successes in this regard have often built on the work of missionaries from other faiths who had previously introduced American Indians to Christianity through the Bible.

That these earlier efforts to teach Lamanite remnants about Christ were neither accidental nor unimportant is demonstrated by the prophet Nephi, who, through vision and angelic tutoring, learned that the latter-day restoration of Book of Mormon peoples

Andrew H. Hedges is an associate professor of Church history and doctrine at Brigham Young University.

to the gospel would involve "the book of the Lamb of God"—the Bible—going forth "from the Gentiles unto the remnant of the seed of my brethren," after which "other books" would go forth that would "establish the truth of the first, which are of the twelve apostles of the Lamb" (1 Nephi 13:38–40). In many areas in the New World, this introductory work with the Bible started centuries before the coming forth of the Book of Mormon, but was clearly— if Nephi's vision means anything—an important step toward these people's eventual restoration to the fulness of the gospel. To discuss the latter-day redemption of the Lamanites only in terms of Latter-day Saint missionary efforts after 1830, is in short, to miss half the story.

This important but somewhat neglected phase of the restoration of the Lamanites to the gospel in the latter days comprised the missionary efforts of several Protestant missionaries who worked with various tribes of Indians during the colonial period in what is today Massachusetts, New Jersey, Delaware, and Pennsylvania, and who collectively converted thousands of Indians to Christianity. Impressive as the immediate results of their labors may have been, however, these missionaries' real contribution to the Restoration lies in their position as the first Protestants to make a sustained effort to teach the American Indians Christianity on American soil and in the inspiration they provided for future generations of missionary-minded men and women representing a variety of Protestant denominations. Detailed accounts of their efforts and successes were published and republished over the course of the seventeenth, eighteenth, and early nineteenth centuries, helping to inspire hundreds of Presbyterian, Baptist, and Methodist missionaries to direct their energies toward converting Native Americans to Christianity rather than fellow Europeans only. Although the labors of these later missionaries met with mixed results, thousands of Native people, hailing from tribes living across the continent, were nevertheless introduced to the Bible to one degree or another, thereby setting the stage for the debut of the "other books" Nephi saw going forth among the remnants of the Lamanites. Their efforts, in short, both inaugurated and helped sustain—through the published, well-read accounts of their successes—the fulfillment of an important, prophesied step toward the restoration of Book of Mormon peoples to the fulness of the gospel.

JOHN ELIOT

By far the best-known of American colonists who tried their hand at establishing Christianity among the American Indians is John Eliot. In spite of his fame, relatively little is known of Eliot's early life; that he was born in England in 1604 is certain, but some doubt remains as to which county he was born in and the status of his family. After earning his degree at Jesus College, Cambridge, in 1622, Eliot, who became good friends with the Reverend Thomas Hooker,[1] joined the exodus of Puritan divines from England in 1631. After having served as teacher of the First Church of Roxbury for a time, he was made that body's pastor in 1633, a post he kept for the rest of his eventful life, which ended in 1690. Active in the proceedings against Anne Hutchinson,[2] Eliot was known by his contemporaries as an honest, devout, zealous man, whose occasional idiosyncracies—he preached vehemently against the growing use of wigs, as well as against the evils of tobacco use—were more than offset by his almost boundless charity.[3]

But it was his unceasing efforts to convert the American Indians of the surrounding countryside to Christianity that made Eliot a household name for several generations of colonists.[4] His interests in the Native Americans seems to have begun during the Pequot War in 1637,[5] when he spoke so strongly against the colony's proceedings against the New England tribe that colonial officials branded him another Roger Williams[6] and asked that he publicly recant. Ten years later, in the fall of 1646, he began instructing the natives living near Roxbury in the fundamentals of Christianity, motivated, he told his friend and colleague Daniel Gookin, by his desire to glorify God, his "compassion and ardent affection" for the American Indians, and his obligation to fulfill the "covenant and promise" New Englanders had made to their king to "communicate the gospel unto the native Indians."[7]

Once he had begun, there was no turning back for Eliot. Braving debilitating sicknesses, fatigue, weather, hostile tribesmen, and apathetic colonists, the "Apostle to the Indians," as he came to be known, prosecuted his designs until he was so feeble that the Honorable Corporation for the Propagation of the Gospel to the Indians in New England and Parts Adjacent, which began funding his and similar efforts in 1649, was forced to find money with which to pay a servant to accompany him on his missionary forays into the New England countryside.[8] Under Eliot's direction, fourteen "praying towns" were established, where praying American Indians seeking Church membership could live apart from their unconverted brethren and practice the arts of civilization, community, and Christianity. Colonial jealousies and suspicions during King Philip's War[9] emptied the praying towns of their inhabitants, and only four were resettled following the end of hostilities. Eliot persevered, however, and by 1687 most of the eighteen congregations of praying Indians in New England were on the mainland, as were three of the six established American Indian churches. Some have estimated that five thousand Native Americans in the region had embraced Christianity to one degree or another by this time—fully one quarter of the estimated twenty thousand American Indians living in New England and her adjoining islands at the time.[10] By the turn of the century, Increase Mather reported that the number of established American Indian congregations in the area had swelled to "thirty several," many of whom were holding midweek lectures as well as Sabbath meetings.[11]

Eliot had some help in bringing all this about. One of his closest friends and staunchest allies was Daniel Gookin, who, four years after being elected a magistrate, was appointed by the Massachusetts Court to be superintendent of those American Indians in the colony who had submitted to English rule. In this capacity, Gookin frequently attended Eliot on his tours through the praying towns, and he stood alone among the magistrates in excoriating the colony's treatment of the Christian Indians during King Philip's War. Through the use of interpreters, he became a well-respected lecturer to the American Indians and was quite popular with those among whom he worked.[12] Other ministers with whom Eliot occasionally coordinated his efforts included the younger John Cotton, son of the great Puritan divine by the same name, and Richard Bourne and William Leverich, who taught the Native Americans living around Sandwich and Mashpee in Plymouth Colony. Leverich had turned to the American Indians at Eliot's request after abandoning his English congregation to the "spirit of Pharisaisme and formality" that had overcome them.[13] Eliot's and most other missionaries' willingness to learn the American Indian language was a tremendous help as well, making it unnecessary for Christian Indians to learn the English language in order to learn the essentials of the English religion. So, too, did Eliot's willingness to translate a variety of religious materials into the Massachusetts dialect, including the entire Bible (in 1663), two catechisms, a grammar, a primer, a singing psalm book, Lewis Bayly's "Practice of Piety," Richard Baxter's "Call to the Unconverted," and Thomas Shepard's "Sincere Convert and Sound Believer."[14] This is all the more significant because the literacy rate among the natives in their own language was relatively high; fully one-third of the men, women, and children Richard Bourne and John Cotton were working with in 1674, for example, could read their own American Indian language, and others were clamoring to learn.[15]

Eliot's liberality toward the American Indians was due, at least in part, to his personal beliefs about their basic humanity, their history, and the role he saw them playing in sacred history. In accordance with the numerous biblical passages that emphasize the ultimate brotherhood of mankind, Eliot and the others frequently referred to the natives as nothing less than the "sons of Adam," among whom lived many every bit as predestined to eternal salvation as the best of England's elect.[16] Holding the Native Americans as "men of the same mould, [God's] offspring as well as we," these missionaries placed them squarely within the scheme of sacred history by identifying them as peoples discussed at length in the Bible, and so heirs to the blessings promised those groups. Most felt that America's native inhabitants were descendants of the Tartars or

Scythians who lived, in ancient times, in northeast Asia, and who at some point in the murky past had been "spilt by some revenging hand of God" onto America.[17] As such, they were the "Gentiles" mentioned so prominently by the Psalmist, Isaiah, and writers and characters of the New Testament—including Christ Himself—whose conversion to Christianity was perhaps to precede, perhaps to follow, the conversion of the Jews, prior to the establishment of the kingdom of God on the earth.[18]

Others, citing similarities between the traditions and religious beliefs of the Bible's Hebrews and the Native Americans, argued that the Native Americans actually belonged to the house of Israel and could even legitimately be called Jews themselves, an opinion that gained ground with some after Rabbi Manasseh Ben Israel of Amsterdam endorsed it.[19] For John Eliot, it was "as clear in the Scripture, that these are the children of *Shem* as we of *Japhet*," and just as clear from more recent developments that the day of "these lost and scattered Israelites" had arrived, a thought which gave this frequently beleaguered missionary the strength to go on.[20]

THE MAYHEWS OF MARTHA'S VINEYARD

For all their fame, John Eliot and his companions were neither the first nor the most successful of the English missionaries working with the Native Americans of colonial New England. Those honors, rather, belong to several members of the Mayhew family, whose ministry of more than eighty years to the Algonquins living on Martha's Vineyard and Nantucket, begun in 1642, resulted in thousands of Indians converting to Christianity. The Mayhews were relative latecomers to the northern English colonies; indeed, by the time twenty-one-year-old Thomas Mayhew Jr. arrived on the island in 1642, Puritans had been in parts of Massachusetts for twenty-two years and had established towns around Narragansett Bay and in the Connecticut River Valley. Despite his late start, however, the young Thomas, "having no small Degree of Knowledge in the *Latin* and *Greek* Languages, and being not wholly a Stranger to the *Hebrew*," quickly made an impression on his countrymen and was soon appointed minister of the "eight or ten English families" that had settled the east end of the island some years before.[21] As zealous a Puritan as he was talented, and finding his responsibilities relatively light over so small a congregation, Thomas Jr. quickly turned his attention toward converting the Native Americans with whom he and his countrymen shared the island. The work proceeded slowly at first; even after learning their language and becoming acquainted with several individual Native Americans, the young missionary had only managed to convert one American Indian by 1643, and another three years passed before he delivered his first public sermon. With his tongue loosed, however, things began to heat up for the young missionary, and by 1650, thirty-nine Native American men, and an even greater number of women, had embraced the new religion. By mid-October of the following year, the number had swelled to 199 men, women, and children, who were meeting in two congregations, and by the end of October 1652, a decade after his first halting attempts to "express his great Concern and Pity for their *immortal Souls*," Mayhew counted 282 adult American Indians in his fold.[22]

Thomas Jr. perished at sea five years later en route to England, where he had hoped to be able to "give a more particular Account of the State of the *Indians* than he could well do by Letters."[23] Upon his death, Thomas Mayhew Sr., the young minister's seventy-year-old father, took over the mission. The elder Mayhew, who had acquired rights not only to Martha's Vineyard after his business prospects had failed on the mainland but to the neighboring Nantucket and Elizabeth Islands as well, had arrived on the island shortly after his son and had been serving as the islands' governor ever since—a post he kept for the rest of his life and which he reportedly filled with unparalleled justice and equity. Despite his advanced years, Thomas Sr. resolved to visit at least some of the Native American congregations at least once a week—no small task, since some were located almost twenty miles away on the other side of the island from where he lived.[24]

The old man's efforts paid off, however, and the gospel's progress among the natives of the islands he governed was nothing short of phenomenal under his enlightened direction. A small number of

Native Americans were admitted to full communion in 1659, and, with John Eliot on the mainland nodding his approval, they formed themselves into a church in 1670, complete with Native American officers.[25] By 1674, Martha's Vineyard was home to two American Indian churches, where almost fifty communicants regularly partook of the Lord's Supper. Virtually all of the island's other Native Americans were regularly attending Sunday services in six different congregations—presided over by ten Native American pastors—by this time; indeed, the elder Mayhew wrote Daniel Gookin that of the some three hundred Native American families inhabiting Chappaquidick and Martha's Vineyard, there was "but one of them that prays not to God."[26] Nearby Nantucket experienced similar growth. The ninety or so families that had converted to Christianity on that island by 1670 had swelled to include "about three hundred Indians, young and old," by 1674, who, under the watchful eyes of four native preachers, were meeting in three different congregations—one of which included thirty communicants.[27]

Due largely to the respect afforded the aged Mayhew by Native Americans and English alike, King Philip's War left the islands virtually unscathed. Indeed, while colonists on the mainland were confining the praying Indians there to a few well-watched towns or to Deer Island, Thomas Sr. actually armed the natives of Martha's Vineyard and the nearby islands—who, at approximately 3,000 adults, outnumbered the English colonists there twenty to one— and had them function as a guard for the English living there. Native Americans, accordingly, continued to convert both during and after the hostilities, and by the time the governor-missionary died in 1682, at the ripe old age of ninety-three, most of the Native Americans on Martha's Vineyard and the surrounding islands had embraced Christianity to one degree or another.[28]

The Reverend John Cotton spent two years instructing the Native Americans on the Vineyard in the mid-1660s, but it was Thomas Mayhew Jr.'s son, John Mayhew, who took over when the aged governor, his grandfather, died. At the end of his short ministry—he died in 1689 of a "heavy Pain in his Stomach"— ten American Indian congregations, boasting one hundred communicants in three churches, were meeting on Martha's Vineyard "in a very orderly Way," while the number of congregations on Nantucket had swelled to five.[29] The American Indians were without any English overseers for five years following John's death until his son Experience Mayhew, who was fluent in the Indian language but a mere sixteen years old when his father died, was finally old enough to minister to them. The lack of English ministers, however, did not stop Christianity's progress during this time. Cotton Mather estimated the number of Christian Indians inhabiting Martha's Vineyard and Nantucket in 1694—the year Experience started preaching to them—at a full three thousand individuals, or virtually every American Indian on the islands.[30]

JOHN SERGEANT, DAVID BRAINERD, AND JOHN BRAINERD

Due in part to the highly publicized efforts of Eliot and the Mayhews, interest in converting the Native Americans to Christianity continued throughout the eighteenth century as European colonists slowly, yet inexorably, displaced Native Americans to the colonies' western frontiers. This interest spawned a number of attempts to send missionaries to tribes who had not yet heard the word of God, most of whom, by this time, were living relatively more remote from the English than Eliot's charges had. Unforeseen events prevented a number of these missions from ever getting off the ground, while others proved highly successful for a time; the increasing ferocity of colonial wars wreaked havoc with most of them at one time or another, however, and none came close to matching the success Eliot and the Mayhews had enjoyed earlier. In this period of deteriorating relationships between Indians and Europeans, however, their labors among various tribes played an essential role in keeping Christianity alive among the Native Americans and, ultimately, in paving the way for the Book of Mormon.

John Sergeant's fifteen-year mission to the small group of "River Indians" living on the Housatonic River in southwest Massachusetts was one of the more successful of these efforts. Noted for his

"Ingenuity, Learning and Piety" by his contemporaries, this young Congregationalist sought an appointment to the American Indians early in his ministerial career, feeling, he wrote in his journal, "asham'd to own myself a Christian, or even a Man, and yet utterly refuse doing what lay in my power to . . . promote the salvation of souls perishing in the Dark." His chance came in 1734 while he was working as a tutor at Yale, when the Society in Scotland for Propagating Christian Knowledge (SSPCK), organized in 1698 and looking for a likely young man whom it could support on a mission to a tractable group of American Indians, heard of Sergeant's wish to "rather be employ'd as a Missionary to the natives . . . than accept a call any English parish might give him" and offered him the job.[31] The Society's choice of both missionary and tribe was apparently a good one, although neither had any previous experience with missionary work; by the time a "nervous fever, attended with Canker," hustled the thirty-nine-year-old Sergeant from this world to a better in 1749, the missionary had baptized 182 men, women, and children, established a church of forty-two communicants, helped create a school where Timothy Woodbridge taught fifty-five children, and settled 218 individuals in the Native American town of Stockbridge—up dramatically from the "short of fifty" Sergeant had first found in the area.[32]

During the course of his labors on the Massachusetts frontier, Sergeant learned of a group of American Indians living twenty miles to the west of Stockbridge who might be interested in Christianity. Hoping to duplicate Sergeant's success at Stockbridge, the SSPCK sent another aspiring missionary, David Brainerd, to sound these natives out in their town of Kaunameek. A disciple of Gilbert Tennent and an early "New Light" Presbyterian who had recently been expelled from Yale for indiscreetly opining that one of his tutors had no more grace than a chair, Brainerd spent a year working with the natives at Kaunameek and learning Mahican—with the help of Sergeant—before leaving them in Sergeant's care and moving to the American Indian town of Crossweeksung, located at the Forks of the Delaware River, in 1744. Subject to bouts of depression, and occasionally so ill he was forced to present his sermons while sitting down, Brainerd labored with the Delaware Indians and sought to make inroads with the numerous tribes living on the upper Susquehanna until consumption drove him from the field in the spring of 1747. Long enamoured with the idea of death and returning to God, Brainerd died that fall at the house of Jonathan Edwards, where the great theologian's eighteen-year-old daughter Jerusha— to whom the twenty-nine-year-old missionary was apparently engaged and who died a mere six months later—"almost overstepped the proprieties of her sex" while trying to nurse him back to health.[33] His efforts, although relatively short-lived and plagued with infirmities, nevertheless produced results; by the time he left for the East, Brainerd had gathered some 130 natives to the Indian town of Bethel, thirty-seven of whom were in full church communion.[34]

David Brainerd's mission did not die with him, however. John Brainerd, David's younger brother, filled in for David the summer he lay dying in Northampton and took over the mission after his death that fall. Every bit as devout and "New Light" as his older brother, and much more stable and healthy, John converted a number of natives to the faith over the next eight years and was happy to report an ongoing reformation in the lives and habits of the "sundry" American Indians whom he had "persuaded . . . to come from distant parts and settle" at Bethel. Disease, however, undermined his efforts to an extent; although some forty natives had joined the Christians at Bethel under John's hand by 1752, John estimated that at least one-third of the town's original inhabitants had died by then, leaving the overall numbers there virtually the same as when David had left.[35] Never enjoying anything even approaching the almost pentecostal season his older brother had enjoyed at Crossweeksung, John's mission nevertheless hummed steadily along until May 1755, when rising French power in the West overawed enough American Indians living on the colonies' frontiers that the SSPCK, fearing for John's safety, recalled him.

CONCLUSION

Despite all that these missionaries accomplished among the Indians in Massachusetts, Delaware, New Jersey, and Pennsylvania, disease, war, land conflicts, and intermarriage took their toll on the Native American congregations—and on the Native American population in general—throughout the course of the colonial period. By the early years of the nineteenth century, the once thriving communities and congregations of Eliot and the Mayhews had been reduced to a few families and individuals,[36] and by 1830 most of New England's seaboard Algonquins had lost, for all intents and purposes, their tribal identities. Converts of Sergeant and the Brainerds suffered similar losses, and in 1824, bereft of any white advocate in the East who might plead their cause, they began a journey westward that ultimately took them to the Indian Territory in 1832.[37] Yet to conclude from this that these missionaries' efforts were ultimately in vain would be a failure to understand the Lord's plan of restoring the Lamanites to the fulness of the gospel in the latter days. Restoration scriptures make it clear that the Book of Mormon would be a *second* witness of Christ to the remnants of the Lamanites—not the first witness, and by no means the only witness. The Bible was to be the first witness, and someone in America had to take the first halting steps in making its contents known to the natives of the land. While the specific tribes with whom these men labored had largely died out by the time the Book of Mormon arrived on the scene, the work they started among the Lamanites at large had not. Indeed, it had successfully set the stage for the fulfillment of prophecies and promises that had been in place for over two thousand years. Like William Tyndale's Bible, these missionaries' efforts were an essential prerequisite to greater things; and just as any reference to an English translation of the Bible today is a quiet acknowledgment of Tyndale's efforts, so much of the success the gospel enjoys among many Native Americans today is an implicit salute to the missionaries who taught the Native Americans of colonial America.

NOTES

   1. Thomas Hooker (ca. 1586–1647) led his congregation out of Massachusetts in 1635 and settled the town of Hartford on the Connecticut River, the first permanent European settlement in what would become Connecticut.

2. Anne Hutchinson (ca. 1590–1643) immigrated to Boston in 1634, where she openly challenged ministerial authority by asserting that God communicated with individual men and women and could, through revelation, give them assurance of personal salvation (the so-called "Antinomian heresy"). Tried and convicted for heresy and sedition in 1638, she and her family, with some followers, moved south to Narragansett Bay as some of Rhode Island's earliest European settlers.

3. For brief overviews of Eliot's life and character, see John W. Ford, *Some Correspondence between the Governors and Treasurers of the New England Company in London and the Commissioners of the United Colonies in America, the Missionaries of the Company, and Others between the Years 1657 and 1712* (New York: Burt Franklin, 1970), xvi–xvii; "The Historical Account of John Eliot, the First Minister of the Church at Roxbury," in *Collections of the Massachusetts Historical Society,* 1st series, 8 (1802): 5–34; "Anecdote of Rev. John Eliot, of Roxbury," in *Collections of the Massachusetts Historical Society,* 1st series, 10 (1809): 186–87. For a more detailed account, see Ola Elizabeth Winslow, *John Eliot: "Apostle to the Indians"* (Boston: Houghton Mifflin, 1968).

4. For in-depth studies of Eliot's efforts among the Indians in eastern Massachusetts, see Andrew H. Hedges, "Setting the Stage: John Eliot and the Algonquins of Eastern Massachusetts, 1646–90," *Regional Studies in Latter-day Saint Church History: The New England States,* ed. Donald Q. Cannon, Arnold K. Garr, Bruce A. Van Orden (Provo, Utah: Department of Church History and Doctrine, Brigham Young University, 2004); Richard W. Cogley, *John Eliot's Mission to the Indians Before King Philip's War* (Cambridge, Mass.: Harvard University Press, 1999); Dane A. Morrison, *A Praying People: Massachusetts Acculteration and the Failure of the Puritan Mission, 1600–1690* (New York: P. Lang, 1995).

5. The Pequots were a tribe of American Indians inhabiting the lower Connecticut River Valley. Some 400 Pequots were killed in 1637 after colonists set fire to a fort in which the Indians had taken refuge following an outbreak of hostilities between the two groups.

6. Roger Williams (ca. 1604–83) argued with the Massachusetts Puritan clergy over Indian land rights, relations with the Church of England, and child baptism. Escaping deportation, he traveled to Narrangansett Bay and founded Providence, Rhode Island, in 1636.

7. Daniel Gookin, *Historical Collections of the Indians in New England [1674],* in *Collections of the Massachusetts Historical Society,* 1st series, 1 (1792): 170; see also "Historical Account of John Eliot," 28–29.

8. See Ford, *Correspondence,* 1, 68.

9. King Philip's War was the costliest and bloodiest of the seventeenth-century

colonial Indian wars. The war began when the Wampanoag Indians—led by Metacomet, or "King Philip," as the colonists called him—began resisting settlers' encroachment on their lands in 1675. By the end of the war three years later, more than one thousand colonists and an untold number of American Indians had lost their lives.

10. See "History of Newton," in *Collections of the Massachusetts Historical Society*, 1st series, 5 (1798): 261.

11. Ford, *Correspondence*, 83.

12. For brief overviews of Gookin's life, see Gookin, *Historical Collections*, 228–29, and *Archaeologia Americana, Transactions and Collections of the American Antiquarian Society* (Cambridge, Mass.: Harvard University Press, 1836), 2:425–28. For Gookin's popularity, see Ford, *Correspondence*, 74–76.

13. Henry Whitfield, *Strength Out of Weaknesse; or, A Glorious Manifestation of the further Progresse of the Gospel among the Indians in New-England* (London: M. Simmons, 1652), in *Collections of the Massachusetts Historical Society*, 3d series, 4 (1834): 180–81; see also Ford, *Correspondence*, x–xi, xiv.

14. See Gookin, *Historical Collections*, 169, 172. Such religious publications in the Indian language continued after Eliot's death; for a complete list and discussion, see William Kellaway, *The New England Company, 1649–1776* (New York: Barnes & Noble, 1962).

15. See Gookin, *Historical Collections*, 197–200.

16. Gookin, *Historical Collections*, 143, 147, 152, 181; see also Whitfield, *Strength out of Weaknesse*, 161, 156.

17. Thomas Shepard, *The Clear Sun-shine of the Gospell Breaking Forth upon the Indians in New-England* (London: n.p., 1648), in *Collections of the Massachusetts Historical Society*, 3d series, 4 (1834): 33; [Shepard], *The Day-Breaking, if not the Sun-Rising of the Gospell with the Indians in New-England* (London: Rich Cotes, 1647), in *Collections of the Massachusetts Historical Society*, 3d series, 4 (1834): 14; see also Gookin, *Historical Collections*, 145.

18. See Whitfield, *Strength Out of Weaknesse*, 155–57; Gookin, *Historical Collections*, 143, 154, 160, 223. For a discussion of seventeenth-century ideas concerning the order in which various groups of people would be converted before the Millennium, see Richard W. Cogley, "John Eliot and the Origins of the American Indians," *Early American Literature* 21, no. 3 (Winter 1986–87), 211.

19. See Gookin, *Historical Collections*, 145–46; Edward Winslow, *The Glorious Progress of the Gospel, amongst the Indians in New England* (London: Edward Winslow, 1649) in *Collections of the Massachusetts Historical Society*, 3d series, 4 (1834): 72–74, 93–95.

20. Henry Whitfield, *The Light Appearing More and More towards the Perfect Day; or, A Farther Discovery of the Present State of the Indians in New-England,*

Concerning the Progresse of the Gospel amongst Them (London: n.p., 1651), in *Collections of the Massachusetts Historical Society*, 3d series, 4 (1834): 119–20; emphasis in original. Eliot initially subscribed to John Cotton's theory that the American Indians were displaced Tartars from Asia. By 1649, however, he was entertaining ideas that at least some of the American Indians were descendants of the tribes of Israel, and that all were Hebrews. He also subscribed to the idea that the Jews would be converted before the Gentiles would; see Cogley, "Origins of the American Indians," 212–17. Over the course of the colonial and early national periods, various authors—notably James Adair and Elias Boudinot—tried their hand at identifying the American Indians' Israelite origins. This effort found its fullest expression in Ethan Smith's *View of the Hebrews*, where Smith argues that the Native Americans were actually remnants of the lost tribes. See Richard L. Bushman, *Joseph Smith and the Beginnings of Mormonism* (Urbana and Chicago: University of Illinois Press, 1988), 133–39, for an excellent discussion of this topic.

21. Thomas Prince, *Some Account of those English Ministers who have successfully presided over the Work of Gospelizing the Indians on Martha's Vineyard, and the adjacent Islands*, in Experience Mayhew, *Indian Converts; or, Some Account of the Lives and Dying Speeches of a Considerable Number of the Christianized Indians of Martha's Vineyard, in New-England* (London: n.p., 1727), 280; emphasis in original.

22. Prince, *Some Account*, 281, 286, 289–90; emphasis in original.

23. Prince, *Some Account*, 291–92; emphasis in original.

24. See Prince, *Some Account*, 280, 292–95, 297–98.

25. See Daniel Gookin, *Historical Collections*, 203–4; Prince, *Some Account*, 299–300.

26. Gookin, *Historical Collections*, 205.

27. Gookin, *Historical Collections*, 206–7; see also John Eliot, "Letter from Eliot to Hon. Robert Boyle," in *Old South Leaflets* 1, no. 21 (Boston: Directors of the Old South Work, Old South Meeting House, n.d.), 2–3.

28. Prince, *Some Account*, 295–97, 299, 301. For an overview of Thomas Mayhew Sr.'s life, see Lloyd C. M. Hare, *Thomas Mayhew: Patriarch to the Indians, 1593–1682* (New York: D. Appleton, 1932).

29. Prince, *Some Account*, 305; [Eliot], "Letters From Rev. John Eliot of Roxbury, to Hon. Robert Boyle, 1670–1688," in *Collections of the Massachusetts Historical Society*, 1st series, 3 (1794): 185. Thomas Prince reported that at John Mayhew's death, the Indians were meeting in only "four or five several Places" across the island, rather than the ten Eliot reported. As Eliot was a contemporary of John Mayhew, and his estimate makes much more sense than Prince's in light of the number of congregations reported by others both before and after John's death, I have opted to cite his figure in the text.

30. See Prince, *Some Account,* 306–7.

31. Samuel Hopkins, *Historical Memoirs Relating to the Housatonic Indians* (Boston: S. Kneeland, 1753), reprinted in *The Magazine of History with Notes and Queries, Extra Numbers 17–20, Volume V* (New York: William Abbatt, 1912), 19–21.

32. Hopkins, *Historical Memoirs,* 14, 158, 11–12. For brief overviews of Sergeant's missionary career, see Henry Warner Bowden, *American Indians and Christian Missions: Studies in Cultural Conflict* (Chicago: University of Chicago Press, 1981), 137–38, and James Axtell, *The Invasion Within: The Contest of Cultures in Colonial North America* (New York: Oxford University Press, 1985), 197–200. For a detailed account of the Housatonic Indians, see Patrick Frazier, *The Mohicans of Stockbridge* (Lincoln: University of Nebraska Press, 1992).

33. Thomas Brainerd, *The Life of John Brainerd, the Brother of David Brainerd, and His Successor as Missionary to the Indians of New Jersey* (Philadelphia: Presbyterian Publication Company, 1865), 132. Brainerd's desire to leave this world of sin occasionally expressed itself rather morbidly. Once, while visiting a house "where was one dead and laid out," Brainerd "looked on the corpse," he wrote, "and longed that my time might come to *depart.*" Reflecting on still another death, Brainerd thrilled at seeing himself "dead, and laid out, and inclosed in my coffin, and put down into the cold grave, with the greatest solemnity" (Sereno Edwards Dwight, *Memoirs of the Rev. David Brainerd; Missionary to the Indians on the Borders of New-York, New-Jersey, and Pennsylvania* [New Haven, Conn.: S. Converse, 1822; reprint, St. Clair Shores, Mich.: Scholarly Press, 1970], 180, 192).

34. See Brainerd, *The Life of John Brainerd,* 117–18. For a brief overview of Brainerd's missionary career, see Bowden, *American Indians and Christian Missions,* 152–55.

35. Brainerd, *Life of John Brainerd,* 255–57.

36. See Gookin, *Historical Collections,* 195 n., 201 n.

37. See Bowden, *American Indians and Christian Missions,* 138–39, 156–57.

7

"COME, FOLLOW ME"

THE IMITATION OF CHRIST IN THE LATER MIDDLE AGES

Jennifer C. Lane

As Latter-day Saints we most often look to the Reformation as the preparation for the Restoration. In my studies of medieval history, however, I have come to realize that the way was also prepared for the Reformation itself, and that preparation occurred in the later Middle Ages. Earlier in the Middle Ages, active participation in religious devotion was the role of religious specialists such as monks and priests. Religious movements in the thirteenth, fourteenth, and fifteenth centuries changed this pattern and created a widespread interest in religion, bringing about a dramatic rise in common people's participation in religious devotion. Concurrent with this was an increased focus on the life and suffering of Jesus Christ.

As late medieval devotion increasingly focused on the life and sacrifice of Jesus Christ, laypeople throughout Europe sought both to meditate on His life and suffering and to follow His example. The efforts to follow in Christ's footsteps took many forms. Pilgrims in

Jennifer C. Lane is an adjunct assistant professor of religion at Brigham Young University–Hawaii.

·Jerusalem sought to stand physically in the places of His suffering.
·Those in Europe believed they could experience His pain through
.meditation on accounts and images of His scourging, His carrying
.the cross, and His crucifixion. Some even scourged themselves to
·feel closer to His suffering.

While I believe we can learn much from this desire to meditate
on Christ's atoning sacrifice, some of these devotional practices may
strike us as missing the full meaning of the Savior's invitation to
"come, follow me" (Luke 18:22). Their enthusiasm for practices that
we would not encourage today grew out of the contemporary belief
that sharing Christ's suffering was necessary to receive the benefits
of the Atonement. The impact of doctrinal understanding on devotional practices illustrates one effect of missing "plain and precious"
parts of the gospel. Nevertheless, I believe that the widespread late
medieval enthusiasm to follow the Savior demonstrates how
through the Spirit of Christ people were gradually prepared for the
Father to teach of the covenant through the Restoration (D&C
84:44–48).

Imitation of Christ through Devotional Literature

One of the ways in which people in the later Middle Ages
learned about the life of Christ was through devotional texts that
told stories about His life and sufferings. As Europe became
increasingly urbanized in the central and later Middle Ages, the
merchant classes grew in size and importance. With this rise came
higher levels of literacy and an increased demand for book production, first in manuscript form and then in printed form, starting in
the mid-fifteenth century with Gutenberg's movable type. While
there was also a widespread interest in chivalric romance literature
and other secular genres, the demand for devotional literature was
very significant. In part this demand had developed under the influence of the mendicant orders of monks, such as the Franciscans and
Dominicans, who encouraged the spread of lay religiosity.[1]

The Franciscans are particularly important in understanding the widespread late medieval interest in meditation on the life of Christ. Their efforts to promote Christ-centered piety and encourage broad participation in these devotional practices can be considered a religious revolution.[2]

During this era the Bible was not generally available in vernacular languages and the laity were not encouraged to own and study the Bible. The devotional texts of the Franciscans, however, written in both Latin and the languages of the people, made the biblical narrative of Christ's life available to a large public.[3] Although the retelling of these stories reflects the Franciscans' theological concerns and in some cases goes beyond the text of the Bible, these efforts created and reinforced a widespread European familiarity and interest in the biblical narrative. These texts also helped to spread and strengthen a widespread European focus on Christ-centered devotion.

To this day one of these texts, Thomas à Kempis's *Imitation of Christ,* has remained well known. Rather than being a unique literary text, the *Imitation of Christ* is part of a body of literature that had been earlier developed and disseminated throughout Europe. Some other early and influential devotional texts include the *Meditationes vitae Christi,* which was believed to have been written by Bonaventure, Richard Rolle's *Mediations on the Passion,* and Ludoph of Saxony's *Vita Christi.* These various meditations on the life of Christ enjoyed widespread popularity and were translated into many languages.

As the titles of these devotional works suggest, their focus was on encouraging individuals to meditate on the life and suffering of Christ. The approach of these works differed from modern scripture commentaries. They were not concerned with the historical context of the life of Jesus in Roman-occupied Judea in the first century. Likewise, the central focus of these texts was not the teachings of the Savior on a sunny hillside in Galilee. Instead they focused on the miracle of the birth of Immanuel ("God with us") and the terrible humiliation and suffering manifest in Christ's expiatory sacrifice on our behalf.

These devotional works followed the general biblical accounts but made them accessible by encouraging readers to see and experience the scriptural events as if they were actually present. In some ways they might be seen as similar to modern Latter-day Saint historical fiction in that they were based on actual events but then made more personal and vivid by retelling them with added details. These devotional texts sought to make the Passion vividly immediate by narrating the events in graphic detail.

These vivid images were designed to evoke intense emotional reactions to the events of Christ's suffering. The devotional texts would also directly address the audience, telling them to behold Christ's suffering and to feel His pain as though they were there with Him. This personal connection of imagination and feeling with the suffering of Christ was seen as a means to participate in the Passion, a participation believed to be necessary to allow individuals to fully receive the benefits of His suffering. This participation allowed individuals a means to know, through their own experience, the love of God manifest in the suffering of Christ.[4]

The experience of participation was seen as a means of following Christ. A fourteenth-century writer from the Netherlands, Gerard Zerbold of Zutphen, explained the effect that this personal connection to the Passion should have: "For He suffered for your personal redemption. Therefore apply all that you read of Christ's doings to yourself, as if they were done for you alone, and always imagine that Christ is saying to you: 'I did this that you might follow Me.'"[5] The devotional accounts of Christ's suffering pointed individuals to Christ and made the invitation to follow Him widely available.

As these devotional texts told the stories of Christ's life and suffering, they encouraged the readers to follow His example. This imitation of Christ was often referred to as "being conformed to Christ." These texts not only encouraged the readers' imitation but they also explained how to participate in Christ's sufferings and gave examples of those who had done so.

While the phrase "being conformed to Christ" did, in some cases, include sharing the physical suffering with Christ, the means through which individuals were encouraged to "take up their cross" and follow Christ varied widely. These different means of following Christ and being conformed to Him also included moral action in living a virtuous Christian life, emotional connection in feeling His suffering and His love, and mental remembrance and meditation on the events of His life and suffering. These different ways of following Christ are illustrated here in this passage of Ludoph of Saxony's *Vita Christi:* "We ought to carry the Cross of our Lord and help Him to bear it, with our hearts by pious remembrance and compassion, with our lips by frequent and devout thanksgiving, with our whole body by mortification and penance, and thus give thanks to our Saviour by our affections, words and deeds."[6] Participation, whether physical, moral, mental, or emotional, was the experience of feeling the love of God manifest in Christ's sufferings. Ludolph explicitly lays out how being conformed to Christ's suffering changes the individual. "Now in order to enter into the sweet savour of our Lord's Passion and to compassionate Jesus crucified, attend to the following things. First strive, as much as thou canst, to unite thyself to Him by fervent love; for the more fervently thou lovest Him, the more thou wilt compassionate His sufferings, and the more thou dost compassionate Him, so much the more will thine affection be enkindled, so that love and pity will thus mutually increase, until thou comest to perfection."[7] For Christians in the later Middle Ages, the desire to follow Christ and become like Him focused primarily on His suffering, believing that this focus would move them to love and perfection.

As Latter-day Saints we also seek to always remember the Savior and His suffering on our behalf. We also believe that remembering His love will increase our love for Him and our desire to obey and follow Him. At the same time, there are aspects of the late medieval devotional emphasis that do not resonate with our sensibilities or doctrinal understanding. One point in particular is the theological question of how the benefits of Christ's suffering are made available for us. I will discuss this in greater depth in the conclusion, but is it important to note that while the Restoration and Book of Mormon have emphasized faith, repentance, baptism, and gift of the Holy Ghost as the path to receiving the blessings of the

Atonement, late medieval Christians did not have this clarity of understanding. They also sincerely wanted to receive the blessings of Christ's suffering on their behalf, but the doctrinal interpretation of their day emphasized that sharing Christ's suffering was the gate. This desire to participate in Christ's suffering was often understood very literally, and this interpretation can be seen in the experience of pilgrims in Jerusalem.

Imitation of Christ through Pilgrimage

Those devout Europeans who had the opportunity to travel to Jerusalem during the later Middle Ages found an extension of the Franciscan-inspired devotional literature and imagery that they were familiar with at home. In the early part of the fourteenth century the Franciscans became the custodians of Jerusalem for Western Christianity and, as such, they were the guides of European pilgrims through the holy places.

The Franciscans' theological focus on Christ's suffering reshaped the Jerusalem pilgrimage from its previous random assortment of holy places of Old and New Testament events.[8] Much like the devotional literature that told the events of the Passion and then encouraged a personal response, the Franciscans shaped pilgrimage into a meditation on the Passion. They focused their tours on the Jerusalem of the New Testament, specifically on the places of Christ's suffering and death, and encouraged the pilgrims to meditate and respond. As the pilgrims walked in Christ's footsteps, they believed that their presence and their compassionate response allowed them to receive the benefits of Christ's suffering, benefits that were quantified by the Franciscans as indulgences.

Although as Latter-day Saints we do not quantify the spiritual benefits available through these acts of remembrance and imitation, many who have visited historical sites have spoken of a feeling of participation. Whether in walking the path of the Savior in Jerusalem or following the steps of the early Saints down Parley Street in Nauvoo, remembering the sacrifices made on our behalf can bring spiritual renewal and rededication.

For many today it is surprising to learn that the fourteenth- and fifteenth-century pilgrims did not follow the historical narrative directly, starting at either the site of the arrest in Gethsemane or the judgment by Pilate and then progressing towards Calvary. Instead, because of the pressures from the governing Muslim authorities of the Mamluk dynasty, the pilgrims started at the Church of the Holy Sepulchre and then moved their way out of the city. This has been seen as a reverse direction because it meant that the pilgrims *began*, rather than ended, their path at what they believed to be the site of the Crucifixion.

When pilgrims returned to Europe a number of them tried to reproduce the experience of Jerusalem pilgrimage in their home cities. This was accomplished by setting up stations or markers that indicated the different sites along the Savior's road to Calvary. The influence of the devotional literature and its Passion narration was so strong that these substitute paths did not reproduce the Jerusalem pilgrimage's reverse direction, but instead followed the biblical narrative. While these stations or markers originally led virtual pilgrims through city streets, they were also set up in churches where the devout would move from one image to another contemplating the experience of Christ's suffering.

These practices of following the Stations of the Cross spread widely throughout Europe, and the stations were eventually formalized into the fourteen stations that continue to be practiced throughout the Roman Catholic world. By the sixteenth and seventeenth centuries, the European experiences of pilgrims led them to demand that the order of the pilgrimage in Jerusalem be changed to follow the order of the biblical narrative. With the institution of the modern-day Via Dolorosa (or Way of Sorrow) Jerusalem pilgrims were able to literally accept the invitation to take up their cross and "come, follow me" (Luke 18:22).

Christ's invitation to "come, follow me" was widely extended throughout the later Middle Ages. Individuals heard this call through devotional literature recounting Christ's life and sufferings, devotional art that illustrated Christ's Passion and death, and devotional practices such as Jerusalem pilgrimage and the Stations of the

Cross. During the fourteenth and fifteenth centuries, meditation on and participation in Christ's sufferings became a widespread concern, creating a large base of interest in questions of religious practice and belief. During the sixteenth century, the Reformers challenged some aspects of these practices, as well as the theology behind many of these practices and beliefs. These challenges to the institutional monopoly of the Roman Catholic Church in Western Europe created multiple churches that, when later combined with the freedom of religion available in the United States, provided the necessary conditions for the Restoration through the prophet Joseph Smith.

IMPLICATIONS FOR LATTER-DAY SAINTS

As grateful as we are as Latter-day Saints for the religious diversity and renewed emphasis on the Bible that the Protestant Reformation brought about, we owe a similar debt of gratitude to the theologians and pious inhabitants in medieval Europe for gradually teaching and embracing a doctrinal focus on the mercy and love manifest in the suffering of Christ. While they did not possess the covenant made possible by the restored authority of the priesthood, I believe that the Spirit was moving upon the people of this era, helping them move closer to coming unto God (D&C 84:45–47). Through the Restoration the final step of that process has been accomplished as "the Father teacheth . . . of the covenant" (D&C 84:48). A fresh examination of the doctrines and practices of late medieval piety can clarify the central saving doctrines revealed through the Restoration.

For pious individuals in the later Middle Ages, the desire to participate in the suffering of Christ was shaped by Franciscan theology's focus on the need to suffer with Christ in order to receive the benefits of Christ's suffering. While in many cases this desire to participate took the form of remembrance, emotional experience, or moral living, it also promoted acts of physical imitation such as flagellation and other forms of self-inflicted suffering.

The emphasis on participation was expressed by Bonaventure,

an important Franciscan theologian: "Christ, the King of Kings, makes a decree that none may see him, unless he is crucified with him. And this decree is applicable to all without exception; moreover it is binding on all, and none may ignore it. And whosoever holds back from accepting the mortification of the cross in his body so that the life of the Lord Jesus in his own body is not manifest in imitation, is not worthy in other respects, without that banner of victory, to follow him to the crown."[9]

This emphasis on participation in Christ's suffering as the means to receive His glory is implicitly stated by Paul in Romans 8:17: "We suffer with him, that we may be also glorified together." The Franciscans' insistence on suffering with Christ to receive Christ's glory was established by the example of their founder, Saint Francis of Assisi, who was believed to have received the stigmata, or wounds of Christ. In Bonaventure's words, Francis was "totally transformed into the likeness of Christ crucified, not by the martyrdom of his flesh, but by the fire of his love consuming his soul."[10] Faith and love led here to literal imitation.

Franciscan theologians and the devout of the later Middle Ages were convinced that Christ was their intermediary with God, but they also believed that the intensity of their faith and love could best be shown by voluntarily imitating Christ's suffering. As Latter-day Saints we also recognize that undergoing suffering may be a necessary part of our process of coming unto Christ (D&C 101:4–5). Elder Neal A. Maxwell has noted, however, that we need not volunteer for suffering: "There are many who suffer so much more than the rest of us: some go agonizingly; some go quickly; some are healed; some are given more time; some seem to linger. There are variations in our trials but no immunities. Thus, the scriptures cite the fiery furnace and fiery trials [Daniel 3:6–26; 1 Peter 4:12]. Those who emerge successfully from their varied and fiery furnaces have experienced the grace of the Lord, which He says is sufficient [Ether 12:27]. Even so, brothers and sisters, such emerging individuals do not rush to line up in front of another fiery furnace in order to get an extra turn!"[11] One of the greatest clarifications of the Restoration is not only the reaffirmation that Christ has suffered for us but the further witness that He has truly suffered *with* us in all things (Alma 7:11–13). With this added confidence in the infinite and personal scope of Christ's Atonement we can gain comfort and strength in moments of personal Gethsemane-like experiences.

While clearly emphasizing Christ's suffering with us, rather than our need to suffer with Him to receive the blessings of the Atonement, both the teachings and experiences of modern prophets and apostles point to how the Lord may use our experiences of suffering to help us more fully come unto Christ. The Prophet Joseph Smith taught, "Men have to suffer that they may come upon Mount Zion and be exalted above the heavens."[12] President Marion G. Romney commented on this, saying, "This does not mean that we crave suffering. We avoid all we can. However, we now know, and we all knew when we elected to come into mortality, that we would here be proved in the crucible of adversity and affliction."[13] In recent times we have heard many of the Lord's prophets and apostles testify both of Christ's suffering with us and how their own sufferings have been sanctified to bring them closer to Christ and to enable them to testify of Him.[14]

As Latter-day Saints we can rightly rejoice to know that receiving of the merits of Christ's atonement requires only faith, repentance, baptism, the gift of the Holy Ghost, and enduring in faith on His name (D&C 20:29). At the same time, the late medieval understanding of the imitation of Christ as participating in His suffering can open up new insights for us into the fulness of the Restoration. A noted scholar of late medieval piety has observed that "for ordinary Christian as well as saint, devotion to Christ entailed ritual identification with him."[15] For late medieval Christians, ritual identification with Christ included a physical, mental, or emotional imitation of His suffering, in the belief that "if it so be that we suffer with him, that we may be also glorified together" (Romans 8:17).

I have previously discussed our shared recognition of the spiritual benefits of always remembering Christ through meditation on devotional readings and participation in retracing the events of sacred history. As helpful and beneficial as these practices can be, I believe that as we ponder this less-familiar notion of ritual

identification with Christ, our appreciation and understanding of
the Restoration will be further deepened.

Latter-day Saint scholars' study of the world of the ancient Near
East has helped us to appreciate aspects of temple worship by clari-
fying how sacred time and space allow us to participate in sacred
history. I believe that the late medieval practice of ritual identification can likewise provide helpful insights as we ponder ordinances
such as partaking of the sacrament or baptism. A useful illustration
of this idea of ritual identification can be seen in the ordinance of
baptism. At baptism we take upon ourselves the name of Christ
(Mosiah 5:5–12), a covenant that we renew weekly when we take
the sacrament (D&C 20:77).

An aspect of taking the name of Christ upon us is ritual identification. Paul described baptism in terms of ritual identification:
"For as many of you as have been baptized into Christ have put on
Christ" (Galatians 3:27). When we "put on Christ" through this ordinance, we ritually identify ourselves with Christ. We *imitate* or *participate* in Christ's death, burial, and resurrection. Paul describes
this participation, saying: "Know ye not, that so many of us as were
baptized into Jesus Christ were baptized into his death? Therefore
we are buried with him by baptism into death: that like as Christ
was raised up from the dead by the glory of the Father, even so we
also should walk in newness of life. For if we have been planted
together in the likeness of his death, we shall be also in the likeness
of his resurrection: Knowing this, that our old man is crucified with
him, that the body of sin might be destroyed, that henceforth we
should not serve sin" (Romans 6:3–6). Through our baptism we are
ritually "baptized into his death" and "buried with him by baptism
into death." Likewise, through our baptism we are ritually lifted up
from this death through Christ's atonement and resurrection. Our
submersion also represents the crucifixion of our "old man" of sin
before our ritual "resurrection" that shows how "we also should walk
in newness of life."

There is a clear sense that our ritual participation in Christ's suffering through the ordinance of baptism is an absolute prerequisite
for our receiving all the blessings of the Atonement. We can live in

the world in a different way, in "newness of life," because of the power of the Atonement that is made available through the ordinance of baptism. As we ritually participate in Christ's death, we also ritually receive the blessings of His atoning sacrifice—the ability to rise in the resurrection of the just "in the likeness of his resurrection" and return back to our Father in Heaven.

Let us now return to Paul's statement in Romans 8:17: "We suffer with him, that we may be also glorified together."[16] Unlike the late medieval Christians, we do not interpret this passage to promote the active pursuit of suffering in imitation of Christ. We can, however, see in this connection a model for the participation in sacred history that the ordinances make available to us. Through ritually suffering with Christ, we receive promises that "we may be also glorified together."

Seeing the ordinances as a means to participate in the atonement of Christ not only helps us to appreciate the ordinance of baptism, but it also can increase our understanding of participation in the sacrament and in the ordinances of the temple. In the sacrament we covenant to take the name of Christ upon us, and we literally partake of emblems of Christ's suffering—His body and blood. Our participation in His sacrifice allows us to receive the blessing to "always have his Spirit to be with [us]" (Moroni 4:3). As with baptism, this participation in Christ's suffering prepares and equips us to go forward and live differently in the world, having "put on Christ" (Galatians 3:27).

The temple ordinances can be seen to offer us similar opportunities to participate in the Atonement so that we may receive Christ's glory. President Harold B. Lee commented that "the receiving of the endowment requires the assuming of obligations by covenants which in reality are but an embodiment or an unfolding of the covenants each person should have assumed at baptism."[17] As we ponder the endowment as "an embodiment or an unfolding" of the baptismal covenant, we can begin to more deeply appreciate Christ's invitation to come unto Him and be perfected in Him (Moroni 10:32). Paul suggests how the ordinances make participation possible when he says that "as many of you as have been baptized into Christ have put on Christ" (Galatians 3:27). This "put[ting] on Christ" can be glimpsed in the dedication of the Kirtland Temple when Joseph Smith prayed that "thy servants may go forth from this house armed with thy power, and that thy name may be upon them, and thy glory be round about them" (D&C 109:22). Through the ritual identification of the ordinances, "we suffer with him, that we may be also glorified together" (Romans 8:17).

Christ has invited us, "Come, follow me." We often place the entire burden of this invitation on our own shoulders and thus grow "weary in well-doing" (D&C 64:33). Instead, we should see His invitation as an offer to yoke ourselves to Him through His restored ordinances. When we understand the imitation of Christ as participating in His expiatory suffering and glorious resurrection, His invitation allows us to learn of Him and find rest unto our souls (Matthew 11:28–30). As we take the name of Christ upon us through the ordinances, we are truly connected with the "newness of life" flowing from His atoning sacrifice and victory over the grave.

NOTES

1. An excellent introduction to late medieval piety can be found in Richard Kieckhefer, "Major Currents in Late Medieval Devotion," in *Christian Spirituality: High Middle Ages and Reformation*, ed. Jill Raitt, World Spirituality 17 (New York: Crossroad, 1989), 75–108.

2. See, for example, Gail McMurray Gibson, *The Theater of Devotion: East Anglian Drama and Society in the Late Middle Ages* (Chicago: University of Chicago Press, 1989), 8. A similar assessment of the Franciscans and additional background on the mendicant movements can be found in C. H. Lawrence, *The Friars: The Impact of the Early Mendicant Movement on Western Society* (London: Longman, 1994).

3. Valuable discussion of this literature can be found in Thomas H. Bestul, *Texts of the Passion: Latin Devotional Literature and Medieval Society*, Middle Ages Series (Philadelphia: University of Pennsylvania Press, 1996); see also Denise L. Despres, *Ghostly Sights: Visual Meditation in Late Medieval Literature* (Norman, Okla.: Pilgrim Books, 1989); John V. Fleming, *An Introduction to the Franciscan Literature of the Middle Ages* (Chicago: Franciscan Herald Press, 1977).

4. A helpful discussion of the role of experiential knowledge in late medieval

piety can be found in David Morgan, *Visual Piety: A History and Theory and Popular Religious Images* (Berkeley: University of California Press, 1998), 60–66. I develop the discussion of the theology of participation in the Passion and the spread of this practice in *"Compassio:* Participation in the Passion and Late Medieval Jerusalem Pilgrimage" (Ph.D. diss., Claremont Graduate University, 2003).

5. Ed. M. de la Bigne, *De Spiritualibus Ascensionibus* (Maxima Bibliotheca Veterum Patrum et Antiquorum Scriptorum Ecclesiasticorum, XXVI), Lyons 1677, 273B; quoted in and translated by Eugène Honée, "Image and Imagination in the Medieval Culture of Prayer: A Historical Perspective," in *The Art of Devotion in the Late Middle Ages in Europe, 1300–1500,* ed. Henk van Os (Princeton: Princeton University Press, 1994), 165.

6. Ludolph of Saxony, *The Hours of the Passion taken from* The Life of Christ *by Ludoph the Saxon,* ed. Henry J. Coleridge (London: Burns and Oates, 1887), 7.

7. Ludolph, *Hours of the Passion,* 22.

8. A recent introduction to late medieval Jerusalem pilgrimage can be found in Nine Miedema's "Following the Footsteps of Christ: Pilgrimage and Passion Devotion," in *The Broken Body: Passion Devotion in Late-Medieval Culture,* ed. A. A. MacDonald, H. N. B. Ridderbos and R. M. Schlusemann (Groningen: Egbert Forsten, 1998), 73–92.

9. Bonaventure, "Dominica IV in Quadragesima, Sermo I" in *Opera Omnia,* ed. Peltier, 13:170–71; quoted in and translated by David L. Jeffrey, *The Early English Lyric and Franciscan Spirituality* (Lincoln, Nebr.: University of Nebraska Press, 1975), 55.

10. Bonaventure, *The Soul's Journey into God—The Tree of Life—The Life of St. Francis,* trans. Ewert Cousins (Mahwah, N.J.: Paulist Press, 1978), 306.

11. Neal A. Maxwell, "From Whom All Blessings Flow," *Ensign,* May 1997, 11–12.

12. Joseph Smith, *History of The Church of Jesus Christ of Latter-day Saints,* ed. B. H. Roberts, 2d ed. rev., 7 vols. (Salt Lake City: The Church of Jesus Christ of Latter-day Saints, 1932–51), 5:556.

13. Marion G. Romney, in Conference Report, October 1969, 57; as cited in Howard W. Hunter, "The Opening and Closing of Doors," *Ensign,* November 1987, 59. President Hunter, who knew much suffering in his life, shared these comments: "Being childlike and submitting to our Father's will is not always easy. President Spencer W. Kimball, who also knew a good deal about suffering, disappointment, and circumstances beyond his control, once wrote: 'Being human, we would expel from our lives physical pain and mental anguish and assure ourselves of continual ease and comfort, but if we were to close the doors upon sorrow and distress, we might be excluding our greatest friends and benefactors. Suffering can

make saints of people as they learn patience, long-suffering, and self-mastery' (*Faith Precedes the Miracle,* Salt Lake City: Deseret Book Co., 1972, 98)" (cited in Hunter, "The Opening and Closing of Doors," 54).

14. In addition to Presidents Howard W. Hunter and Spencer W. Kimball, recent examples come to mind in the experiences and statements by such apostles as Elder David B. Haight, Elder Neal A. Maxwell, and Elder Robert D. Hales.

15. Richard Kieckhefer, *Unquiet Souls: Fourteenth-Century Saints and Their Religious Milieu* (Chicago: University of Chicago Press, 1984), 192.

16. The full context of this passage discusses the covenant of baptism. It refers to our adoption as the children of God and our becoming joint-heirs with Christ. This specifically refers to baptism as an adoptive covenant. See my article, "Hebrew Concepts of Adoption and Redemption in the Writings of Paul," in *The Apostle Paul: His Life and His Testimony, The 23d Annual Sidney B. Sperry Symposium,* ed. Paul Y. Hoskisson (Salt Lake City: Deseret Book, 1994), 80–95.

17. Harold B. Lee, *The Teachings of Harold B. Lee: Eleventh President of The Church of Jesus Christ of Latter-day Saints,* ed. Clyde J. Williams (Salt Lake City: Bookcraft, 1996), 574.

8

PRELUDE TO THE PEARL

SWEEPING EVENTS LEADING TO THE DISCOVERY OF THE BOOK OF ABRAHAM

Kerry Muhlestein

In a general conference, Elder John A. Widtsoe of the Quorum of the Twelve Apostles taught that "throughout all the ages of history the hand of God has overruled the actions of mankind, that nothing is done except as the Lord may use it for the accomplishment of his mighty purposes. . . . The things accomplished by humanity become in the end God's accomplishments, as he makes use of them in working out his infinite purposes."[1] Even the great movements of nations and armies often serve to accomplish the workings of the Lord, such as when the empire of Assyria rose to great heights in order that the Lord could "send him against an hypocritical nation [Israel]" (Isaiah 10:6). While Isaiah prophetically informed us of such divine involvement, we are frequently unable to see how the Lord has shaped human affairs to further His work until sufficient time has passed to give us a more keen hindsight. Such retrospection seems to indicate that a series of large and sweeping events opened a window of time in which conditions were

---

Kerry Muhlestein is an assistant professor of history and religion at Brigham Young University–Hawaii.

most suitable for the discovery and transport of the papyri that contained the book of Abraham, and thus the wonderful flood of light
which its doctrine cast upon the gospel. In much the same way that
the Lord prepared the New World so a freedom of religious expression allowed for the Restoration, He also prepared other countries
and peoples so the book of Abraham could further the restoration
of gospel principles.

It is indisputable that the book of Abraham and its attendant
doctrines proved to be a great boon to the fledgling Church and
served to deepen our early leaders' understanding of the gospel. Of
the acquisition of the papyri, the Prophet Joseph wrote that "much
to our joy [we] found that one of the rolls contained the writings of
Abraham, another the writings of Joseph of Egypt, etc.—a more full
account of which will appear in its place, as I proceed to examine or
unfold them. Truly we can say, the Lord is beginning to reveal the
abundance of peace and truth."[2] While the book's value to the Saints
is well known, what is not as clear is that just a short time before
Joseph's reception of the papyri it would have been extremely
unlikely that such a find would be available. Furthermore, not long
after the purchase of the papyri, conditions in Egypt changed such
as to make circumstances less favorable for them to wend their way
out of Egypt and into the American frontier. In the large scheme of
things, there was only a small window of time in which an environment was fostered that lent itself to a set of papyri from Thebes
making its way into the hands of a small group of people in Ohio.

EARLY EXCAVATIONS

The papyri that Joseph Smith purchased seem to have come
from a tomb near Thebes, deep in southern, or Upper, Egypt,[3] and
most likely started their journey from Egypt to America in the early
to mid-1820s.[4] The exportation of goods from Thebes had, until just
before this time, been a rare event. After the conquest of Egypt by
Muslims in the mid-seventh century, access to the country by non-
Muslims was restricted to Cairo and Alexandria. While the addition
of Egypt to the Ottoman Empire in the early sixteenth century

eventually made entrance to the southern portions of the country theoretically possible, in reality no one dared venture south of Giza.[5] Because of a belief in the medicinal qualities of mummies, or at least parts of them, they were regularly exported from at least the thirteenth century onward;[6] but access to Upper Egypt was limited. It was not until 1589 that a record was made of a European traveling to Upper Egypt.[7] From this point onward, a slow trickle of European explorers made their way into Egypt while a similarly minuscule rivulet of Egyptian artifacts made their way to Europe. Pietro de Valle brought back a few intact mummies for display in the early 1600s.[8] The beginnings of small collections of artifacts appeared in the early 1700s. Between 1717 and 1738, men such as Lucas, Pococke, and Norden explored Egypt, brought back some meager antiquities, and published maps and other accounts of their findings.[9] Whole mummies for display also began to make appearances after this. The site of these mummies' excavation is now unknown, but it seems very unlikely that they came from Upper Egypt. Although the intellectual involvement with Egypt and her past increased dramatically during the eighteenth century, the number of expeditions that brought antiquities into Europe before 1790 was still negligible. Certainly, European elite had been prying into Egypt's past for some time via a variety of academic exercises, yet Europe's increasing fascination with and musing about Egypt's ancient intellectual and spiritual culture had not yet brought in a sizeable amount of her material culture.[10]

NAPOLEON'S INVASION OF EGYPT

The watershed event that turned the trickle of antiquities into a surging flood was Napoleon's invasion of Egypt in 1798, just years before the First Vision. Egypt's history and Europe's involvement with Egypt were dramatically and unalterably changed by the Napoleonic naval landing. Napoleon's motivations for his invasion of Egypt were both bold and complicated. Certainly he meant to strike at British dominance in access to the exotic. Egypt controlled the way to India, the jewelstone of Britain's far-flung empire.[11]

Additionally, Napoleon had reportedly become intrigued with pharaonic culture, a near-passion that intertwined itself with a desire to offset a perceived British superiority in the study of Egypt.[12] This influenced Napoleon's decision to make the expedition a scientific exploration as well as a military mission. It also seems certain that part of his aim was to bring Egyptian artifacts back to France, probably as a show of cultural acumen.[13] Moreover, the able general seems to have been partially modeling himself after Alexander the Great, who "liberated" Egypt from foreign rule.[14]

Under the influence of these motivations, Napoleon mounted not only a military force but also an army of intellectual elites, known as the savants, to accompany him on his expedition to Egypt. Thirty-eight thousand men were transported to the coasts of Egypt in 328 ships. Among these were 150 members of the Commission on Arts and Sciences, consisting of civil engineers, mining engineers, physicians, cartographers, zoologists, mathematicians, chemists, botanists, astronomers, archaeologists, artists, printers, geologists, and ancient historians. Most of these did not know of their destination until they were well out to sea.[15]

Napoleon's army easily defeated the adversaries they encountered, and they marched to Thebes and beyond. They fought battles within view of the pyramids, while the ever-dramatic Bonaparte reminded them that forty centuries of history looked down upon them.[16] Upon first beholding the temples of Karnak and Luxor, his soldiers were so impressed that they spontaneously burst into applause and then presented arms to the ancient buildings. Napoleon's savants experienced no lack of material to study. As they traveled up and down the Nile, they busied themselves in both acquiring and copying Egyptian inscriptions and other artifacts. Chief among these inscriptions was the Rosetta stone, an inscription in Greek and two phases of the Egyptian language which would eventually prove to be the key in cracking hieroglyphs and unlocking the voluminous texts of ancient Egypt.

However, not all was fortuitous for this expedition. Exactly a month after the arrival of the French in Egypt, the British located the French fleet of ships and destroyed them. Meanwhile, British diplomats quickly opened communication with the Ottomans, reminding them that Egypt was part of the Ottoman Empire, and volunteering to help wrest it back from French control. A year after his arrival in Egypt, Napoleon abandoned his men and fled from the country. The French force remained for some time, during which the savants continued their frenzied study. Eventually the Ottoman sultan sent a military force, which was accompanied by an eager British expedition, to oust the French. Nearly three years after their arrival, the French army surrendered in 1801.

The disposition of gathered antiquities became an important part of the terms of surrender. Article 16 of the formal capitulation agreement dictated that all artifacts collected by the French would become the property of the combined armies of the Ottomans and the British. A few antiquities were allowed to return to France, along with the drawings and papers of the savants.[17] The Ottoman Turks seemed to have had no interest in the larger Egyptian artifacts and were apparently surprised that possession of such was the only demand of the British for their part in the conflict. And so, the great prizes were claimed by the British, who seemed to want them as much to demonstrate that they had taken France's goods as for their own sake.[18] The Rosetta stone was apparently recognized for its value and was sent to England on a ship of its own.

The three years of study did not prove to be a complete disappointment to the French intellectuals. A member of the commission was soon able to publish an account of the expedition. Some time thereafter the official publication of the Commission on Arts and Sciences was made available. It was called *Description de l'Égypte* and consisted of several volumes. One volume contained giant-sized folio pages with drawings of Egypt and her architecture and artifacts. An atlas also accompanied the publication, and all these works received a wide circulation. With the release of the maps, stories, and images, public interest in Egypt exploded. European imagination was caught up in the seeming romance and mystery of such an ancient and splendor-filled culture. Soon many of the European countries were involved in frenzied efforts to satisfy the intellectual demand for knowledge of Egypt. The information about Egypt that was made available via the publications of the French expedition made such efforts all the more possible.

MUHAMMAD ALI'S INFLUENCE

The increased knowledge of Egypt and incessant curiosity about it were not the only outcomes of Napoleon's infiltration that fostered an environment of artifact export and exploitation. "It happened that in the expeditionary force sent by the sultan to Egypt was a young man, Muhammad Ali, who changed the history of Egypt. Napoleon's expedition revealed the might of Europe, but Muhammad Ali was one of the few who understood the source of that might and attempted to bring Egypt into the modern world by borrowing from the West."[19] Ali was an Albanian with an acumen for political maneuvering who, shortly after serving as an important officer in the force that expelled the French, became de facto ruler of Egypt; within four years he managed to get himself appointed pasha, or high official, of Egypt. Ali wanted very much to modernize Egypt, and he engaged in a game of playing countries against each other. He was largely successful in this endeavor because the contest for Egypt between France and Britain continued, but the battlefield had shifted to artifact acquisition—and Ali held all the currency for the contest. It was to Ali that Champollion—the man who eventually deciphered hieroglyphs—went for permission to study inscriptions in Egypt. It was through Ali that permission was obtained to bring major monuments out of Egypt and into France and England. For example, in exchange for help in modernizing his country, Ali negotiated the acquisition of several obelisks by these two countries, who engaged in a number of dealings with the Egyptian leader in an effort to obtain whatever obelisk the other country had desired.[20] As the fascination with Egyptian antiquities increased, Ali, who was puzzled over interest in such ancient pieces, was liberal in granting requests for artifacts, since these Europeans "were thereby indebted, at no perceived cost, to Mohammed Ali and his government."[21]

The desire for Egyptian collections was not restricted to competition between France and Britain, though they were often the major players. Many other countries, most notably Austria and Italy, also vied for pieces of Egyptian history. Most modern European countries sent a consul to Egypt, and these consuls competed so fiercely in collecting Egyptian antiquities that the period came to be known as the War of the Consuls.[22] "The Consuls and their collections began the process that would culminate in the Egyptian Museum and the Egyptian Antiquities Service in the second half of the century, but Egypt in the early 1800s was regarded as a source of antiquities for European (and later American) national museums whose displays would reflect the prestige of the home state, not of Egypt."[23] The widespread, frantic, and unrestrained deportation of artifacts that ensued was closer to wholesale looting than to excavation.

Excavators of Artifacts

Napoleon's military expeditions had another curious effect that contributed to the climate of the War of the Consuls. Because of the reaction in France against men who were seen as loyal to Napoleon—the so-called Bonapartists—a great many men who had served with Napoleon were unable to return to their home countries. For example, Bernardino Drovetti, who was appointed by Napoleon as the French consul to Egypt, decided to remain in Egypt due to his fear of the French royal family after the French government changed hands. He became a trusted adviser to Ali. Another Bonapartist refugee was Antonio Lebolo, the man who would exhume the papyri that later came into the possession of Joseph Smith.

Drovetti proved to be one of the most energetic of Egyptian exporters. He competed first and foremost with Henry Salt, the consul for Britain. These two men employed a number of people in their efforts to obtain Egyptian artifacts. The competition between them and other consuls gave rise to some of the most colorful characters of Egyptology and an era of uncontrolled and chaotic extraction and exchange of Egyptian goods. Between the two of them, Salt and Drovetti acquired enough artifacts to create the foundation of the Egyptian collection in the British Museum, the Louvre, the Turin Museum, and countless "curiosity cabinets" and private collections.[24] This was a period of excavation by explosion and coat-closet conservation.

Inexplicably, many of the most famous and successful of these hired "excavators" were Italians. Salt hired Giovanni Battista Caviglia, a Genoan who spent a great deal of time exploring the pyramids and Sphinx of Giza.[25] Salt later hired a man who would become the most famous of these maverick explorer-excavators: Giovanni Belzoni. This Italian giant had served as a strongman in a circus before embarking on one of the most successful careers of Egyptian treasure hunting that the world has known.

More apropos to our subject was Drovetti's hiring of the Italian Antonio Lebolo, who was also a political refugee.[26] Lebolo directed excavations under Drovetti's behest for a number of years. As Drovetti turned his attention towards helping Ali in his role as adviser to the pasha, he left much of the acquisition of Egyptian antiquities to Lebolo. It was Lebolo who played official host to visitors in Upper Egypt, and in his work he sometimes oversaw hundreds of men. Lebolo became so ensconced in this role, especially in Thebes, that he was even referred to by some as the new king of Thebes.[27] Apparently wanting to leave his mark behind, Lebolo went so far as to carve his name into one of the pillars of Karnak, much as ancient Egyptian kings had done. While thus employed, Lebolo was able to send off a host of goods to European countries.

Lebolo's fortunes took something of a downturn when Drovetti lost his post as consul due to the political reversals in France. While Drovetti continued as an adviser to Pasha Ali, he could no longer afford to pay Lebolo. Since both men were aware that the antiquities business was lucrative and a viable option for political refugees such as themselves, Lebolo agreed to continue working for Drovetti under the conditions that after meeting quotas of goods which were under Drovetti's control, Lebolo could then extricate as many goods

as he could for personal profit.[28] Thus, the pace of chaotic excavation increased.

The sheer quantity of goods available made a great many of
them commonplace among such excavators as Lebolo. He reportedly lived in a tomb that was filled with mummies, statues, and
papyri, and used a bas-relief stone for his door. He burned ancient
coffins for his firewood and bought goods that local Arabs sold willy-
nilly.[29] He was not alone in this type of behavior. We know of other
excavators who destroyed anything similar to the antiquities they
were trying to sell, in order to increase their value.[30] Almost certainly
it was during these days as "king of Thebes" that Lebolo exhumed
the mummies in which the papyri containing the book of Abraham
were found.

The fascination with Egyptian things that held sway in Europe
also captured the American imagination. With fewer antiquities
entering the New World than Europe, those that did come drew
considerable public attention. It was just such circumstances that
prompted a later owner of the papyri, Michael Chandler, to purchase the mummies and scrolls in America in an attempt to earn a
living off of them. Chandler traveled with his mummies and papyri
throughout the countryside, charging admission to any who would
come to see them. After some time he tired of the lifestyle this produced and determined to sell them. While exhibiting the collection
in Ohio, Chandler came into contact with the Prophet Joseph
Smith, who felt inspired to purchase the collection, and soon thereafter made the happy discovery outlined above—the Lord had
brought another prophetic record to the Church. Thus the demand
for Egyptian antiquities had drawn the book of Abraham out of
Egypt, into Europe, through the United States, and into the
Prophet's keeping, for the purpose of enlightening the Lord's
covenant people.

Fortunately for the field of Egyptology, the heyday of chaotic
excavation and exchange was short-lived. While the battle for
museum prestige pieces continued, some control was brought to the
deportation of antiquities. In the mid-nineteenth century, the pasha
created a National Antiquities Service, and soon Auguste Mariette

was put in charge. About this same time the Egyptian Museum was founded, and Mariette ensured that most of Egypt's finds thenceforth remained in Egypt. To be sure, black-market antiquities have never been completely curtailed; but the War of the Consuls was over, and the flood of exiting artifacts began to be dammed.

IMPLICATIONS

During the roughly fifty years we have just examined, conditions in Egypt were such that scores of mummies, papyri, and other artifacts flowed almost completely uninhibited from Egypt to Europe and America. This small window of time was concurrent with the infant days of the Church. Undoubtedly, had the Lord intended to bring the book of Abraham to the Prophet Joseph in other circumstances, He could have. Yet it seems that the swirling movements of the nations swept that which was much needed by the Church into the hands of the Prophet at a crucial time. As Elder Widtsoe said, "The hand of God has overruled the actions of mankind. . . . Nothing is done except as the Lord may use it for the accomplishment of his mighty purposes."[31]

We cannot assume that as the Lord accomplishes His work, all the specific actions of individuals involved in that work are thus justified. Even as the Lord said He used the king of Assyria in order to punish Israel, He also stipulated that the king did not have righteous intentions nor did he give credit to the Lord (Isaiah 10:7–15). As a result, this instrument of the Lord was punished, even for actions that fulfilled the Lord's will. In a similar manner, we are not safe in construing that Napoleon, Lebolo, Drovetti, or Ali, though they all played some role in the appearance of the book of Abraham, were doing so with righteous intent nor that all their actions were acceptable. Certainly, much of the climate that allowed Lebolo to extricate and export mummies and papyri was full of self-serving and ignoble acts. As Latter-day Saints we need not condone any of the actions that led to the discovery of the book of Abraham by our beloved Prophet. Yet, equally certainly, the large events and chaotic circumstances of the time made it possible for such a blessing to take place. For this, we are grateful.

NOTES

1. John A. Widtsoe, in Conference Report, October 1927, 25.

2. Joseph Smith, *History of The Church of Jesus Christ of Latter-day Saints,* ed. B. H. Roberts, 2d ed. rev., 7 vols. (Salt Lake City: The Church of Jesus Christ of Latter-day Saints, 1932–51), 2:236.

3. For information about the original location of the mummies and papyri, see H. Donl Peterson, *The Story of the Book of Abraham: Mummies, Manuscripts, and Mormonism* (Salt Lake City: Deseret Book, 1995), 53–62.

4. See Peterson, *Story of the Book of Abraham,* 70.

5. See Giovanni Belzoni, *Belzoni's Travels: Narrative of the Operations and Recent Discoveries in Egypt and Nubia,* ed. Alberto Siliotti, trans. Richard Pierce (London: The British Museum Press, 2001), 13.

6. See Kerry Muhlestein, "European Views of Egyptian Magic and Mystery," *BYU Studies* (forthcoming).

7. See Anonimo Veneziano (Anonymous Venetian), *Viagio Che O Fato L'anno 1589, dal Caiero in Ebrin navigando su per el nilo* (n.p., 1589).

8. See John Baines and Jaromir Malek, *Cultural Atlas of Ancient Egypt,* rev. ed. (New York: Checkmark Books, 2000), 22.

9. See Muhlestein, "European Views," 3; see also Belzoni, *Travels,* 14, 18.

10. See Muhlestein, "European Views," 3, 7–8.

11. See Fekri A. Hassan, "Imperialist Appropriations of Egyptian Obelisks," in *Views of Ancient Egypt Since Napoleon Bonaparte: Imperialism, Colonialism and Modern Appropriations,* ed. David Jeffreys (London: University College London Press, 2003), 23.

12. See David Jeffreys, "Two Hundred Years of Ancient Egypt: Modern History and Ancient Archaeology," in *Views of Ancient Egypt Since Napoleon Bonaparte: Imperialism, Colonialism and Modern Appropriations,* ed. David Jeffreys (London: University College London Press, 2003), 1–2.

13. See Morris L. Bierbrier, "Art and Antiquities for Government's Sake," in *Views of Ancient Egypt since Napoleon Bonaparte: Imperialism, Colonialism and Modern Appropriations,* ed. David Jeffreys (London: University College London Press, 2003), 70. See also J. C. Herold, *Bonaparte in Egypt* (London: Hamish Hamilton, 1963).

14. Jeffreys, "Two Hundred Years," 1.

15. See Mark Lehner, *The Complete Pyramids* (London: Thames and Hudson, Ltd., 1997), 46; Peterson, *Story of the Book of Abraham,* 38.

16. See Napoleon Bonaparte, Correspondance de Napoléon Ier; publiée par ordre de l'empereur Napoléon III (Paris: Impr. Imprériale, 1858–69), 29:450.

17. See Bierbrier, "Art and Antiquities," 71–73.

18. See Bierbrier, "Art and Antiquities," 73–74.

19. Yahya Armajani and Thomas M. Ricks, *Middle East: Past and Present* (Englewood Cliffs, N.J.: Prentice-Hall, 1986), 177. For an example of British help in modernizing Egypt, see Albert Hourani, *A History of the Arab Peoples* (Cambridge, Mass.: Harvard University Press, 1991), 267.

20. See Hassan, "Imperialist Appropriations," 61.

21. Bierbrier, "Art and Antiquities," 74.

22. See Belzoni, *Belzoni's Travels,* 26.

23. Bierbrier, "Art and Antiquities," 75.

24. See Nicolas-Christophe Grimal, *A History of Ancient Egypt* (Cambridge: Blackwell, 1992), 9; see also Lehner, *Complete Pyramids,* 48; Jeffreys, "Two Hundred Years," 4.

25. See Lehner, *Complete Pyramids,* 48–49.

26. The reason for this situation is not understood. We only gather it from a letter from a journal entry of Belzoni, in which he records that Lebolo had "left Piedmont after the fall of the late government," meaning the Napoleonic government. See Belzoni, *Travels,* 197. See also Peterson, *Story of the Book of Abraham,* 44.

27. See Peterson, *Story of the Book of Abraham,* 47.

28. See Peterson, *Story of the Book of Abraham,* 54.

29. See Peterson, *Story of the Book of Abraham,* 47–48.

30. See Muhlestein, "European Views," 7.

31. Widtsoe, in Conference Report, October 1927, 25.

9

WHAT WE HOLD SO DEAR

RELIGIOUS TOLERATION AS A PRECONDITION TO THE RESTORATION

David Pigott

*C*onsidering the widespread religious intolerance and intense persecution during the early years of the Latter-day Saint Church, many may be surprised to learn that the United States in the early 1800s was a religiously tolerant place, relatively speaking. The Restoration of the gospel occurred at the dawn of an era when most people agreed that religious pluralism was a positive attribute of an increasingly complex society. Indeed, the increasing complexity of society led to the necessary acceptance of religious toleration, making the United States in the early nineteenth century the most religiously diverse and tolerant nation on earth. However, the widespread acceptance of religious toleration as a civic virtue is a relatively modern development. Barely two generations before Joseph Smith's First Vision, religious toleration was the exception rather than the norm among the vast majority of Christians, both in America and in Europe, where the idea of toleration among a growing number of Christian faiths began.

David Pigott is a history professor at Brigham Young University–Idaho.

Despite the risk of oversimplification, even a cursory study of some of the contributing ideas concerning the development of religious toleration may be of use in our continued efforts to understand modern religious pluralism. Religious toleration is so fundamental to our own culture and so necessary to peace abroad, yet few understand its precarious origins and the innumerable sacrifices made to contribute to its eventual acceptance. Nor do we fully understand the ideas of toleration within the context of the restored gospel.

The most striking reason for the relatively widespread level of religious toleration in America around the time of Joseph Smith was the First Amendment to the Constitution of the United States, which had been written by the Founding Fathers. They, as we know through modern revelation, received divine inspiration in creating this nation: "for this purpose have I established the Constitution of this land, by the hands of wise men whom I raised up unto this very purpose" (D&C 101:80). Such men as Thomas Jefferson, James Madison, Benjamin Franklin, and John Adams learned from and built upon liberal ideas percolating in Europe, specifically France and England. Those ideas argued for equality before the law, an end to feudal privilege, religious toleration, and the need for a secular government detached from religious affinity. Religious toleration was an idea that influenced these inspired men and others like them. It was an idea that gradually gained wide acceptance.

LONG-STANDING INTOLERANCE

Religious toleration today does not have the same meaning it did fifteen hundred (or even five hundred) years ago. Today it connotes a type of noble compassion, an acknowledgment of nonessential differences allowed to exist for the sake of civility; "to bear or endure; to nourish, sustain or preserve."[1] This modern definition of *toleration* was widely accepted only in the late 1700s as the accepted definition of *tolerance;* the concept evolved into a positive meaning in an effort to maintain social unity at the expense of religious unity which had been shattered in the previous two centuries. *Toleration* had an ambiguous and indeterminable definition throughout the Middle Ages. The medieval precept expressed by Pope Stephen V in 817 summed up the general mentality throughout the Middle Ages: *quaedum tolerantur, non imperantur* ("whatsoever is tolerated, is not ruled").[2] Centuries later, during the Protestant Reformation, religious toleration was seen as a form of weakness and as tacit approval for illicit actions, or, as religious historian Elisabeth Labrousse asserts, "a distasteful habit of lax complacency."[3]

A consistent theme in the development of religious toleration within Christianity was the tendency for those institutions that held predominant power (either religious or political) to exercise prejudice towards dissenting ideologies. This tradition received imperial support when Emperor Constantine empowered Catholic bishops with judicial authority at the Council of Nicaea (325). From this point onward, a repeating pattern of intolerance toward dissenting beliefs (especially within Christianity but later targeted also toward non-Christians) became common.[4] This tradition continued largely unabated throughout the Middle Ages, when persecution of dissident faiths or beliefs was a common occurrence. Among other methods of coercion for the sake of political and social unity were the various crusades against rival forms of Christianity in the thirteenth and fourteenth centuries and the Inquisition.

Things changed during the Reformation, however, as new ideas (and the religions they spawned) became so widespread that resources proved insufficient to suppress them any longer. During the Protestant Reformation, experimental attempts were made to mediate the growing hostilities between Protestants and Catholics and to offer some form of legitimacy to the upstart religions. These attempts included the Peace of Augsburg (1555) and later the Peace of Westphalia (1648) which ended the Thirty Years' War. However, these treaties proved more political truces rather than long-term solutions to the problem of tolerating a minority religion, and hostilities resumed.[5] This pattern was broken only after the Protestant Reformation proved too formidable an adversary, one which medieval Christianity could not overpower.

COLONIAL AMERICA

Central to the development of toleration was the rise of secular governments, weary of the violence and destruction attached to religious dogmatism. Indeed, no such thing as religious liberty existed before colonial America—and there, only in the colony of Rhode Island, which was established by Roger Williams, who insisted on the distinct separation of church and state. Williams had been cast out of the Massachusetts Bay Colony and labeled an atheist for his desire to take God out of government.[6] Religious freedom was the primary reason behind the *Mayflower* expedition to the New World. True to the pattern mentioned above, however, once these freedoms had been attained through the establishment of a state-church hierarchy, the Pilgrims promptly denied the same freedoms to those Europeans who followed, unless they were of the same religion.[7] Nathaniel Ward, a pastor in the early years of the Massachusetts Bay Colony, proudly declared the general mentality of the American settlers of the seventeenth century: "God does nowhere in his world tolerate Christian states to give toleration to such aversaries [sic] of his truth, if they have power in their hands to suppress them."[8]

Such was the general attitude towards religious diversity in a land destined to serve as a beacon to future nations of toleration and freedom. Each colonial government was closely linked to the majority religion which had founded it: Anglicanism in Virginia, Dutch Reformed in New York, Catholicism in Maryland, Congregationalism in Massachusetts, and so forth. Other than Rhode Island, only Pennsylvania showed any tolerance for immigrants of different faiths, as it was not linked to a state-sponsored church.[9] Throughout most of the colonies, Catholics were particularly discriminated against. Indeed, the Massachusetts Bay Colony statute of 1647 specifically targeted "Jesuits, priests, and missionaries" to be "treated as 'an enemy to the true Christian religion.'"[10]

Where did the Puritans who settled this continent get these ideas that tolerance was something to be avoided at all costs? From their homelands in Europe. We will begin here with the development of toleration theories stemming from the Protestant Reformation.

CONFLICT DURING THE REFORMATION

One of the earliest to understand the importance of religious toleration to the stability of society was the great humanist Sir Thomas More. In his *Utopia* More described a land where "everyone was free to practise what religion he liked, and to try and convert other people to his own faith, provided he did it quietly and politely, by rational argument."[11] More wrote *Utopia* in 1516, just before society was torn apart because of the actions of Martin Luther. More remained a devout Catholic his entire life and should not be considered a "reformer" per se. However, his *Utopia* contains many elements of religious toleration and moderation, influencing future theorists on the subject. Religious toleration in the "Land of Nowhere" (Utopia) stood in stark contrast to the long-held tradition of religious intolerance and persecution in medieval Europe. Unaware of the profound effect *Utopia* would have on future thinkers, Thomas More ironically turned out to be one of the many "great religious reformers [who] began to throw off the rituals and dogmas that had been attached to Christianity during the dark ages and sought to return to the pure and simple truths of the New Testament," as Elder L. Tom Perry reminds us.[12]

Another of these reformers was Desiderius Erasmus. In his voluminous writings Erasmus only rarely mentions religious toleration directly. However, throughout his works "certain major themes . . . implied a tolerant attitude toward religious differences. . . . His philosophy of Christ made him oppose violence and fanaticism of any kind."[13] Writing to a colleague about the endemic violence erupting from Luther's movement, Erasmus emphasized the need for continued vigilance in the pursuit of truth, "not by taunts and threats, not by force of arms and injustice, but by simple discretion . . . by gentleness and tolerance."[14] Erasmus's most famous work, *The Praise of Folly* (1509), offered a satirical look at humanity's weaknesses, poking particular fun at the many eccentricities that had crept into the various monastic orders, while at the same time reminding the reader how far off course the current form of Christianity had deviated:

"One monk will point to his paunch, distended by eating every conceivable variety of fish; another will pour forth psalms by the bushel. Another will number up his myriads of fasts, and account for his bursting belly by the fact that he eats only one meal at mid-day. Another points to his huge pile of ceremonies performed, so many they couldn't be laden on seven naval transports. Another brags that for sixty years he has never touched money except with fingers protected by two pairs of gloves. Still another wears a cowl so dirty and slimy that no sailor would let it touch his body. Another boasts that for more than half a century he has led the life of a sponge, always fixed to the same spot. . . . But Christ, interrupting their boasts (which otherwise would never end) will ask, 'Where did this new race of Jews come from? I recognize no law but my own, and about it I hear nothing whatever. Long ago, speaking openly and using no intricate parables, I promised that my father's kingdom would be granted, not to cowls, prayers, or fasts, but to works of faith and charity.'"[15]

Sadly, Erasmus's message of reform within Catholicism often fell on deaf ears, and he became embroiled in the religious controversies that shook European life to its very foundations. An early supporter of Martin Luther's actions in Germany, Erasmus saw Luther become increasingly dogmatic and intolerant toward differing interpretations of scripture. As a result, Erasmus distanced himself from the German reformer and father of the Reformation and remained wholly devoted to changing Christian devotion from within the Catholic Church.

Usually, when one thinks of the great leaders of the Reformation, Martin Luther and John Calvin are the first to come to mind. It may seem ironic that as mature leaders of the two most powerful Protestant movements (later termed Lutheranism and Calvinism), both Luther and Calvin proved just as intolerant—and in the case of Calvin, perhaps more so—than the Catholic Church had been toward their reforms. Early in Luther's career as a reformer, his attitude toward heretics was mild, condemning the killing of heretics to solve the problem of discord—he was, after all, a heretic himself in the eyes of the Catholic Church. Indeed, in 1523 Luther argued that no authority other than God Himself can hold sway over a man's beliefs: "Since, then, belief or unbelief is a matter of every one's conscience, and since this is no lessening of the secular power, the latter should be content and attend to its own affairs and permit men to believe one thing or another, as they are able and willing, and constrain no one by force."[16] This and similar references to the separation of the secular from the religious have led many to interpret in Luther the seedlings of the eventual separation of church and state, and he did remain consistent on his views that no authority can force a person to believe what that person does not believe voluntarily. However, for Luther, the freedom afforded the Christian was purely spiritual. Put bluntly, one could believe anything but could not act on those beliefs unless they were consistent with societal, political, and religious conventions.

Luther's early views on the role of secular authority contrast sharply with his later writings after his movement had taken shape and he had plenty of support from the German nobility in his struggle against Rome. Shortly after Luther witnessed the violent uprisings in Germany (after 1524) following his official break with Rome and he saw the many sects that followed his lead and formed their own communities (specifically the Anabaptists), his attitude toward religious dissenters echoed that of his Catholic rivals. Due to continued frustrations at establishing the kingdom of God on earth, by 1536 Luther insisted in his typically vitriolic tone that "secular authority is held to reprimand blasphemy, false doctrines and heresy and to inflict corporal pain on those who support such" (author's translation).[17] We should not read too much into Luther's refusal to condone a religiously pluralistic society. As a product of feudal Germany, Luther still retained the medieval concept that Christian society must be unified, that the Christian princes of western Europe held a fundamental obligation to uphold the Christian faith—naturally, as Luther interpreted how that faith should be practiced. With few exceptions, the rest of Europe generally agreed.

The separation of church and state, a value held dear today, was ·
inconceivable. The idea of religious coexistence, that one could be ·
of a different religion and still be a loyal subject of one's sovereign,
was considered too radical a notion for nearly all sixteenth-century
society. Again with few exceptions, the vast majority of Protestants,
themselves products of Catholicism in more ways than not,
enforced conformity on their various members, just as Catholics had
done for centuries previously.

As the Saints did in the early years of the restored Church, so
the persecuted sects of the sixteenth and seventeenth centuries
interpreted intolerance towards their beliefs as a sign of election.
The New Testament is replete with the Lord's description of persecution being a hallmark of the true church: "Blessed are ye, when
men shall hate you" (Luke 6:22); "And ye shall be hated of all men
for my name's sake" (Mark 13:13; Luke 21:17). What is alarming
compared to the persecutions inflicted on members of the restored
Church in the mid-nineteenth century is that the Reformation
churches tended to return the abuse in kind—hatred for hatred,
resentment for resentment—against the Catholic Church trying to
stem the tide of religious change, as well as against breakaway sects
from within Protestantism. Nephi saw this era in his vision of "a
church which is most abominable above all other churches which
slayeth the saints of God" (1 Nephi 13:5).

There were during these times of trouble, however, a few
calmer minds who felt that even the Catholic Church had no right
passing judgment on a man's conscience; only Christ personally held
that power. One of the earliest defenders of man's inherent right to
"the privilege of worshiping Almighty God according to the dictates
of [his] own conscience," as we read in the eleventh Article of Faith,
was Sebastien Castellio, a man of great historical significance in the
development of religious toleration. The life of Castellio (1515–63)
is indelibly linked to that of John Calvin, the great father of the reformation that was then occurring in Geneva and that within a few
decades spread to France, the Netherlands, Scotland, and finally
America under the Puritans.

Castellio gained some acclaim in his attack on the methods

Calvin used to govern in Geneva, which he ruled essentially as a theocracy. (Rival Catholics across the border in France called Calvin the "Pope of Geneva.") In 1553 Calvin ordered the execution of Michael Servetus, with whom Calvin had corresponded for years beforehand. Servetus was extremely outspoken in his beliefs: He doubted the divinity of Christ and the relationship between Him and the Father, and he was involved in other heresies. For these beliefs, the last few years of Servetus's life were spent fleeing the Inquisition, living in secret as he was pursued by Protestant and Catholic authorities alike. He passed through Geneva on his way to Italy to seek refuge only to be recognized, imprisoned, tried, and burned at the stake at Calvin's order.[18]

Immediately after Servetus's painful death, Castellio published an attack on the methods used to convict him, accusing Calvin and all religions of participating in a thousand years of hypocrisy and intolerance, correctly noting that after the pagans stopped persecuting Christians in the Roman era, the Christians, emboldened by imperial support, began to persecute pagans and other Christians; the tradition had only worsened since the Reformation: "I can discover no more than this, that we regard those as heretics with whom we disagree. This is evident from the fact that today there is scarcely one of our innumerable sects that does not look upon the rest as heretics, so that if you are orthodox in one city or region, you are held for a heretic in the next."[19]

A continuous theme throughout Castellio's refutation of Calvin was that all people believe in the truth of their religion and that one's beliefs are personal, as is the interpretation of scripture. The Prophet Joseph Smith took a similar stance in the heat of severe persecutions against him when he declared, "If any man is authorized to take away my life because he thinks and says I am a false teacher, then, upon the same principle, we should be justified in taking away the life of every false teacher, and where would be the end of blood?"[20]

Castellio concluded his tract against Calvin by asserting that constraint in religion forces people to pretend to believe so as to avoid public condemnation and that the Lord hated hypocrisy more

than any of man's other vices.[21] In a time when priesthood authority was taken from the earth and men and women were left to
search for the truth using only their limited understanding of scripture, Castellio advocated charity and tolerance in the name of
peace. In this respect he anticipated our modern governments.

In our modern and "enlightened" society, Castellio's ideas seem
obvious, even puerile. However, put in a sixteenth-century context,
his views on toleration were revolutionary. His idea that a person's
religion did not necessarily infringe upon his loyalty as a subject to
the king had a great influence on future mediators in the widening
religious conflict, especially in France, which had experienced
nearly forty years of continuous religious bloodshed. As early as
1561, at the beginning of these wars of religion in France, the small
minority of religious moderates known as the *politiques* and led by
Chancellor Michel de l'Hôpital realized that what was at stake with
the Huguenots' (French Calvinists) insistence to worship freely was
"not a question of constituting a religion, but of constituting a
republic; and some can be citizens without being [Catholics]: even
the excommunicated do not cease to be citizens."[22] L'Hôpital's ability to separate religion from government anticipated the *philosophes*
of the French Enlightenment by more than a hundred years.

The French wars of religion lasted nearly forty years and dev-
astated Europe's most powerful kingdom. Hostilities temporarily
ended at the signing of the Edict of Nantes (1598), which allowed
limited toleration of the estimated one million Huguenots living in
France.[23] The Edict of Nantes was relatively short-lived and was
revoked under the absolutist rule of Louis XIV in 1685 for the sake
of religious and political unity. Huguenot ministers were given the
choice of exile or death; laypeople were required to convert to the
French Catholic Church (often at gunpoint) or die for their faith.
Virtually all converted publicly while continuing to worship in the
Calvinist tradition in secret. Although they were prohibited from
fleeing the kingdom by order of Louis XIV, an estimated two hundred thousand skilled Huguenot craftsmen and merchants fled
France for lands where they could worship without persecution:
Holland, England, America, Prussia, and even South Africa profited

from this exodus. The French kingdom under Louis XIV was perhaps the least tolerant of all "civilized" nations of its day: Jacques-Benigne Bossuet, the great Catholic apologist under Louis XIV, boasted in 1691 that Catholicism was the least tolerant of all religions.[24]

ENLIGHTENMENT IDEALS

Louis's infamous Revocation of the Edict of Nantes inspired one of the greatest contributors to the eventually accepted notion that peace can be attained amidst religious diversity: John Locke (1632–1704). When news of the Revocation was released, Locke was exiled to Holland. Locke was a Puritan who had fled the resurgent Catholic monarchy in England. He had already gained significant recognition in England and France as a philosopher, and he would become one of the founding fathers of the Enlightenment. After the widespread distribution of Locke's works, the ideas formulated by men like Castellio in the sixteenth century would come to maturity and gain general acceptance by the educated minds of Europe.[25]

Locke's *Letter Concerning Toleration* (1689) was the culmination of decades of deep reflection on the role of the magistrate in religious matters and was influenced by the political and religious uncertainties taking place in England under the overtly Catholic James II. Locke wrote the *Letter* while in exile in Holland, which at that time was a haven for exiles due to its liberal policies toward religious dissidents. Although the constitution in Holland still officially maintained a state-sponsored church (Dutch Reformed), the Low Countries were perhaps the best example in early-modern Europe of religious coexistence because dogmatism and intolerance were overlooked in the name of peace and commerce. Locke begins his *Letter* with a summation of its message: "I esteem that toleration to be the chief characteristical mark of the true church . . . for every one is orthodox to himself."[26] He defends this point throughout in typically Lockean prose: "The toleration of those that differ from others in matters of religion, is so agreeable to the Gospel of Jesus

Christ, and to the genuine reason of mankind, that it seems monstrous for men to be so blind." Locke was more clear in expressing the need for separating church and state than any of his predecessors, and he anticipates Doctrine and Covenants 134 concerning the relationship between religious institutions and civil government: "It is not my business to inquire here into the original of the power or dignity of the clergy. This only I say, that whencesoever their authority be sprung, since it is ecclesiastical, it ought to be confined within the bounds of the church, nor can it in any manner be extended to civil affairs; because the church itself is a thing absolutely separate and distinct from the commonwealth. The boundaries on both sides are fixed and immoveable. He jumbles heaven and earth together, the things most remote and opposite, who mixes these societies, which are, in their origin, end, business, and in every thing, perfectly distinct, and infinitely different from each other."[27]

Therefore, according to Locke, the sovereign was required to tolerate all religions that did not threaten the civil government. In Locke's view, toleration was much more effective at safeguarding the people than was repression, which bred recriminations and long-standing rivalries detrimental to the general prosperity. As Castellio argued, a government that mandated conformity to one religion merely reinforced hypocrisy among its subjects.[28] Along these lines, Locke echoes the sentiments of Roger Williams in colonial America, advocating toleration for all within the bounds of civil law.

More than any other event, the eventual acceptance of religious toleration was due to the long-lasting effect of the Protestant Reformation. The creation of several rival religions in short succession made it impossible for the Catholic Church to suppress them as it had successfully done before. What made the Protestant Reformation different from previous schisms within Christianity was the rapid growth in converts made possible by the effectiveness of the printing press, invented in the previous century. Greater access to printed materials made it impossible for the Church to control the growing number of readers of inflammatory pamphlets attacking the clergy; Luther's *Ninety-five Theses* was only one of many dozens that soon followed, attacking clerical abuses and fomenting rebellion.[29]

As the number of sects grew, so too did the need for peaceful coexistence among them and a government that was above the fray of disputes. Enlightenment thinkers such as Montesquieu, Voltaire, Jefferson, Franklin, and Thomas Paine all insisted on the innate freedom to follow one's conscience unrestrained by political pressures. Some of these great leaders were antagonistic toward any form of organized religion but fought vehemently for the freedom to believe according to one's conscience, even if they might not agree with those beliefs.

Thus, the centuries of religious conflict resulted in the development of a healthy skepticism as to the veracity of any one religion over another one—healthy because without this skepticism from the Founding Fathers, it is likely that the newly formed United States would have continued in the tradition of state-sponsored churches, thus perpetuating intolerance. Voltaire, perhaps the greatest writer of his day, commented insightfully on the need for religious diversity. Concerned over the atrocities he witnessed committed against Huguenots worshiping clandestinely to avoid penalties, Voltaire defined religious tolerance as "the endowment of humanity . . . the first law of nature." Advocating greater, not less religious diversity, he continued: "If there are two religions in your country, they will cut one another's throats; if there are thirty of them, they will live in peace."[30]

Secularization was a positive development in advancing the idea of religious toleration. It was also a necessary environment for the gospel to be restored. If there had been only one state religion in America in the early 1800s, Joseph Smith's efforts would have had a much more concentrated opposition. That there were dozens of sects allowed the restored gospel to take root. This is not to minimize the harsh persecutions experienced by the early Saints. However, it could have been worse. As we have seen, when only two religions exist, they will usually become rivals; when many religions exist, a climate of toleration is much more likely.

CONCLUSION

Why consider the idea of tolerance as a priority at a time when The Church of Jesus Christ of Latter-day Saints is well established in the developed world and when religion in general seems to be falling prey to the growing skepticism of absolute truth? As the Church grows, its members will continue to come in contact with cultural traditions they must treat with respect and dignity. Religious coexistence—harmony among differing faiths—has been a common theme in several of the most recent addresses of the General Authorities. President Hinckley has maintained a consistent word of counsel to "cultivate a spirit of tolerance for those of varying religious and philosophical persuasions," confirming that it is "possible to disagree without being disagreeable."[31] Applying this idea to our surroundings, Elder Russell M. Nelson said that "this broadly includes neighbors in our own family, our community, our nation, and our world."[32]

We must remember that toleration should not spill over into complacency. As Elder Dallin H. Oaks has stated, "Carried to an undisciplined excess, love and tolerance can produce indifference to truth and justice."[33] We must never compromise our beliefs in an effort to "fit in." Nor must we appear self-righteous and judgmental toward the beliefs and practices of those with whom we may disagree. As Joshua told the elders of Israel, "Choose you this day whom ye will serve . . . but as for me and my house, we will serve the Lord" (Joshua 24:15). It is indeed possible to disagree without being disagreeable. The true application of religious toleration can be achieved only under the direction of the Holy Ghost as we try to understand those with whom we may not see eye to eye. In short, religious toleration is a form of compassion and charity. It is in one aspect the true love of Christ. It will always yield the results intended by the Lord if practiced under the influence of His Spirit.

We are indeed "a chosen generation . . . a peculiar people" (1 Peter 2:9). Our peculiarity in a historic sense will be manifested if, when we achieve a majority in numbers or economic power (already present in some areas), we remain tolerant rather than falling into the age-old trap of persecuting others simply because we can. President Gordon B. Hinckley has counseled: "We can be a little more tolerant and friendly to those not of our faith, going out of our way to show our respect for them. We cannot afford to be arrogant or self-righteous."[34]

NOTES

1. The Oxford English Dictionary defines toleration as "the action of allow-ing" (*Oxford English Dictionary, Abridged Version* [Oxford: Oxford University Press, 1971], s.v. "toleration").

2. Quoted in Mario Turchetti, "Une question mal posée: La qualification de 'perpetuel et irrévocable' appliquée à l'Edit de Nantes," *Bulletin de la société de l'histoire du protestantisme français* 139 (1993): 68.

3. Philip P. Wiener, ed., *Dictionary of the History of Ideas* (New York: Scribner's, 1973), 4:113; see also Edmond Huguet, *Dictionnaire de la langue française du XVIème siècle* (Paris: Didier, 1961), 7:1026.

4. In addition to the examples given on medieval and early modern attitudes toward tolerance, one could offer ample illustrations of religious fundamentalism in all of its variations today: Christian, Islamic, Jewish, and so forth.

5. Augsburg gave princes authority to declare the religion of their subjects (either Lutheran or Catholic). Augsburg was a step in the right direction, but we should remember that there was no concept of religious toleration in 1555, as Catholics were forced from Lutheran lands and vice versa, according to the declared religion of the feudal prince. Rather, Augsburg is remembered for "legiti-mizing" Lutheranism. The Peace of Westphalia hastened a long trend of separat-ing religious from political interests; however, religious persecutions continued thereafter well into the eighteenth century. See Jeffrey Parker, *The Thirty Years' War* (London: Routledge, 1984); DeLamar Jensen, *Reformation Europe: Age of Reform and Revolution* (Lexington, Mass.: D. C. Heath, 1992), 88, 152, 215.

6. For a brief overview of religious toleration in colonial America, see George M. Marsden, *Religion and American Culture* (New York: Harcourt, Brace, Jovanovich, 1990).

7. The most well-known example is the state church established by the Massachusetts Bay Company in 1629–30 under the auspices of John Winthrop. See his "Little Speech on Liberty" in Paul Johnson, *A History of the American People* (New York: Harper Collins, 1997), 41–46.

8. Quoted in Johnson, *History of the American People*, 41.

9. Quakers were, however, the majority faith in Pennsylvania and wielded the bulk of the political and economic power of the colony (Marsden, *Religion and American Culture*, 23).

10. Ralph Pyle and James D. Davidson, "The Origins of Religious Stratification in Colonial America," *Journal for the Scientific Study of Religion* 42 (2003): 60. My thanks to Professor John Thomas for leading me to this article.

11. Thomas More, *Utopia*, trans. Paul Turner (London: Penguin, 1965), 119.

12. L. Tom Perry, "God's Hand in the Founding of America," *New Era*, July 1976, 45.

13. Perez Zagorin, *How the Idea of Religious Toleration Came to the West* (Princeton: Princeton University Press, 2002).

14. Quoted in Johann Huizinga, *Erasmus and the Age of Reformation* (Princeton: Princeton University Press, 1984), 152.

15. Desiderius Erasmus, *The Praise of Folly and Other Writings*, ed. amd trans. Robert M. Adams (New York: Norton, 1988), 63.

16. Martin Luther, *Secular Authority: To What Extent It Should Be Obeyed*, in *Martin Luther: Selections from His Writings*, ed. John Dillenberger (New York: Doubleday, 1961), 385.

17. See Henry Kamen, *L'Éveil de la tolérance*, Jeanine Carlander, trans. (Paris: Hachette, 1967), 41.

18. Calvin based his judgment to execute Servetus on anachronistic reading of Roman Emperor Justinian's seventh-century law mandating the death penalty for those who denied the official Church doctrine of the Trinity and for those who rejected the practice of infant baptism (Zagorin, *Religious Toleration*, 93–99). Servetus, Castellio, and many others like them who criticized Christian orthodoxy (either Catholic or Protestant) and the authority of religious leaders were usually labeled as *heretics*, an ironic word of Greek origin meaning one "able to choose"— ironic because of the fundamental role choice (or agency, as we call it) plays in the divine plan of eternal progression (Walter W. Skeat, ed. *A Concise Etymological Dictionary of the English Language* [Oxford: Oxford University Press, 1961], s.v. "toleration," 238; see also the *Oxford English Dictionary*). Although central to the divine plan as explained in the restored gospel, in times past one's freedom to choose was not at the personal level but at the communal level and was directed by those leaders charged with keeping not only order but orthodoxy. Individualism, what we might consider a social norm today, would not become visible for the historian until the Renaissance humanists reintroduced it beginning in the mid-fourteenth century.

19. Quoted in Zagorin, *Religious Toleration*, 107.

20. Joseph Smith, *Teachings of the Prophet Joseph Smith*, sel. Joseph Fielding Smith (Salt Lake City: Deseret Book, 1976), 344.

21. Castellio seems to be echoing the spirit of Doctrine and Covenants 121:37 in his condemnation of Calvin's actions toward Servetus. "But when we undertake to cover our sins, or to gratify our pride, our vain ambition, or to exercise control

or dominion or compulsion upon the souls of the children of men, in any degree of unrighteousness, behold, the heavens withdraw themselves: the Spirit of the Lord is grieved; and when it is withdrawn, Amen to the priesthood or the authority of that man" (D&C 121:37).

22. Quoted in Donald Nugent, *Ecumenism in the Age of the Reformation: The Colloquy of Poissy* (Cambridge: Cambridge University Press, 1974), 84.

23. See Philip Benedict, *The Huguenot Population of France, 1600–1685: The Demographic Fate and Customs of a Religious Minority* (Philadelphia: Transactions of the American Philosophical Society, 1991); Elisabeth Labrousse, *L'édit de Nantes et sa revocation: histoire d'une intolerance* (Paris: Seuil, 1985); Warren C. Scoville, *The Persecution of the Huguenots and French Economic Development, 1680–1720* (Berkeley: University of California Press, 1960).

24. See Wiener, *Dictionary of the History of Ideas*, 4:112.

25. It should be noted that several other influential authors wrote on religious toleration in the late seventeenth century. Most notable besides Locke was Pierre Bayle, an exiled Huguenot living in Holland at the same time as Locke. Bayle's most influential work was his *Philosophical Commentary on Christ's Words 'Compel Them to Come'* (*Commentaire philosophique sur ces paroles de Jesus-Christ 'contrains-les d'entrer'*, 4 vols. [Amsterdam, 1686–88]), in which a rising tone of secularism can be discerned.

26. John Locke, *A Letter Concerning Toleration,* ed. John Horton and Susan Mendus (London: Routledge, 1991), 15–16.

27. Locke, *Letter,* 26.

28. Locke reportedly had in his library at his death works from Castellio, as well as anti-Trinitarian works, which would have made him sympathetic to Michael Servetus's beliefs and worthy to be burned at the stake in John Calvin's Geneva (John Harrison and Peter Laslett, *The Library Catalog of John Locke* [Oxford: Oxford University Press, 1965]).

29. See Elizabeth Eisenstein, *The Printing Press in Early Modern Europe* (Cambridge: Cambridge University Press, 1983).

30. Voltaire, *Philosophical Dictionary,* trans. Peter Gay (New York: Basic Books, 1962) 2:482, 485.

31. Quoted in Sheri L. Dew, *Go Forward with Faith: The Biography of Gordon B. Hinckley* (Salt Lake City: Deseret Book, 1996), 536.

32. Russell M. Nelson, "Teach Us Tolerance and Love," *Ensign,* May 1994, 70.

33. Dallin H. Oaks, "Our Strengths Can Become Our Downfall," *Ensign,* October 1994, 12.

34. Gordon B. Hinckley, "Thanks to the Lord for His Blessings," *Ensign,* May 1999, 88.

10

RECOVERING THE WORLD OF THE BIBLE

Dana M. Pike

The pillar of light that fell upon Joseph Smith in the woods near Palmyra, New York, in the spring of 1820 ushered in a new dispensation of the gospel.[1] But that light, which shone "above the brightness of the sun" (Joseph Smith–History 1:16), did not *just* enlighten the world as far as religion is concerned. The light emanating from the pillar in which the Father and Son stood symbolically represents the latter-day, divine illumination of many aspects of life on this earth—past, present, and future.

The Lord did not restore His gospel in a historical, cultural, or political vacuum. He provided a world-context into which He restored His Church so as to facilitate the spread and acceptance of His gospel. Given the accumulation of discoveries and decipherments during the past two centuries, it is easy to forget that before 1800 very little was known about the ancient world of the Bible.[2] The avalanche of historical and linguistic knowledge relating to that ancient world that began in the early 1800s, *at the same time* the

---

Dana M. Pike is an associate professor of ancient scripture at Brigham Young University.

Lord was restoring doctrine and authority to the earth through Joseph Smith, is part of the Lord's work in "the fulness of times" to "gather together in one all things, both which are in heaven, and which are on earth" (D&C 27:13; see also Ephesians 1:10).[3] The recovery of the world of the Bible was an integral part of the world-context of the Restoration and of the gathering together of all things in one.[4] As such, this recovery informs and reinforces many aspects of the Restoration, providing us with a much greater understanding of the background and contents of the Bible and other Restoration scriptures and of the Lord's work in all dispensations. The Book of Mormon, the book of Abraham, and the world of the Bible all literally came forth "out of the dust" at the same time (Isaiah 29:4).

The world of the Bible consists of the countries and cultures with which the ancient Israelites interacted, as recorded in the Bible. Geographically, this region is known as the Near East or Middle East. It stretches from Turkey in the west through Iraq (ancient Assyria and Babylonia) to Iran (ancient Persia) in the east, and down through the eastern Mediterranean countries of Syria, Lebanon (ancient Phoenicia), Israel/Palestine, and Jordan, to Egypt and the Arabian peninsula. A very brief sketch of the political and religious situation in the Middle East from the 1790s to 1850 points up important aspects of the early recovery of the world of the Bible.[5] And there are fascinating correlations between these discoveries and the Restoration through Joseph Smith.

The Middle East from the 1790s to 1850

Following a series of impressive victories, Napoleon Bonaparte became a general in the French military in 1794, five years after the outbreak of the French Revolution in 1789. By 1797 the French had trained their sites on Great Britain, their only serious European competition. Rather than attempt an invasion of England, as many expected, Napoleon took his forces to Egypt to impede British trade and communication opportunities through the strategic Isthmus of Suez. This one-hundred-mile stretch of land provided an important alternative to circumnavigating Africa to reach expanding British interests in India and the Far East.[6] The local Egyptian forces were no match for Napoleon's far better trained and better equipped troops, and he quickly took control of the country in July 1798.

In 1798 Egypt was part of the Turkish Ottoman Empire, the capital of which was Constantinople (now Istanbul). Although within the orbit of the Ottoman Empire, Egypt had always enjoyed a certain amount of autonomy. The Ottoman Empire had reached its peak during the 1500s, controlling much of the Middle East and eastern Europe.[7] A decline in military and economic development and a series of military defeats during the late 1600s and the 1700s foreshadowed the long-lived empire's demise.

Napoleon's expedition to Egypt dramatically changed relations between the West and Middle East forever, as the Ottoman Empire became much more involved in a political and economic dance with several European powers—especially Britain, France, and Russia—in which each partner tried to maintain a certain balance of power but also to gain an individual advantage. The political developments cited below help demonstrate this situation. Similar political circumstances existed between several European powers and Persia, the Ottomans' rival to the east.

A few weeks following Napoleon's invasion of Egypt, the British Admiral Nelson destroyed much of the French fleet off Alexandria, Egypt, after which the Ottomans and the British began negotiating to expel the French from Egypt. Five months later, in January 1799, Napoleon invaded Palestine from Egypt, planning to go on to Syria. He got as far north as Acre (now Acco, Israel, just north of Haifa), where he laid siege to the city. But by that time, his diminished troops were too weary, ill, and insufficiently equipped to capture the well-fortified Acre, the protection of which was ensured by British ships anchored off the coast. Experiencing his first career defeat, Napoleon headed back to Egypt in late May. The French defeated Ottoman forces near Alexandria, and Napoleon returned to France later in 1799 to become its new leader. In 1801 an Ottoman-British coalition drove the remaining French forces from Egypt.

Later, in 1827, Europeans were dissatisfied with the Ottoman response to the Greek revolution against the Ottoman Empire. The British took the lead in destroying the Ottoman naval fleet, which included Egyptian vessels. For several reasons, including lack of compensation for participation in efforts to quell the Greek rebellion, the Egyptian *pasha* (governor), Muhammad Ali, took advantage of his military strength and relative autonomy to seize control of Syria and Palestine in 1831. In 1840 Britain helped the Ottomans drive the Egyptians out of Syria and Palestine.

As a result of such political dynamics, three important developments occurred that significantly affected the recovery of the world of the Bible. First, in addition to troops, Napoleon took with him about 170 savants—French scientists, engineers, naturalists, draftsmen, and geographers. They studied, mapped, and recorded the human and natural wonders of Egypt (and to a lesser extent, Palestine) in an unprecedented way.[8] Their multivolume report, *Description de l'Egypte,* published from 1809 onward, helped precipitate a considerable new interest in contemporary Egypt and in its ancient inhabitants.[9] Second, in July 1799, French soldiers who were enlarging their fort near the port town of Rashid, Egypt (ancient Rosetta, about thirty-five miles east of Alexandria), discovered an inscribed stone that had been reused in an old wall. Now known as the Rosetta stone, the stone and its inscription played a key role in deciphering Egyptian hieroglyphics. Third, from 1831 to 1840, Palestine was under the independent control of the Egyptian pasha, not the Ottoman Empire. This situation provided much more favorable conditions than in previous decades for Westerners who were traveling to Egypt and Palestine for adventure or for economic or religious reasons.

Although many European Christian pilgrims had traveled to the Holy Land from the fourth through the fifteenth centuries, the rate greatly diminished after 1500 with the dominance of the Ottoman Empire, and it remained low until the late 1700s. However, after Napoleon's exploits dramatically brought the world of the Bible into the public consciousness of Europeans and Americans, the Middle East became a destination for many Western travelers with varied interests and backgrounds, just as lesser-known parts of Africa and central Asia had so become.[10] Some of these new travelers to the Middle East published travelogues and journals that were very popular in Europe and in the United States.

Thus, the increased interaction between European governments and the Ottomans and Persians coincided with a spirit of adventurism that produced a vastly increased European and American awareness of the Middle East. These factors in turn provided new vistas for both historical discovery and religious outreach in the early 1800s. The majority of the Middle Eastern population at that time was Muslim, but communities of Jews and Christians were scattered throughout the region. The Christians were mainly Eastern Orthodox, but there were Roman Catholics as well. Protestant Christianity was not legally recognized in the Ottoman Empire at that time, and Protestants in general had previously exhibited little interest in the land and holy sites of the Bible. But that significantly changed in the early 1800s.

RECOVERING THE WORLD OF THE BIBLE
FROM THE 1790s TO 1850

Some of the notable accomplishments in the exciting story of the early recovery of the world of the Bible will now be recounted to demonstrate how remarkable and influential these achievements were. Not surprisingly, most of the individuals involved in this recovery process were possessed of a natural curiosity, a great deal of energy, or gifts in language. Each region of the Middle East deserves its own individual treatment, but only three can be highlighted here: Egypt,[11] Mesopotamia (modern Iraq; with slight attention to Persia/Iran),[12] and Israel/Palestine.[13]

Egypt. By the early Christian centuries, the ability to read any of the ancient Egyptian scripts was entirely lost. Most people already presumed hieroglyphics represented a symbolic, mythic code that required interpretation rather than decipherment.[14] A few Europeans attempted to make sense of hieroglyphics in the seventeenth and eighteenth centuries, but they made little progress until the discovery of the Rosetta stone by some of Napoleon's soldiers stationed in the western Nile delta in 1799.[15] This partially damaged, monumental inscription had originally been erected at an Egyptian temple in 196 B.C. by the Macedonian Greek king of Egypt, Ptolemy V, to commemorate the first anniversary of his reign and to publicize privileges he had granted to priests. Its great value lies in the fact that the text was written in two languages—Egyptian and Greek—and in three scripts—Egyptian hieroglyphics, Egyptian demotic (a cursive form of hieroglyphics), and the Greek alphabet. The Greek version, readable by European scholars, provided the means to eventually decipher the Egyptian versions. When the British defeated the French in Egypt in 1801, the Rosetta stone was ceded to the British, who shipped it to London in 1802. It is still on display in the British Museum. Though not the only inscription involved in the decipherment of Egyptian hieroglyphics and demotic, the Rosetta stone was especially significant and appropriately symbolizes the accomplishment.

Several people were involved in deciphering Egyptian scripts. Important contributions came from the Englishman Thomas Young (1773–1829), a pioneer in the decipherment of demotic, and Jean-François Champollion (1790–1832), the brilliant young Frenchman, born December 23, 1790, who first successfully deciphered hieroglyphics (on a rudimentary level; the "complete" work of decipherment extended many decades beyond Champollion's life).

A group of competitive plunderers who essentially ransacked Egyptian tombs and temples were primarily responsible for the early recovery of ancient Egypt's material culture. Prominent in this group were the British consul Henry Salt (1785–1827); Bernardino Drovetti (1776–1852), French consul in Egypt from 1803 to 1814 and then commercial advisor to the pasha; and Giovanni Battista Belzoni (1778–1823), a former circus strongman known as the "Italian giant." Destructive "excavations" were allowed by the Egyptian pasha Muhammed Ali, who exhibited little concern for Egyptian antiquities and who no doubt benefited from the arrangements. The German Karl Richard Lepsius (1810–84) sent many valuable Egyptian artifacts back to the Berlin Museum, but he is also remembered for his efforts to preserve inscriptions and reliefs in copies and casts.

The following highlights demonstrate the significant way in which the Egyptian portion of the world of the Bible began to be recovered in the early 1800s.

1799. The Rosetta stone was discovered by French troops near Rashid, Egypt (ancient Rosetta).

1802. The British shipped the Rosetta stone to London; the Greek portion was translated.

1802. Sylvester de Sacy and J. H. Åkerblad succeeded in identifying some names and other words in the demotic text of the Rosetta stone.

1809–16. Napoleon's scholars published a multivolume report dealing with the antiquities of Egypt: *Description de l'Egypte.*

1813. James Lewis Burckhardt was the first European to discover the monumental statues of Ramses II and Nefertari carved into the side of a cliff at Abu Simbel, about 170 miles south of the modern Aswan Dam. Belzoni excavated the temple beneath the statues in 1817.

1814–19. Thomas Young had further success with demotic and early success in identifying some of the hieroglyphs in the name Ptolemy. He summarized his efforts in an *Encyclopedia Britannica* supplement entry (1819).

1817. Belzoni discovered the tomb of Egyptian pharaoh Seti I, father of Ramses II, in the Valley of the Kings. "Excavations" were ongoing for years in several parts of the Valley.

1818. Belzoni opened the second pyramid of Giza, tomb of Chephren, and entered its royal burial chamber.

1820. Belzoni mounted an exhibition of Egyptian artifacts in London.

1822. Champollion, building on the work of Young, publicized his initial success in deciphering hieroglyphics, in a report completed September 22 and publicly read September 27, entitled *Lettre à M. Dacier relative à l'alphabet des hiéroglyphs phonétiques.*

1824. Champollion published his *Précis du système hiéroglyphique dans anciens égyptiens,* decisively demonstrating that he had rudimentarily deciphered the basic system of hieroglyphics.

1836. One of two obelisks in front of the Luxor temple was transported to Paris and erected in the Place de la Concorde.

1837. John Gardiner Wilkinson published his *Manners and Customs of the Ancient Egyptians,* the first modern book of its kind on ancient Egypt.

1842. Karl Richard Lepsius published the Turin copy of the Egyptian Book of the Dead.

1842–46. Lepsius led a very productive German expedition to Egypt.

1847. Irishman Edward Hincks published further advances in understanding hieroglyphics.

1849–56. Lepsius published his twelve-volume *Monuments of Egypt and Ethiopia* (in German), which included further advances in understanding hieroglyphics as well as more accurate copies of many Egyptian inscriptions than were previously available. Some of the nine hundred plates in this work preserve inscriptions which have since been destroyed.

Mesopotamia and Persia. The region known as Mesopotamia (modern Iraq and northeast Syria) was home to the ancient Assyrians and Babylonians. Mesopotamia comprised the eastern flank of the Ottoman Empire, bordering the empire's Middle East rivals, the Persians (modern Iran). The wonders of ancient Assyria and Babylonia lay under a greater blanket of obscurity than did those of ancient Egypt. About all that was left of these distant, great civilizations were large, flat-topped mounds—destroyed cities covered by the dust of ages—that dotted the fairly flat countryside between the Tigris and Euphrates rivers. While the Mesopotamian ruins were less immediately spectacular than many Egyptian ruins, Austen Henry Layard expressed the profound emotion that they stirred within him (and others like him): "These huge mounds of Assyria made a deeper impression upon me, gave rise to more serious thought and more earnest reflection, than the [Roman] temples of Balbec [in Lebanon] or the theaters of Ionia."[16]

The writing system used by the ancient Assyrians, Babylonians, Persians, and Hittites (in eastern Turkey) is called "cuneiform"— wedge-shaped inscriptions. Each sign represents one or more syllabic values; some signs also represent words. Carved into rock and pressed into soft clay tablets, this stylized script was employed in one form or another for almost three thousand years. A few seventeenth- and eighteenth-century travelers brought small cuneiform inscriptions or partial transcriptions from Mesopotamia and Persia back to Europe, and fledgling efforts were made to decipher this arcane script. But only in the early 1800s did scholars and amateurs alike inaugurate the large-scale recovery of Mesopotamian and Persian texts and artifacts.

Important individuals involved in this recovery include a young German academic named Georg Friedrich Grotefend (1775–1853), who in 1802 made important advances in the decipherment of Persian cuneiform; Claudius J. Rich (1787–1820), a British agent whose travels throughout Mesopotamia produced artifacts and accurate accounts of ruins that were foundational for British Mesopotamian studies; Henry Creswicke Rawlinson (1810–95), British consul in Baghdad from 1843 to 1855 who copied the monumental, mountainside trilingual cuneiform inscription of Persian King Darius I (522–486 B.C.) at Bisitun in western Persia/Iran, and who played a major role in the decipherment of cuneiform;[17] Paul Émile Botta (1802–70), French consul in Mosul, in northern Mesopotamia, who excavated at Nineveh and Khorsabad in the mid-1840s;[18] and Englishman Austen Henry Layard (1817–94), who excavated at Nineveh and Nimrud (biblical Calah) in the late 1840s.[19]

The following highlights demonstrate the significant way in which the Mesopotamian and Persian portion of the world of the Bible began to be recovered in the early 1800s.

1802. Georg Friedrich Grotefend successfully deciphered some of the characters used in Persian cuneiform, focusing on personal names in a bilingual inscription.

1807–16. Claudius J. Rich collected artifacts and mapped Mesopotamia, providing reliable accounts of the ruins of Babylon, Nineveh, and other ancient cities in such publications as *Memoir on the Ruins of Babylon* (1815) and *Second Memoir on Babylon* (1818).

1835. Henry Rawlinson began copying the trilingual Darius inscription at Bisitun, Persia.

1836. Eugene Burnouf and Christian Lasson independently established the value of all signs in Persian cuneiform script and worked out readings of geographic names.

1842. The American Oriental Society was founded. Still in existence, it is dedicated to studying the languages and literatures of Asia, including the Middle East.

1843–44. Paul Émile Botta excavated and made amazing discoveries at Khorsabad (Assyrian Dur Sharrukin, in northern Iraq), the ruins of a capital city built by King Sargon II of Assyria (721–705 B.C.).

1844 and 1847. Rawlinson copied the Elamite and Babylonian cuneiform versions of the trilingual Darius inscription at Bisitun, Persia.

1845–51. Austen Henry Layard excavated at Nimrud (Assyrian Kalhu; northern Iraq). Major finds included the Black Obelisk of Shalmaneser III, which depicts Jehu, king of Israel (2 Kings 9–10).

1846–51. Layard excavated at Nineveh (Tell Kuyunjik). His exceptional discoveries include the celebrated library of King Ashurbanipal and the discovery of King Sennacherib's "palace without a rival," the decorations of which included wall carvings depicting the destruction of the Judahite city of Lachish by Sennacherib in 701 B.C. (2 Kings 18:13–19:37).

1846. Rawlinson published the Old Persian cuneiform text from Bisitun. Edward Hincks finished his initial deciphering of Old Persian cuneiform.

1847. The first exhibition of Assyrian sculpture and artifacts in the world was mounted at the Louvre Museum in Paris, displaying Botta's discoveries at Khorsabad.

1847–52. Edward Hincks succeeded in his rudimentary deciphering of Mesopotamian cuneiform, used by the Assyrians and Babylonians.

1849. Layard's publication *Nineveh and Its Remains* was greeted with great public acclaim.

1850. Layard conducted preliminary excavations at Babylon.

1850. Rawlinson's *A Commentary on the Cuneiform Inscriptions of Babylonia and Assyria* was the first description of the Assyrians to employ some of their own texts as sources.

Israel/Palestine. "At the beginning of the 19th century Palestine was but a derelict province of the decaying Ottoman Empire. . . . Its economy was primitive; the sparse, ethnically mixed population subsisted on a dismally low standard; the few towns were small and miserable; the roads were few and neglected."[20] "Many of the ancient cities and towns mentioned in the Scriptures had seemingly vanished without a trace, and even the holy cities of Jerusalem, Bethlehem, and Nazareth were now little more than provincial market towns."[21] These conditions hardly matched the biblical description of a "land flowing with milk and honey" (Exodus 3:8, 17).[22] No wonder so many European and American travelers to Palestine in the early 1800s were surprised and dismayed by what they encountered. Several factors, however, attracted people to the region. These included the desire to explore a relatively unknown area, economically related national interests, and Bible-related interests of various sorts.

Two fascinating early explorers of Palestine (following Napoleon's team in 1799) were the German Ulrich Jasper Seetzen (1767–1811), who journeyed through Syria, Palestine, Egypt, and Arabia from 1805 to 1810; and the Swiss-born James Lewis Burckhardt (1784–1817), who traveled through Syria, Palestine, Egypt, and Arabia from 1809 to 1817. Both spent several years of preparation in Syria learning Arabic and Eastern customs, both traveled dressed as Arabs, and both left accounts of their travels that helped advance Europeans' knowledge of and interest in the land of the Bible.

Some adventurers went to Palestine to investigate potential trade routes through the Jordan Rift between the Red Sea and the Sea of Galilee. Such men, whose motives were primarily economic and nationalistic, include the Englishman James Silk Buckingham (1786–1855), who traveled through Palestine in 1816; and an American officer named William Francis Lynch (1801–65), who led a U.S. Navy expedition from the Sea of Galilee down the Jordan River to the Dead Sea in 1848. While successful in gathering important data about the Dead Sea and its environs, neither the Lynch expedition nor any other could successfully champion Palestine as a competitive trade route. Accounts of their experiences, however, were part of an ongoing stream of publications that maintained a heightened American and European public interest in the land of the Bible.

The Bible itself was another impetus for encountering the Holy Land. In the wake of such developments as eschatological expectations at the turn of the eighteenth to nineteenth century, the Napoleonic Wars in Europe (until 1815), and the Second Great Awakening (second revivalist movement) in the United States, Christian missionary societies in the United States and Great Britain were organized in the early 1800s to carry Bibles and the message of Christ to every corner of the earth. This, of course, included Palestine and the rest of the Middle East. The American Levi Parsons (1792–1822) became the first Protestant Christian missionary to visit Jerusalem, arriving in 1820. He was followed there in 1825 by his earlier missionary traveling companion, Pliny Fisk (1792–1825). Such activity provides another indicator of the new attention given the land of the Bible by many Westerners.

Others who traveled to Palestine were more intent on recovering the ancient world of the Bible than on converting its modern inhabitants. Many biblical sites were no longer identifiable, and some local traditions on site locations were incorrect. "A *flood* of western travelers took advantage of the improved conditions [under the Egyptian pasha, after 1831] to add yet more knowledge to the western understanding of the land of the Bible. During the eighteen-thirties, a number of explorers from France, Germany,

England, and America had roamed among the ancient sites of
Palestine, recording their impressions and theories. None, however,
had the background that Edward Robinson possessed, and the
achievements of all of them would soon pale by comparison."[23]
Robinson (1794–1863), a Bible scholar and linguist, was conservative in his religious orientation and sought to support the historical
reliability of the Bible in a world of increasing skepticism.
Robinson's travels to Palestine in 1838–41 and 1852, and his subsequent publications in 1841 and 1856, not only generated great public interest in the land of the Bible but more importantly laid the
foundations of the serious study of the historical geography of
Palestine and the foundations for the field of biblical archaeology.
He was accompanied and greatly assisted in his efforts by an
American missionary named Eli Smith (1801–57), who spent many
years in Beirut preaching the gospel and preparing an Arabic translation of the Bible. Together they became adept at recognizing
ancient Hebrew place-names in their altered Arabic guise, accurately identifying and mapping dozens of biblical sites for the first
time in the modern era. To this day, "Robinson's Arch" is the name
given to the surviving edge of a two-thousand-year-old monumental archway protruding from a wall near the southwest corner of the
Temple Mount.

The activities of two other men are worth quickly noting. David
Roberts (1796–1864), a Scottish landscape artist, toured Egypt,
Palestine, and Lebanon in 1838–39. Lithographs prepared from his
drawings were published between 1842 and 1849 and became
instantly popular. They are still well known due to their detailed,
albeit somewhat romanticized, depiction of important sites and life
in the Middle East.[24] John Lloyd Stephens (1805–52), an American
explorer and author, is best known for his travels to southern Mexico
and Central America in 1839–41. His books on ancient Mayan
ruins, complete with marvelous illustrations by Englishman
Frederick Catherwood (1799–1854), generated a great deal of interest among Americans, even eliciting a comment in the Latter-day
Saint *Times and Seasons*.[25] Stephens, however, had traveled in the
Middle East in 1836, and his travelogue, *Incidents of Travel in*

Egypt, Arabia Petraea, and the Holy Land, became very popular after its publication in 1837.[26] Of particular interest to Latter-day Saints is that Stephens, who graduated from New York City's Columbia College (now University) in 1822 at the age of seventeen, was the "favorite pupil" of Columbia professor Charles Anthon, "America's most famous classicist" at the time.[27] Also, Stephens, like so many other travelers to Jerusalem, recounts that he stayed at the Latin Convent (now Saint Savior's Convent), just as Elder Orson Hyde did five years later.[28]

The following highlights demonstrate the significant way in which the Israel/Palestine part of the world of the Bible began to attract attention and to be recovered in the early 1800s.

1804. The Palestine Association was formed in England to help fund exploration (and exploitation); it was modeled on other British associations and societies previously formed to explore remote areas of the world. Little actually came of the Association's efforts.

1805–07. Ulrich Seetzen traveled through Syria and Palestine. He rediscovered the ruins of Jerash and Amman (modern Jordan).

1810–12. John Lewis Burckhardt traveled from Syria down the Jordan Rift and rediscovered the fabled ancient city of Petra (southern Jordan), about forty-seven miles southeast of the Dead Sea.

1815. Lady Hester Stanhope "excavated" at Ashkelon (modern Israel) looking for buried treasure on the basis of a purportedly medieval document. Finding no treasure, she destroyed the large statue of a Roman emperor she found in order to discourage other people from plundering the site for artifacts.

1816. James Buckingham traveled through Palestine, exploring a possible trade route in the Jordan Rift.

1820. Levi Parsons became the first Protestant Christian missionary to travel to Jerusalem. He was followed by Pliny Fisk (1825) and many others in the succeeding decades. Parsons and Fisk were supported by the American Board of Commissioners for

Foreign Missions, founded in 1810 to help Protestants prepare the world for the return of Christ.

1829. Henry H. Milman published the first academic history of ancient Israel in his *History of the Jews* (first edition; second edition published in 1830).

1836. Edward Robinson published an English translation of the renowned German scholar William Gesenius's *Hebrew Lexicon* (for the study of biblical Hebrew).

1838–41. Edward Robinson explored Palestine with Eli Smith and correctly identified many biblical sites for the first time in the modern era. Robinson returned to Palestine in 1852.

1839. David Roberts traveled though Palestine, drawing many important sites and later publishing the drawings as lithographs (1842–49).

1841. Robinson and Smith's three-volume *Biblical Researches in Palestine, Mount Sinai, and Arabia Petraea* was published in Boston. Robinson's *Later Biblical Researches in Palestine and the Adjacent Regions* was published in 1856.

1848. A United States naval expedition, led by William Lynch, traveled from the Sea of Galilee down the Jordan River to the Dead Sea, gathering information for a possible trade route.

The Restoration of Christ's Church and the Early Recovery of the World of the Bible

Even this brief sketch of the early recovery of the world of the Bible in the first half of the nineteenth century demonstrates its chronological correlation with the restoration of the Lord's gospel and Church through the Prophet Joseph Smith.[29] One aspect of the divine preparation of the world for restoring the gospel was the initial recovery of the biblical world and the context it provided for understanding the Lord's work in previous dispensations. This correlation is specifically illustrated by the following five items.

1. *The Book of Mormon.* Joseph Smith was first tutored by the angel Moroni in 1823. He received the Book of Mormon plates in September 1827. The bulk of the translation occurred in 1829, and

the book was first published in March 1830. Martin Harris, a friend and early scribe to Joseph Smith, sought confirmation of the young prophet's gift. Traveling to New York City in early 1828 with a copy of some "reformed Egyptian" characters from the gold plates (Mormon 9:32), Harris visited with Columbia College professors Charles Anthon, "a gentleman celebrated for his literary attainments" (Joseph Smith–History 1:64), and Samuel Mitchill (misspelled *Mitchell* in Joseph Smith–History 1:65). According to Harris, Professor Anthon said, among other things, that the characters Harris showed him "were Egyptian, Chaldaic, Assyriac, and Arabic; and he said they were true characters. . . . Dr. Mitchell . . . sanctioned what Professor Anthon had said respecting both the characters and the translation" (Joseph Smith–History 1:64–65). With the initial successful decipherment of some Egyptian demotic and hieroglyphic symbols in Europe by 1824, Harris's consultations with Anthon and Mitchill in 1828 emphasize a general awareness of the contemporary recovery of Egyptian aspects of the world of the Bible.[30] Furthermore, it is striking that Joseph Smith was involved in the decipherment and publication of an ancient text that had roots in the world of the Bible at the same time other ancient languages and texts from that world were beginning to be deciphered and published—the Prophet translating scripture, the scholars translating nonscriptural texts.

As Brigham Young University professor Wilfred Griggs has observed, "Inasmuch as the Book of Mormon is a record of peoples who migrated from the Old World (the Mediterranean and Mesopotamian regions) . . . [to the Americas], the imprint of the ancient Near Eastern cultures from which the peoples originated can still be found within the record." An understanding "of the international currents flowing around the world of Lehi can help explain the presence of Hebrew, Egyptian, Babylonian, and even Greek cultural elements in the records of Lehi and his successors."[31] The recovery of the world of the Bible thus provides a context for the coming forth of the Book of Mormon as well as helping us better understand its content.

2. *The book of Abraham.* The book of Abraham derives from

papyrus documents preserved with four mummies the Prophet Joseph Smith purchased from Michael Chandler in Kirtland, Ohio, in July 1835. These four mummies were part of a group of eleven which were acquired by Chandler in the United States in 1833. He toured them in the eastern states, selling some as he went, until he sold the last four to the Prophet Joseph. The mummies had been removed from Egypt about 1820 by Antonio Lebolo (1781–1830), who had served in the French army from 1799 to 1801 (although not in Egypt) and who later worked from 1817 to 1822 "excavating" Egyptian antiquities for Bernardino Drovetti as well as on his own.

According to his journal entries, Joseph Smith worked on the papyrus texts during the remainder of 1835, and then a little again in 1842 as he prepared them for publication in the *Times and Seasons* in Nauvoo.[32] While "his precise methodology remains unknown," Latter-day Saints accept that "it was principally [by] divine inspiration rather than his knowledge of languages that [Joseph Smith] produced the English text of the book of Abraham."[33]

Of the Abraham material published in the Pearl of Great Price, only Facsimile 1 is preserved on the eleven papyrus fragments known to have survived from what the Prophet had. But all three facsimiles are Egyptian in nature, and they and the content of the book of Abraham itself are more fully understood and appreciated because of the recovery of the world of the Bible that began in the early 1800s.[34] Indeed, the modern availability of the book of Abraham results in part from the role Lebolo played in the initial recovery of the world of the Bible in the early 1800s and the public interest in such matters upon which Chandler capitalized by touring his mummies. Joseph Smith was definitely aware of that recovery process, and he personally participated in the excitement it generated. Not everyone had mummies on display in their city as the Saints in Nauvoo did.

3. *Orson Hyde's mission to Jerusalem.* One of the first apostles in this dispensation, Orson Hyde (1805–78) was charged by Joseph Smith in April 1840 to dedicate "the land of Palestine for the

building up of Jerusalem and the gathering of Abraham's posterity."[35] Elder Hyde arrived in Jerusalem after an eighteen-month journey that included much preaching, many hardships, and divine intervention. He climbed the Mount of Olives on October 24, 1841, and pronounced the first apostolic dedicatory prayer in this dispensation for Jerusalem, the Holy Land, and the gathering of Israel.[36] An account of his experiences—*A Voice from Jerusalem, or a Sketch of the Travels and Ministry of Elder Orson Hyde*—was published in Liverpool and Boston in 1842 and was a significant contribution to the growing number of accounts of travel in the Middle East published at that time. Orson Hyde's mission did not specifically involve the early recovery of the world of the Bible—he was not motivated by sight-seeing, antiquities, or ancient texts.[37] But he traveled a similar route, saw similar sites, and stayed in the same Latin convent in Jerusalem that so many other explorers and missionaries did in that time period. Furthermore, his mission signaled another way in which the Lord's power began to move across the Middle East. The Orson Hyde Memorial Garden on the west slope of the Mount of Olives commemorates his mission.[38]

4. *Joseph Smith and biblical Hebrew.* The Prophet Joseph Smith developed a keen interest in learning languages, including the primary languages of the Bible: Hebrew and Greek. One illustration of this is that, perhaps arising from the acquisition of the mummies and papyri in July 1835, the Prophet procured Hebrew books in November 1835 and commenced his study. Eventually, Professor Joshua Seixas was hired to teach biblical Hebrew in Kirtland from January 6 to March 29, 1836.[39] In his journal entry dated February 17, 1836, the Prophet wrote: "Attended the school and read and translated with my class as usual. My soul delights in reading the word of the Lord in the original [Hebrew], and I am determined to pursue the study of the languages, until I shall become master of them, if I am permitted to live long enough."[40] Such effort and sentiment lends credence to the importance of understanding the Bible and other scripture in their linguistic, historical, and cultural context—something which is much more fully possible due to the recovery of the world of the Bible which began in the early 1800s.

5. *Proposed Nauvoo museum.* The May 15, 1843, edition of the *Times and Seasons,* entitled "To the Saints Among All Nations," contained the following exhortation, apparently from Joseph Smith: "According to a Revelation, received not long since, it appears to be the duty of the members of the Church of Jesus Christ of Latter Day Saints to bring to Nauvoo, their precious things, such as antiquities . . . as well as inscriptions and hieroglyphics, for the purpose of establishing a Museum of the great things of God, and the inventions of men, at Nauvoo." Editor John Taylor stated in an appended comment that this museum should be "a receptacle of every thing new and old, ancient and modern, antique, fanciful and substantial—indeed any thing and every thing that has a tendency to throw light upon ancient nations, their manners, customs, implements of husbandry and of war, their costume, ancient records, manuscripts, paintings, hieroglyphics, . . . any thing that is calculated to enlighten the mind, enlarge the understanding, gratify the curiosity, and give general information."[41] It is striking that Church leaders in 1843 Nauvoo had such a grand and broad vision of the Restoration—a vision that included the value of the ancient texts and artifacts then being recovered in the Middle East. This emphasizes their awareness of the recovery process going on in their own time, their estimation of the importance of knowledge of the world of the Bible for better understanding the scriptures, and their desire to participate in gathering all things together in one.

CONCLUSION

As with any new academic undertaking, there were exaggerated claims and errors in decipherment and interpretation as the recovery of the world of the Bible commenced. And even with the discoveries and advances highlighted above, the recovery of the world of the Bible was still in its infancy in 1850. However, the efforts of hearty, curious, and insightful explorers and decipherers in inaugurating this recovery were instrumental for our present understanding of that ancient world and its value for better understanding our religious and cultural heritage. The recovery of further aspects of the ancient Near East and the refining of the translation of its texts continues to our day.

As outlined above, the beginnings of the recovery of the ancient world of the Bible are closely linked to and provide a revealing context for the Restoration in general and for the book of Abraham and the Book of Mormon in particular.[42] These ancient scriptures were made available by divine will and were translated and published in an age flush with the excitement of great discovery and decipherment. No wonder President John Taylor later taught, "There is nothing hidden but what shall be revealed, says the Lord. He is prepared to unfold all things; all things pertaining to the heavens and the earth, *all things pertaining to the peoples who have existed,* who now exist or will exist, that we may be instructed and taught in every principle of intelligence associated with the world in which we live or with the Gods in the eternal worlds."[43] All this reinforces the significance of the Lord's 1833 injunction that "it is my will that you should . . . obtain a knowledge of history, and of countries, and of kingdoms, of laws of God and man, and all this for the salvation of Zion" (D&C 93:53; see also D&C 90:15).

Shortly after Edward Robinson and Eli Smith published their *Biblical Researches in Palestine, Mount Sinai, and Arabia Petræa* in 1841, a British commentator suggested that divine power influenced their accomplishments: "The gratification of their own curiosity was the only motive perhaps of which they were conscious. . . . Little did they think that they were obeying an impulse from on High, and that Jehovah meant them to be witnesses of His truth to the after-ages of the world.'"[44] This perceptive observation extends not only to Robertson and Smith but to Champollion, Layard, Rawlinson, and many others who were involved in the early recovery of the biblical world and who were (knowingly or unknowingly) moved upon by the Lord as part of His plan to bring about the gathering together of all things in one in this last and greatest gospel dispensation.[45] What a blessing to have the spiritual light of the restored gospel! And what a joy to have knowledge of the world of the Bible, which the Lord has provided in conjunction with the gospel to deepen our understanding and appreciation of His words and His works.

NOTES

I thank my student assistants Matt Gray, Hollie Pollan, and Albert Jarvi for their assistance in the preparation of this paper, and my wife Jane Allis-Pike for carefully reading it and making suggestions for improving it.

1. See the Bible Dictionary, s.v. "Dispensations": "The fulness of times is the final dispensation. . . . It is a dispensation of restoration and of fulfillment of the Lord's plans and purposes since the world began. There are also things reserved for the fulness of times that have not been revealed previously."

2. Before 1800, knowledge of the biblical world was limited to what was preserved in the Bible and by ancient Greek and Roman historians, such as Herodotus, Xenophon, and Strabo.

3. Bruce R. McConkie and Joseph Fielding Smith have made similar points in relation to modern technological advances and inventions (see Bruce R. McConkie, *Mormon Doctrine*, 2d ed. [Salt Lake City: Bookcraft, 1979], 724, s.v. "Signs of the Times"; Joseph Fielding Smith, *Doctrines of Salvation*, comp. Bruce R. McConkie, 3 vols. [Salt Lake City: Bookcraft, 1954–56], 1:180–83).

The term *avalanche* comes from Jean Bottéro, who in his book *Mesopotamia: Writing, Reasoning, and the Gods* (Chicago: University of Chicago, 1992), entitled one of the chapters "The 'Avalanche' of Decipherments in the Ancient Near East between 1800 and 1930."

4. Of course, the recovery of the world of the Bible represents only one part of the Lord's preparation of the world to receive the restored gospel. Latter-day Saints believe that political conditions in the United States were also divinely directed. And the religious climate in the early nineteenth century provided fertile ground for the restored gospel to flourish. On this latter point, see, for example, Grant Underwood, *The Millenarian World of Early Mormonism* (Urbana, Ill.: University of Illinois, 1993), 22–23.

5. So much more could be said on the history of the early 1800s. Rather than reference each point in these introductory comments, I refer interested readers to resources that deal with the history of the Middle East, such as the following: Arthur Goldschmidt Jr., *A Concise History of the Middle East*, 5th ed. (Boulder, Colo.: Westview, 1996); Emory C. Bogle, *The Modern Middle East: From Imperialism to Freedom, 1800–1958* (Upper Saddle River, N.J.: Prentice Hall, 1996); Sydney Nettleton Fisher and William Ochsenwald, *The Middle East: A History*, 5th ed. (New York: McGraw-Hill, 1997), vol. 1; and Bernard Lewis, *The Middle East: A Brief History of the Last 2,000 years* (New York: Scribner, 1995).

See also the history woven into such semipopular accounts as Yehoshua Ben-Arieh, *The Rediscovery of the Holy Land in the Nineteenth Century*, 2d ed. (Jerusalem: Magnes, 1983); and Neil Asher Silberman, *Digging for God and Country: Exploration, Archeology, and Secret Struggle for the Holy Land, 1799–1917* (New York: Alfred A. Knopf, 1982).

6. The Isthmus of Suez lies between the northern end of the Gulf of Suez (Red Sea) and the Mediterranean Sea. Construction of the Suez Canal was completed in 1869. Traveling from England to India around Africa is about five thousand miles longer than going through the Isthmus of Suez.

7. The name *Ottoman* was coined from the name of a Turkish Muslim named Osman (ca. A.D. 1300), whose descendants created an empire through conquest. Suleiman the Magnificent (ca. 1520–66) was the greatest of the Ottoman sultans.

8. A somewhat similar but much smaller and less successful venture sponsored in the 1760s by the Danish government was the first of its kind. Carsten Niebuhr (1733–1815) was the only one of a team of five who returned alive from a mission to map the areas of Egypt and Arabia and catalog features of historical and scientific interest. He published his experiences in German and English: *A Description of Arabia* (1772) and *Travels through Arabia and Other Countries of the East* (1774).

9. This "scientific" aspect of Napoleon's expedition reveals another dimension of his strategy in conquering Egypt. He was not only motivated by immediate political concerns, but by a vision, inherent to a degree in the French Revolution itself, that France was going to restore enlightened civilization to the world. And Egypt, whose ancient splendor and wisdom had long since departed, was a prime, symbolic candidate because of its powerful past and its present weakness. This vision is powerfully communicated in a comment from the French foreign minister Talleyrand, dated February 13, 1798: "Egypt was a province of the Roman Republic; she must become a province of the French Republic. Roman rule saw the decadence of this beautiful country; French rule will bring it prosperity. The Romans wrested Egypt from kings distinguished in arts and science; the French will lift if from the hands of the most appalling tyrants who have ever existed" (quoted in Charles Coulston Gillispie and Michael Dewachter, eds., *Monuments of Egypt: The Napoleonic Edition* [Princeton, N.J.: Princeton Architectural Press, 1987], 3).

10. For an overview of pilgrimage to the Holy Land, see, for example, Teddy Kollack and Moshe Perlman, *Pilgrims to the Holy Land: The Story of Pilgrimage through the Ages* (New York: Harper and Row, 1970).

11. Several citations deal with the recovery of ancient Egypt and the decipherment of Egyptian scripts. See, for example, Richard Parkinson, *Cracking Codes: The Rosetta stone and Decipherment* (Berkeley: University of California Press, 1999); Maurice Pope, *The Story of Decipherment: From Egyptian Hieroglyphs to*

Maya Script, rev. ed. (London: Thames and Hudson, 1999), 11–84; W. V. Davies, "Egyptian Hieroglyphics," in *Reading the Past: Ancient Writing from Cuneiform to the Alphabet* (London: British Museum Press, 1990), 119–28; Johannes Friedrich, *Extinct Languages* (New York: Philosophical Library, 1957), 16–26; Ronald Ridley, *Napoleon's Proconsul in Egypt: The Life and Times of Bernardino Drovetti* (London: Rubicon Press, 1998); and pertinent entries in Donald B. Redford, ed., *The Oxford Encyclopedia of Ancient Egypt*, 3 vols. (New York: Oxford University, 2001). See also more popular accounts such as C. W. Ceram, *Gods, Graves, and Scholars: The Story of Archaeology*, 2d ed. (New York: Alfred A. Knopf, 1967), 75–135; and Leslie Greener, *The Discovery of Egypt* (New York: Viking, 1966). See also "Egyptology Online" at http://www.egyptologyonline.com/index.htm.

12. Rather than reference all the points made in these introductory comments, several citations are provided that deal with the recovery of ancient Mesopotamia and Persia and the decipherment of cuneiform. See, for example, Pope, *Story of Decipherment*, 85–122; Mogens Trolle Larsen, *The Conquest of Assyria: Excavations in an Antique Land, 1840–1860* (London: Routledge, 1996); C. B. F. Walker, "Cuneiform," in *Reading the Past*, 58–62; Seton Lloyd, *Foundations in the Dust: The Story of Mesopotamian Exploration*, rev. ed. (London: Thames and Hudson, 1980); Friedrich, *Extinct Languages*, 50–68; Herman V. Hilprecht, ed., *Explorations in Bible Lands During the 19th Century* (Philadelphia: A. J. Holman, 1903); and pertinent entries in *The Oxford Encyclopedia of Archaeology in the Near East*, 5 vols. (New York: Oxford, 1997), and Sasson, Jack M., ed., *Civilizations of the Ancient Near East*, 5 vols. (New York: Charles Scribner's Sons, 1995), 1:67–120; see also Ceram, *Gods, Graves, and Scholars*, 211–64.

13. As above, all the points made in these introductory comments are not referenced. See such works as Ben-Arieh, *The Rediscovery of the Holy Land in the Nineteenth Century;* and Silberman, *Digging for God and Country.*

14. There were three major Egyptian scripts. The oldest is hieroglyphics. *Hieratic* (priestly) and *demotic* (popular) generally derive from hieroglyphs and are increasingly cursive in nature. Comments in this paper will focus on hieroglyphics and demotic, the first two scripts to be deciphered in the nineteenth century. *Coptic* refers to late Egyptian texts written in the Greek alphabet, with a supplement of demotic signs.

15. The Rosetta stone is a black granite stela that in its present, damaged condition measures about 3 feet 9 inches tall, 2 feet 6 inches wide, and 11 inches thick, and weighs about 1,500 pounds. Originally it was a few feet taller.

16. Quoted in Ceram, *Gods, Graves, and Scholars*, 247.

17. Sometimes dubbed the "father of cuneiform [decipherment]," Rawlinson is more accurately described as one of the main decipherers, since the Irishman Edward Hincks and the Frenchman Jules Oppert made important contributions

to the process. Others associated with deciphering cuneiform include the German Christian Lassen and the Frenchman Émile Burnouf.

Darius's inscription at Bisitun (also spelled Behistun), carved into the side of a mountain along with a huge relief of the king himself, was recorded in Old Persian, Elamite, and Babylonian to commemorate some of his victories.

18. Khorsabad is the ancient Assyrian city of Dur Sharrukin ("fortress of Sargon"), which Sargon II (king from 721 to 705 B.C.) built as his new capital. Sargon is mentioned in Isaiah 20:1 and is the king who deported thousands of Israelites who became "lost" (2 Kings 17:6; 18:11).

19. The modern name *Nimrud* is derived from the name of *Nimrod*, about whom the Bible (Genesis 10:8–12) and the Quran (21:52–69) contain some traditions. Anciently, the city was named Kalhu, the biblical form of which is Calah, attested in Genesis 10:11, 12.

20. Ben-Arieh, *The Rediscovery of the Holy Land in the Nineteenth Century*, 11.

21. Silberman, *Digging for God and Country*, 18.

22. The established holy sites were primarily connected with accounts of Jesus in the New Testament. These were controlled mainly by Eastern Orthodox Christians and to a much lesser extent by Roman Catholics.

23. Silberman, *Digging for God and Country*, 40; emphasis added.

24. The Holy Land lithographs of David Roberts are available in various republications of the original 1842 edition of *Views in the Holy Land, Syria, Idumea, and Arabia.*

25. The suggestion that it would "not be a bad plan to compare Mr. Stephens' ruined cities with those in the Book of Mormon" appeared, along with an extract from Stephens's text, in the October 1, 1842, edition of the *Times and Seasons* (3:927). The comment is often attributed to the Prophet, but it may have come from editor John Taylor. I thank David J. Whittaker at Brigham Young University's Harold B. Lee Library for his conversation with me on this point.

26. Catherwood, an architect and artist, had been in Egypt and Palestine in the 1820s–30s, and his maps of Jerusalem, which he published in 1835, became the standard for years to come. Stephens was introduced to Catherwood's work after buying one of his maps in Jerusalem in 1836. They subsequently met in London and later traveled together to Central America.

27. Victor W. Von Hagen, in his introductory comments to a reprint of John Lloyd Stephens, *Incidents of Travel in Egypt, Arabia Petraea, and the Holy Land* (New York: Dover, 1996), vii–viii. I thank my colleague D. Kelly Ogden for bringing this information about John Lloyd Stephens to my attention and for sharing his file on Stephens with me.

28. Stephens, *Incidents of Travel in Egypt, Arabia Petræa, and the Holy Land,*

342, 412–14. Whether significant or not, it is interesting that Stephens, after spending a few weeks in and around Jerusalem, departed the Holy City on April 3, 1836, the day the great revelations recorded in D&C 110 took place in Kirtland, Ohio.

29. See the relevant entries in such works as Dennis L. Largey, ed., *Book of Mormon Reference Companion* (Salt Lake City: Deseret Book, 2003) and Daniel Ludlow, ed., *Encyclopedia of Mormonism,* 5 vols. (New York: Macmillan, 1992). For the book of Abraham, see also, for example, H. Donl Peterson, *The Story of the Book of Abraham: Mummies, Manuscripts, and Mormonism* (Salt Lake City: Deseret Book, 1995); John Gee, *A Guide to the Joseph Smith Papyri* (Provo, Utah: FARMS, 2000); and Michael D. Rhodes, *The Hor Book of Breathings: A Translation and Commentary* (Provo, Utah: FARMS, 2002).

30. As talented and skilled as they were, Anthon or Mitchill probably could not actually have verified Joseph Smith's translation of the "reformed Egyptian" Book of Mormon characters that Harris showed to them. Nor is it likely that they could have actually read a hieroglyphic or demotic text in 1828. They could, however, have recognized the characters as similar to certain Near Eastern scripts, including then-recently published Egyptian texts. For a fuller account of this "significant and controversial" episode in Church history, see, for example, Milton V. Backman, "Anthon Transcript," in Largey, ed., *Book of Mormon Reference Companion,* 63–66.

31. C. Wilfred Griggs, "Book of Mormon, ancient Near Eastern roots of," in Largey, *Book of Mormon Reference Companion,* 99.

32. John Taylor noted in the February 1, 1843, edition of the *Times and Seasons* that the Prophet had promised "to furnish us with further extracts from the Book of Abraham" (4:95), but this never happened. What was published in 1842 comprises our book of Abraham, but clearly there was more to be had than what is presently available.

33. H. Donl Peterson, "Translation and Publication of the Book of Abraham," in Ludlow, *Encyclopedia of Mormonism,* 134.

34. For further discussion see John Gee, "The Role of the Book of Abraham in the Restoration" (Provo, Utah: FARMS paper, 1997).

35. Quoted in Andrew C. Skinner, "Nineteenth-Century Mormon Pilgrimages to the Holy Land," in Bryan F. Le Beau and Menachem Mor, eds., *Pilgrims & Travelers to the Holy Land* (Omaha, Neb.: Creighton University Press, 1996), 230.

36. Ten dedicatory prayers have been offered on the Holy Land in this dispensation (Skinner, "Nineteenth-Century Mormon Pilgrimages to the Holy Land," 240–42, 246).

37. This important observation is made in Skinner, "Nineteenth-Century Mormon Pilgrimages to the Holy Land," 236.

38. See, for example, "President Spencer W. Kimball Dedicates Orson Hyde Memorial Garden in Jerusalem," *Ensign,* December 1979, 67.

39. References to the study of Hebrew in Kirtland are found in Joseph Smith, *History of The Church of Jesus Christ of Latter-day Saints,* ed. B. H. Roberts, 2d ed. rev., 7 vols. (Salt Lake City: The Church of Jesus Christ of Latter-day Saints, 1932–51), 2:385, 390, 396–97, 428, and so on. For a convenient summary and discussion of this matter, see D. Kelly Ogden, "The Kirtland Hebrew School," in Milton V. Backman, ed., *Regional Studies in Latter-day Saint Church History, Ohio* (Provo, Utah: Department of Church History and Doctrine, Brigham Young University, 1990), 63–87.

40. Smith, *History of the Church,* 2:396.

41. *Times and Seasons,* 4:201.

42. Even the Doctrine and Covenants is replete with biblical vocabulary, expressions, and literary devices. Thus, the recovery of the world of the Bible has also assisted with our understanding of this modern, English-language scripture. See, for example, D. Kelly Ogden, "Biblical Language and Imagery in the Doctrine and Covenants," in *The Doctrine and Covenants: A Book of Answers* (Salt Lake City: Deseret Book, 1996), 169–87.

43. *Deseret News Semi-Weekly,* June 10, 1884, 1; as quoted in *Teachings of the Presidents of the Church: John Taylor* (Salt Lake City: The Church of Jesus Christ of Latter-day Saints, 2001), 185; emphasis added.

44. Silberman, *Digging for God and Country,* 46.

45. This concept should not be challenging to Latter-day Saints, who believe that Columbus and others involved in the rediscovery of the Americas and the development of favorable conditions therein were also brought about according to the will of the Lord (1 Nephi 13:10–23).

11

MEDIEVAL TEXTS IN MORMON HYMNODY

Paul B. Pixton

Three months after the organization of The Church of Jesus Christ of Latter-day Saints, Joseph Smith received a revelation that directed the Prophet's wife, Emma, to make a selection of sacred hymns for the Church (D&C 25:12). The current edition of our hymnbook contains some 341 such hymns, including some that were in the original edition. Many others have been added over the past 150 years. In the preface of our hymnbook we read, "Inspirational music is an essential part of our meetings. The hymns invite the Spirit of the Lord, create a feeling of reverence, unify us as members, and provide a way for us to offer praises to the Lord."[1] Some of these hymns are expressions of a clearly Latter-day Saint theology, such as "The Morning Breaks," "The Spirit of God," "Praise to the Man," "O My Father," and "High on the Mountain Top," while others, such as "Lead, Kindly Light" and "Abide with Me; 'Tis Eventide," have a more general message and have come to us from the greater Christian community.

Paul B. Pixton is a professor of history at Brigham Young University.

Three hymns have, remarkably, come down to us from medieval authors, the earliest of whom flourished in the late eighth century and the latest in the early thirteenth century. A study of these hymns demonstrates some of the subtle changes in medieval Roman Catholic theology while at the same time drawing attention to three individuals who sought to give expression to their deepest spiritual feelings during a time of (as so many believe) limited enlightenment. I have undertaken this study for deep personal reasons, because I am by training a medieval historian who has spent more than forty-five years trying to understand and interpret a thousand-year period that generally receives short shrift in Latter-day Saint discussions: Is this not the period of the Great Apostasy? All too often in our treatment of human history we spring over the medieval centuries in our haste to get from the apostolic period to the age of the Reformation and the so-called forerunners of the Restoration. Indicative of this mindset was a discussion in a meeting of the high priests group in my home ward last year. There we talked about the outpouring of the Holy Ghost upon the earth at various times, and while the group found it easy to believe that such occurred during the Renaissance and Reformation periods, I was alone in proposing that there is ample evidence (for those willing to seek it) of such during the Middle Ages as well.

At a First Presidency Christmas devotional following the coming down of the Berlin Wall and the breakup of the Soviet Bloc, President Gordon B. Hinckley declared that the Spirit of the Lord has been brooding over the earth, including the people of eastern Europe.[2] This marvelous metaphor is also useful in helping us appreciate long historical processes which were going on during the Middle Ages, without which the institutions and conditions which made possible the Restoration of the gospel of Jesus Christ would not have existed in 1820. I invite you to come with me into a world not often entered by Church members, but a world of fascinating people, exciting ideas, enchanting places, and critically important institutions.

Our first stop will be in the world of the late eighth century; the place is northern Spain. Most of Spain had been overrun by

Muslims in 711, and the remaining Christian powers were crowded up against the southern edge of the Pyrenees mountains in the kingdom of the Asturias. Centuries earlier, barbarian Germans known as the Visigoths had migrated from the area of the Black Sea all the way into Spain, where they settled among and in time merged with the Romanized Iberians. Among these hard-pressed Christians lived a man named Theodulf, who somehow managed to acquire a reputation for learning and a familiarity with both Christian and pagan writers. In the year 781, following a military expedition into Spain by the mighty Frankish king Charlemagne, Theodulf fled into Frankish-held territory and offered his services to the Carolingian court, where he quickly gained a reputation as an authority on theological matters. For example, in 787 he was asked to draft a rebuttal to certain decrees recently issued by the Second Council of Nicea regarding the use of images in worship; the result was the theological compendium later known as the *Libri carolini* ("The Books by Charles"). While at the court, Theodulf became part of a small circle of scholars whose collective efforts generated that remarkable cultural flowering we call "the Carolingian Renaissance."[3]

Theodulf was a man of many talents. About 785 he was consecrated bishop of Orleans, and he later served as abbot of Fleury, demonstrating in the process qualities of an able administrator. But he was also a poet, a patron of art, and an architect—his oratory at St. Germigny-des-Prés is still standing, showing a familiarity with churches from the east as well as from Visigothic Spain.

Following Charlemagne's death in 814, Theodulf enjoyed good terms with the new king, Louis the Pious, but about 818 he fell from favor and was imprisoned at Angers. During his confinement he composed several poems, perhaps including one which contains the well-known lines *Gloria laus et honor,* which came to be included in the Palm Sunday processional music of the Catholic Church.[4]

The text by Theodulf[5] has been set to music composed by Melchior Teschner (1584–1635), as found in the Latter-day Saint hymnbook (no. 69). The translation used in the hymnal, the most widely known in English, reads:

All glory, laud, and honor
To thee, Redeemer, King,
To whom the lips of children
Made sweet hosannas ring.
Thou art the King of Israel,
Thou David's royal Son,
Who in the Lord's name comest,
The King and Blessed One.

The company of angels
Are praising thee on high,
And mortal men and all things
Created make reply.
The people of the Hebrews
With palms before thee went;
Our praise and love and anthems
Before thee we present.

To thee, before thy passion,
They sang their hymns of praise;
To thee, now high exalted,
Our melody we raise.
Thou didst accept their praises;
Accept the love we bring,
Who in all good delightest,
Thou good and gracious King.

Another stanza is not included in our hymnal. Sung until the seventeenth century, its omission suggests how tastes have changed since that time:

Be Thou, O Lord, the Rider,
And we the little ass;
That to God's holy city
Together we may pass.[6]

It is significant that in articulating the fundamental doctrines of The Church of Jesus Christ of Latter-day Saints the Prophet Joseph

Smith placed the concept of the Godhead first, followed immediately by the concepts of the Fall and the Atonement. It is also noteworthy that so much of the understanding of these teachings rests on latter-day revelation and that a good portion of each temple session is devoted to a review of them. Clearly, these were truths lost to some degree over the course of the seventeen centuries between the apostolic Church and the Restoration. But it is possible to catch a glimpse of that change as we consider the text of Theodulf's poem; therein we see reflected the social setting of his day. Human institutions later labeled as *feudalism* were in the process of being formed, giving structure to a dangerous and uncertain world. Weaker men voluntarily submitted to the power and authority of stronger men, binding themselves by oaths to serve and obey. The rights and obligations of both the overlord and the subordinate were clearly defined, and breaking this bond was a serious matter.

The prevailing theology in the late eighth to early ninth century is summarized most effectively by Professor Richard W. Southern, who describes the view of theologians before the end of the eleventh century:

They argued that by sin—"disobedience to God and obedience to the will of the Devil—man had voluntarily withdrawn himself from the service of God and committed himself to the service of the Devil. It was rather like the act of *diffidatio* in feudal custom by which a man rejected the authority of his overlord and submitted himself to another. Of course, the overlord did not acquiesce in this state of affairs: it meant war—but still, the rules of *diffidatio* having been observed, the war must be fought according to the rules. So it was in the war between God and the Devil over the soul of Man. God could not fairly use his omnipotence to deprive the Devil of the rights he had acquired over Man by Man's consent: the rule of justice must be observed even in fighting the Devil. The command over Man which the Devil had acquired by voluntary cession, could only be lost in one of two ways: either Man could go back on his choice and voluntarily turn again to God; or the Devil could himself forfeit his claim by abusing his power and breaking the rules by which he held mankind in fee. But Man's tragedy consisted precisely in the impossibility of a voluntary return. The only hope for Man therefore lay in some breach of the rules by the Devil himself."[7]

Man in this drama has a very static role: he is a helpless spectator in a battle between God and Satan, ultimately won by God because He was a superior strategist—He took on flesh and overcame the devil's power. That God should become man was a great mystery to these early Christians, a majestic, awe-inspiring act which Theodulf acclaims in his poem—this is a victory expression, with little or no place for tender compassion for the sufferings of Jesus. The earthly incidents of Jesus' life were swallowed up in a drama enacted between heaven and hell.

Between the death of Theodulf of Orleans in 821 and the early twelfth century, subtle changes occurred in people's social, intellectual, and theological perceptions. No one epitomizes these changes more than Bernard of Clairvaux (1090–1153), a young nobleman from southern France who eschewed the life of the world and in 1113 entered the recently established monastery of Citeaux in Burgundy. Three years later he was directed by the abbot to establish a "daughter-house" on the lands of the count of Troyes in the austere solitude of *Clara vallis*—Clairvaux. At the time of his death he was the dominant personality in all of Latin Christendom (that is, the Roman Catholic Church). He counseled popes and chastised secular rulers; inspired the founding of the Knights Templars; preached a crusade with his unusual oratorical skills; and wrote several hundred sermons, over five hundred letters dealing with a wide range of issues, and numerous treatises on theology and liturgy. Through these writings he had a profound influence on the development of religious sensitivity and practices, not only in his own day but from that time forward.[8]

Religious life as expressed in monasticism had become extremely busy in the centuries since Theodulf. Originally conceived of as providing balance between physical and spiritual activities, it had been transformed in the tenth to eleventh centuries into an intense routine that left the individual little private time for contemplation. In the late eleventh century, however, a trend toward a greater measure of solitude, of introspection and self-knowledge, grew rapidly and found expression in numerous spiritual soliloquies. This same period also saw the birth of a new interest in the human Jesus, a new devotion to Him, and a new concern with all the circumstances of His life. This cult of the human Jesus was closely linked in its origin to the desire to see His earthly home in Palestine (a pilgrimage) and to the crusading ideals. Jesus came to be viewed more and more as a human being, not by the exclusion of His divine nature but by the restoration of a balance strangely lacking in the notions of earlier centuries.

Borrowing from the eloquent declarations of Anselm of Canterbury of the previous generation, St. Bernard and his fellow Cistercians popularized this new view of Christ, one that engendered compassion and tenderness rather than the fear and trembling of Theodulf's age. And it was this image of Christ that passed on into later centuries and is clearly familiar to Latter-day Saints.

Whether rightly attributed to Bernard or not, one of the most popular and successful expressions of this new piety was contained in a long poem, *"Dulcis Jesu memoria,"* which has been made familiar in the translation by J. M. Neale:

> *Jesu! the very thought is sweet;*
> *In that dear Name all heart-joys meet:*
> *But, oh, than honey sweeter far*
> *The glimpses of His presence are.*[9]

In the Latter-day Saint hymnbook (no. 141), this becomes—

> *Jesus, the very thought of thee,*
> *With sweetness fills my breast.*
> *But sweeter far thy face to see,*
> *And in thy presence rest.*

The poetic writings of St. Bernard and other Cistercians paralleled artistic representations of the Crucifixion that began to appear in the late eleventh century. From the time of Theodulf and beyond, the traditional way of representation conveyed a sense of a

majestic and remote act of divine power, but from the time of
Anselm and Bernard it began to explore the limits of human suffering: The dying figure was stripped of its garments, the arms sagged
with the weight of the body, the head hung down to one side, the
eyes were closed, the blood ran down the cross. This new emotion-
alism led to the countless pieces of art depicting the suffering
Christ, whether it be the extremes of Matthias Grünewald's paint-
ing or the tenderness of Michelangelo's.[10]

Born nearly a century after Bernard, Francis of Assisi
(1181–1226) grew up in the rapidly changing world of northern Italy
in the last quarter of the twelfth century. Unlike the aristocratic
Bernard, Francis was the son of a wealthy cloth merchant and spent
his youth reading chivalric romances and dreaming of being another
Lancelot. In 1205, while engaged in military activities, Francis experienced the first stages of an agonizing spiritual "conversion"; that
is, he became aware of the glaring discrepancies between the New
Testament descriptions of how Christ and His disciples lived and
the affluent display of contemporary clergy. In consequence thereof
he renounced his secure but dull life and dedicated himself to complete poverty and service to the poor and needy.

Francis became a legend in his own time, eventually drawing
hundreds into his association, which won papal approval as the
Order of Lesser Brothers (*Ordo Fratrum Minorum*) in 1210. He
was a charismatic preacher about whom stories sprang up. Among
these are some about his communicating with birds, fish, wolves,
and other animals. Thomas of Celano (d. 1260), in his *First Life of
St. Francis (Vita prima sancti Francisci)*, preserves this anecdote:

"During the time [after 1210] when . . . many joined themselves
to the brethren, the most blessed father Francis was journeying
through the valley of Spoleto and came to a spot near Bevagna [and
three miles south of Assisi] where a very great number of birds of
different sorts were gathered together, namely doves, rooks, and
those other birds that are called in the vulgar tongue *monade* [jack-
daws]. When he saw them, being a man of the most fervent temper
and also very tender and affectionate toward all the lower and irra-
tional creatures, Francis, the most blessed servant of God, left his

companions in the way and ran eagerly toward the birds. When he was come close to them and saw that they were awaiting him, he gave them his accustomed greeting. But, not a little surprised that the birds did not fly away (as they are wont to do), he was filled with exceeding joy and humbly begged them to hear the word of God.

"After saying many things to them, he concluded: 'My brother birds, much ought you to praise your Creator and ever to love him who has given you feathers for clothing, wings for flight, and all that you had need of. God has made you noble among his creatures, he has given you a habitation in the purity of the air, and, whereas you neither sow nor reap, he himself does still protect and govern you without any care of your own.'"[11]

A similar theme is found in the "Canticle of Brother Sun," a hymn of praise honoring all creatures, which Francis wrote in Italian in 1225, shortly before his death.[12] We show this in a translation much closer to the original in the left-hand column, while the translation by William H. Draper, found in the Latter-day Saint hymnal as "All Creatures of Our God and King" (no. 62), is in the right-hand column.

Most High Almighty Good Lord,	*All creatures of our God and King,*
Yours are the praises, the glory, the honor, and all blessings!	*Lift up your voice and with us sing,*
To you alone, Most High, do they belong,	*Alleluia! Alleluia!*
And no man is worthy to mention You.	
Be praised, my Lord, with all Your creatures,	*Thou burning sun with golden beam,*
Especially Sir Brother Sun,	*Thou silver moon with softer gleam,*
By whom You give us the light of day!	*Alleluia! Alleluia!*

*And he is beautiful and radiant
  with great splendor.*

*Of you, Most High, he is a
  symbol!*

*Be praised, my Lord, for Sister
  Moon and the Stars!*

*In the sky You formed them
  bright and lovely and fair.*

*Be praised, My Lord, for
  Brother Wind*

*And for the Air and cloudy and
  clear and all Weather,*

*By which You give sustenance
  to Your creatures!*

*Be praised, My Lord, for Sister
  Water,*

*Who is very useful and humble
  and lovely and chaste!*

*Be praised, my Lord, for
  Brother Fire,*

*By whom You give us light at
  night,*

*And he is beautiful and merry
  and mighty and strong!*

*Alleluia! Oh, praise him!
  Alleluia!*

*Thou rushing wind that art so
  strong,*

*Ye clouds that sail in heav'n
  along,*

Alleluia! Alleluia!

*Thou rising morn, in praise
  rejoice;*

*Ye light of evening, find a
  voice,*

Alleluia! Alleluia!

*Alleluia! Oh, praise him!
  Alleluia!*

*Thou flowing water, pure and
  clear,*

*Make music for thy Lord to
  hear,*

Alleluia! Alleluia!

*Thou fire so masterful and
  bright,*

*That gives to man both warmth
  and light,*

Alleluia! Alleluia!

Alleluia! Oh, praise him!
Alleluia!

Be praised, My Lord, for our
Sister Mother Earth,

Dear Mother Earth, who day
by day

Who sustains and governs us,

Unfoldest blessings on our
way,

And produces fruits with color-
ful flowers and leaves!

Alleluia! Alleluia!

The flow'rs and fruit that in
thee grow,

Let them his glory also show,

Alleluia! Alleluia!

Alleluia! Oh, praise him!
Alleluia!

Be praised, my Lord, for those
who forgive for love of You

And endure infirmities and
tribulations.[13]

Francis's love for nature and God's creatures was never an end in itself. Because all creatures reflect the glory of the Creator, his focus on them was intended to ultimately draw human attention to God. Francis saw inanimate nature at the service of man, man striving to live in peace with man, and death as the point where time meets eternity.[14] Whereas earlier ascetics had renounced the world, including the dualistic Cathars (Albigensians), who in the twelfth century had rejected the physical creation as the work of Satan, Francis reflects changes in perceptions as Christians of his generation were learning to cope with materialism; rather than rejecting the physical creation as something evil that was to be shunned, Francis embraced that world and through it praised the Creator of the earth and all that is in it.

The restored gospel of Jesus Christ also testifies that this earth was created by a loving Father through His Son, for a specific purpose (1 Nephi 17:36)—not as a place to punish His children for disobedience but as a testing ground. Once the earth has "answer[ed] the end of its creation" (D&C 49:16), it will "be renewed and receive its paradisiacal glory" (Articles of Faith 1:10). With St. Francis we take delight in the Creation and sing praises to our Father for our place within it.

Our brief journey through five medieval centuries has come to an end. What we have witnessed is a religious world constantly redefining itself, breaking loose from many of the older views that had charted its course from late antiquity through the end of the first millennium of the Common Era. What we have discovered is both individuals and groups whose search for God found religious expression in poetry that has transcended their time and place, has enriched our lives, and has become an integral part of the Latter-day Saints' acceptance of "anything virtuous, lovely, or of good report or praiseworthy" (Articles of Faith 1:13).

NOTES

1. *Hymns of The Church of Jesus Christ of Latter-day Saints* (Salt Lake City: The Church of Jesus Christ of Latter-day Saints, 1985), ix.

2. See Gordon B. Hinckley, First Presidency Christmas devotional, December 1989, 4–5.

3. For detailed insights into the Carolingian Renaissance, see M. L. W. Laistner, *Thought and Letters in Western Europe, A.D. 500 to 900*, rev. ed. (Ithaca, N.Y.: Cornell University Press, 1957); Eleanor Shipley Duckett, *Alcuin, Friend of Charlemagne: His World and His Work* (New York: Macmillan, 1951); Richard E. Sullivan, *Aix-la Chapelle in the Age of Charlemagne* (Norman, Okla.: University of Oklahoma Press, 1963); and Pierre Riché, *The Carolingians: A Family Who Forged Europe* (Philadelphia: University of Pennsylvania Press, 1993), 327, 332, 342–43, 348–49.

4. See William Smith and Henry Wace, eds., *A Dictionary of Christian Biography* (London: John Murray, 1887), 4:983–89. E. L. Dümmler, *Poetae latini aevi Carolini* (Berlin: Weidmann, 1981), 1:558, gives the full text 78 lines, based on the Paris MS 18557 (tenth century). See also J. Kayser, *Beiträge zur Geschichte und Erklärung der alten Kirchenhymnen* (Paderborn: F. Schöningh, 1886),

2:313–22; Albert Hauck, ed., *Realencyklopädie für protestantische Theologie und Kirche* (Leipzig: J. C. Hinrichs'sche Buchhandlung, 1907), 19:622–25.

5. Scriptural inspiration for the hymn is found in Psalms 24:7–10; 118:25–26; Matthew 21:1–17; Luke 19:37–38.

6. See John Julian, ed., *A Dictionary of Hymnology, Setting Forth the Origin and History of Christian Hymns of All Ages and Nations*, 2d ed. rev. (New York: Dover, 1957), 426.

7. Richard W. Southern, *The Making of the Middle Ages* (New Haven, Conn.: Yale University Press, 1953), 234–35.

8. See Robert S. Hoyt, *Europe in the Middle Ages,* 2d ed. (New York: Harcourt, Brace & World, 1966), 345–47. On the life of St. Bernard, see also Watkin Williams, *Saint Bernard of Clairvaux* (Manchester: Manchester University Press, 1935), especially 372–73. Useful in the understanding of Bernard's thought are G. R. Evans, *The Mind of St. Bernard of Clairvaux* (Oxford: Clarendon Press, 1983), and *Bernard of Clairvaux* (Oxford: Oxford University Press, 2000), by the same author.

9. The poem exists in numerous manuscripts from the late twelfth century and is attributed by many to an anonymous English Cistercian, rather than to Bernard himself. The entire poem has been edited by André Wilmart, *Le 'Jubilus' dit de Saint Bernard* (Rome: n.p., 1944); see Southern, *Making of the Middle Ages,* 233–34.

10. See Southern, *Making of the Middle Ages,* 236–38.

11. Thomas of Celano, cited in A. G. Howell, trans., *The Lives of St. Francis of Assisi, by Brother Thomas of Celano* (New York: n.p., 1908), 57–59. Originally published as Thomas of Celano, *Vita prima sancti Francisci* 1.16.42–43, ed. E. d'Alençon (Rome: n.p., 1906).

12. See Marion A. Habig, ed., *St. Francis of Assisi: Writings and Early Biographies: English Omnibus of the Sources for the Life of St. Francis,* 3d ed. (Chicago: Franciscan Herald Press, 1973); see also Edward A. Armstrong, *Saint Francis: Nature Mystic, the Derivation and Significance of the Nature Stories in the Franciscan Legend* (Berkeley: University of California Press, 1973).

13. William R. Cook and Ronald B. Herzman, *The Medieval World View* (Oxford: Oxford University Press, 1983), 309–10, quoting Raphael Brown, trans., *The Little Flowers of St. Francis* (Garden City, N.Y.: Doubleday, 1958), 317–18.

14. See Vincent Moleta, *From St. Francis to Giotto: The Influence of St. Francis on Early Italian Art and Literature* (Chicago: Franciscan Herald Press, 1983), 5–10.

12

THE ROAD THROUGH PALMYRA

CONNECTING THE RESTORATION'S WITNESSES

Matthew O. Richardson

With enthusiastic anticipation, Isaiah prophesied of "a marvellous work and a wonder" (Isaiah 29:14) that would come forth following certain apostasy. Interestingly enough, this restorative work, marvelous in scope and significance, was not conceived in notable circles of theologians, scholars, or philosophers. It would have been utterly impossible for this movement to take place at any recognizable location, as did other notable events in human history. In fact, this prophesied restorative work could begin only at one place in the world, a region that relatively few knew—Palmyra, New York. In this light, the marvelous work of the Restoration was truly a wonder.

The Restoration was inseparably linked to Palmyra because within a relatively unobtrusive and common-looking hill nearby a sacred record was buried. This record, written and deposited in the hill by ancient prophets, would become known as the keystone to the doctrine of the Church and was directly associated with the

---

Matthew O. Richardson is associate dean of Religious Education at Brigham Young University.

miraculous restorative events during 1820–30.[1] Another fixed facet of the Restoration to consider was the foretold participation of a "seer" who would be raised up with the power to bring forth the word of God (Joseph Smith Translation, Genesis 50:30). Joseph of Egypt prophesied that this seer would be a deliverer "like unto Moses" (2 Nephi 3:9) and that "his name shall be called after me; and it shall be after the name of his father" (2 Nephi 3:15). President Brigham Young later clarified that it was Joseph Smith Jr. who would be the seer, for "it was decreed in the counsels of eternity, long before the foundations of the earth were laid, that he should be the man, in the last dispensation of this world, to bring forth the word of God to the people, and receive the fulness of the keys and power of the Priesthood of the Son of God."[2] Thus, a specific man and a specific hill had to meet.

As incredible as these foretold events were, there is still more to consider. There were those who would provide invaluable assistance in bringing forth the Restoration. They were the "means" to further the work (D&C 5:34), those whom Nephi described as "three witnesses" who would see Cumorah's record and "testify to the truth of the book and the things therein" (2 Nephi 27:12). Thus, Martin Harris, Oliver Cowdery, and David Whitmer also had to converge within reasonable proximity to the fixed geographical region of Palmyra, where they would be connected to the foretold seer. Their connection was necessary for the Restoration to be set in motion. The story of how the seer and three witnesses of the marvelous Restoration would meet in the proper place at the proper time is a fascinating one.

JOSEPH SMITH

The Prophet Joseph Smith's road to Palmyra was a lengthy journey of delays, detours, disappointments, and, at times, heartwrenching trials. It was a journey that began long before his birth. While some may consider the Smiths' eventual move to Palmyra as coincidence or fate, it is wise to consider President Thomas S. Monson's feeling that "there is a guiding hand above all things.

Often when things happen, it's not by accident. One day, when we look back at the seeming coincidences of our lives, we will realize that perhaps they weren't so coincidental after all."³ In this light, the hardships, trials, and mishaps experienced by the Smith family members not only molded their characters but served to move them in certain directions. Perhaps even the Smiths were surprised to find themselves in Palmyra, for there is no record of a divine manifestation directing them there. Unlike Moses or Lehi, who were foretold of a promised destination, it seems that the Smiths were able to make sense of the long journey to Palmyra only after they had arrived. And then it was difficult to ignore the "guiding hand above all things."

The Smiths' road to Palmyra was a generational journey. Perhaps a good starting point would be Ebenezer Mack (Joseph Smith Jr.'s maternal great-grandfather). He was "a man of considerable property, and lived in good style."⁴ He was in a position to leave his family in security with both property and style. Yet through a series of "misfortunes," he was reduced to poverty, and his son, Solomon, was "boundout" (apprenticed) as a youth. Apparently, this influenced Solomon to spend his lifetime consumed with obtaining riches.⁵ His quest to find comfort and prosperity was never realized, and Solomon finally concluded that "the Lord would not suffer me to prosper."⁶ Rather than sinking deep roots on a spacious family farm, Solomon's attempts to secure reasonable means to make a living eventually led him and his family to Gilsum, New Hampshire. It was while Solomon was living in Gilsum that his son Stephen, a successful businessman, sought to have his sister, Lucy, live with him and help care for his growing family.⁷ Lucy Mack returned with her brother Stephen to Tunbridge, Vermont, in 1795 while her parents, Solomon and Lydia Gates Mack, remained in Gilsum.⁸

Joseph Smith's father's family was of Puritan stock with deep generational roots in Topsfield, Massachusetts. Samuel Smith (Joseph Jr.'s paternal great-grandfather) was well respected and even served in community positions. Samuel's second son, Asael (Joseph Jr.'s grandfather), left the family farm only to return to Topsfield in hopes of saving the family farm from the burden of debt.[9] Asael's attempts to save the farm were in vain, and after spending time in Ipswich, Massachusetts, Asael sought inexpensive land in Vermont. He took his sons, Jesse and Joseph, with him to clear land, and in 1791 the Smith family moved to Tunbridge, Vermont. It was in Tunbridge that Joseph Smith and Lucy Mack met and eventually married in 1796.

Joseph Smith Sr. and Lucy Mack Smith began their married life under reasonably favorable circumstances. With modest business success, Joseph Sr. became interested in investing in ginseng.[10] Unfortunately, he was cheated in the venture and was left financially ruined. For the next fourteen years, the Smiths worked day labor and resorted to tenancy rather than land ownership. It was under such conditions that Joseph Smith Jr. was born on December 23, 1805, in Sharon, Vermont. After enduring the typhoid outbreak in 1812, the Smiths began farming in Norwich, Vermont, on Esquire Murdock's property. Lucy Mack Smith wrote, "The first year our crops failed; yet, by selling fruit which grew on the place, we succeeded in obtaining bread for the family."[11] Unfortunately, the second year of crops also failed, and the last straw came in 1816. Often called the "year without a summer," 1816 saw unusual wintry conditions throughout the spring and summer making it impossible to raise crops.[12] When the crops failed for a third time, Joseph Smith Sr., discouraged and broken, determined to leave Vermont. His brothers had already moved to New York by 1815, and Joseph thought it might be well to follow in their footsteps. Joseph Sr.'s desire to leave Vermont was not singular. In fact, in 1816 Vermont experienced a mass exodus of those hoping to find more favorable conditions elsewhere.[13]

The Smiths found their way to the village of Palmyra, New York, in 1816. Through sheer determination and a united effort by parents and children, the Smiths worked to secure a tract of land in Manchester (on the borders of the township of Palmyra) sometime in 1818.[14] After building a "snug" cabin, the Smiths continued to work the land and secure odd jobs to make ends meet. At this point they were located less than three miles from a drumlin that would later be called the "Hill Cumorah."[15]

Now that the Smiths were living just off Stafford Road bordering Palmyra and Manchester, conditions were set for unfolding the Restoration. Granted, the road to Palmyra had been arduous and long, but now the chosen seer was present. In 1820 Joseph would enter the grove of trees that surrounded the Smith log home, and this experience would set in motion a series of marvelous events. In 1827, after yearly visits to the Hill Cumorah, Joseph would obtain the sacred record and begin translating the contents. Three years later, the Church of Jesus Christ would be restored again in Fayette, New York, less than thirty miles from Cumorah. It is interesting that the Lord's hand in moving Joseph into the position to receive the plates was wrought not only upon him but upon previous generations of his family. While circumstances of the moment, poor personal decisions, and even decisions made by others seemed unfortunate and surely unbearable at the time, the Smiths and the Macks were influenced by such experiences that comfort might have otherwise eclipsed. Likewise, some may conclude that the desperate ice summer of 1816 was bereft of godliness, and they may be surprised to find God in the event upon further inspection. This was the culminating event, after all, that persuaded the Smiths to leave Vermont and seemed to direct them further along the road to the area of Palmyra. Upon later reflection, Brigham Young said, "The Lord had his eye upon him [Joseph Smith], and upon his father, and upon his father's father, and upon their progenitors. . . . He has watched that family and that blood as it has circulated from its fountain to the birth of that man."[16]

MARTIN HARRIS

The road to Palmyra was much shorter for Martin Harris than for the Smiths. This does not discount the influences on or reasons for earlier members of the Harris family to immigrate to a new country and settle in Palmyra. But much of Martin Harris's pre-Palmyra history is only slightly known.[17] Martin Harris was born

May 18, 1783, in Easttown, New York. He was described by one of his early contemporaries as an "industrious, hard-working farmer, shrewd in his business calculations, frugal in his habits, and what was termed a prosperous man in the world."[18] He married his cousin Lucy Harris in 1808 and, over the next several decades, managed over 240 acres of productive land. In addition to his farming skills, Martin was a man of varied talent. He won prizes in local fairs, produced textiles, and raised animals. He was also active in civic affairs, participating in local defensive campaigns during the War of 1812 and serving as a town manager and the overseer of highways. It is clear by almost every account that Martin Harris maintained a respectable reputation.

With Harris already established in Palmyra, it is how his path intersected that of Joseph Smith that is of particular interest and importance. Harris became acquainted with the Smith family sometime after their arrival in Palmyra in 1816. It seems that he first became associated with the Smiths when he employed some of the members of their family.[19] This makes sense since the Smiths were eager to find means to support themselves and better their circumstances. Beyond this scope, the depth and frequency of their association is uncertain. According to Harris, it was well after Joseph's vision in 1820 that he began to personally investigate the religious claims of the young prophet. Although it is certain that Harris knew the Smiths by this time, at least through their business association, he was initially cautious in his involvement with the Restoration. In fact, he first waited for his wife and daughter to make inquiries about Joseph's experiences before he began his own investigation.[20] But by 1828 Martin was confident enough in his opinion of the Restoration that he found himself helping Joseph by acting as his scribe in the translation.

The path to the Restoration for Martin Harris was not predictable, nor was it easy. By 1829 it was well known in Palmyra that Martin Harris was directly connected with the Restoration and even though he was a Palmyra local with an essentially impeccable character, he was publicly criticized and scorned for this connection. In spite of the scorn, Harris was unafraid to show public support of

Joseph and the Restoration.[21] In addition to giving personal assistance, Harris was also a financier of both Prophet and the work of the Restoration. Little did he realize that the very land he successfully cultivated would one day become the ransom for publishing Cumorah's record.[22]

OLIVER COWDERY

Like Joseph Smith's path, Oliver Cowdery's road to Palmyra can be traced to generations before his birth. Unlike the Smith family, where financial ruin, unfortunate mishap, and even natural disaster uprooted and moved the family, Oliver's heritage was moved by different means. Oliver Cowdery's fourth-great-grandfather William Cowdery was "staunch in his belief of personal religious freedom and the right of free worship."[23] Inspired by personal beliefs, William pursued a quest of religious worship by coming to America with the Pilgrim movement in 1630. For several generations, the Cowderys made their home in Massachusetts, and then Nathaniel Cowdery moved to Reading, Vermont, in 1786. Nathaniel's grandson William Cowdery Jr. married Rebecca Fuller and became the father of Oliver Cowdery on October 3, 1806. It is interesting to note that Oliver's mother, Rebecca Fuller, was the great-granddaughter of John Fuller and Mehitbel Rowley, who were the second-great-grandparents of Lucy Mack Smith (mother of Joseph Smith Jr.). This made Oliver Cowdery and Lucy Mack Smith third cousins.[24] There is no evidence, however, that Oliver knew of his family relationship with the Smiths.[25]

Oliver Cowdery was raised in Vermont, and although some of his brothers left the family home in search of better situations in New York, Oliver stayed until 1825. In 1828 Oliver's brother Lyman was hired to teach at a rural school in Manchester, New York. Unfortunately, Lyman could not fulfill the assignment and suggested to the trustees that his younger brother, Oliver, might be given the post. The trustees of the school (which included Hyrum Smith) approved Oliver as a replacement, and he began his employ in 1828.[26] At this point, Oliver not only had found the road to

Palmyra but was himself the master of a schoolhouse located on Stafford Road, only a mile east of the Smith home. With such close proximity, it was only a matter of time before his path intersected the Prophet's.

It was the general custom of the day that the master of the rural school would board with families of his students in lieu of charging tuition.[27] Thus, Oliver met the Smiths under this circumstance. Remember that Joseph was in Harmony, Pennsylvania, at this time and not at the Smith homestead. According to Lucy Mack Smith, it was while Oliver was staying with them that "he began to hear from all quarters concerning the plates."[28] Rumors of the miraculous events had been circulating in Palmyra since the First Vision in 1820. To think that Oliver would not hear of the rumors, especially when he was actually boarding with the Smiths, would be odd indeed. With piqued curiosity, Oliver began to petition Father Smith for more information about the incredible experiences. Naturally, the Smiths were cautious in sharing tales of visions, angels, and golden plates—especially with strangers. Lucy Smith admits that after a "considerable length of time," Oliver gained the confidence of Joseph Sr. and was given "a sketch of the facts relative to the plates."[29]

The accounts of the Restoration that Father Smith shared with Oliver made a deep impression on him. He couldn't seem to escape thinking about the events and finally determined that he must meet Joseph. After making it "a subject of prayer," Oliver firmly believed that it was "the will the Lord" that he should go to Harmony, Pennsylvania. With that sense of a "guiding hand above all things," Cowdery was resolute in his desire to leave for Harmony, and he related to Lucy Mack Smith, "If there is a work for me to do in this thing, I am determined to do it."[30] Thus, in late March 1829, Oliver Cowdery and Samuel Smith left Manchester to meet the Prophet Joseph in Harmony, Pennsylvania. Granted, to some, Oliver's generational journey to Palmyra may have been surprising, but in truth his arrival and intersection with the promised seer were foreseen.

For Joseph, Oliver's arrival was none too soon. In March 1829 the Lord assured Joseph, "I will provide means whereby thou mayest accomplish the thing which I have commanded thee" (D&C 5:34). Only weeks later, Joseph met Oliver, the promised "means" to the restorative end. Almost immediately after his arrival, Oliver Cowdery began working as Joseph's scribe in the translation of the Book of Mormon and was also witness to the marvelous work of the Restoration. With Oliver at Joseph's side, the restorative events began to unfold at a wondrous pace.

David Whitmer

David Whitmer was born January 7, 1805, near Harrisburg, Pennsylvania. His journey to Palmyra began when his parents, Peter and Mary Musselman Whitmer, left Pennsylvania for New York in 1809. The Whitmers settled with other Pennsylvanian Germans in Fayette, New York, which happened to be only thirty miles from Palmyra. The eventual parents of eight children, the Whitmers were respected citizens in the area.[31]

According to David Whitmer, he arrived in Palmyra because of business dealings. His initial connection to the Restoration, however, was through Oliver Cowdery. In 1828 David Whitmer was on business in Palmyra when he heard townsfolk discussing golden plates found by local resident Joseph Smith. Initially, Whitmer dismissed the claims as gossip, but then he talked further with Oliver Cowdery, who was living in Palmyra at the time. Oliver Cowdery said that he knew the Smith family and believed that there was some truth to the story and that he planned to investigate further.[32]

David, who was twenty-three years old at the time, returned to Fayette with a promise that Oliver Cowdery would advise him of his investigation. David was informed months later that Oliver intended to visit Joseph in Harmony, Pennsylvania, where the Prophet was living near his in-laws.[33] In the spring of 1829, Oliver Cowdery and Samuel Smith made their way to Harmony. Both Oliver and Samuel visited the Whitmers in Fayette on their way to visit Joseph in Pennsylvania. Little did anyone realize at this point that within a year's time, the Church of Jesus Christ would be organized at that very spot in Fayette.

Oliver and Samuel departed to visit Joseph, and shortly afterward, David received another letter from Oliver giving a positive testimony to his inquiries regarding Joseph and the plates. In a later communication, Oliver told David that he was acting as a scribe for Joseph as they translated the plates from Cumorah. Oliver even included several lines from the translated work, which David shared with his family in Fayette. A later communication from Oliver requested David to come to Harmony and bring Oliver and Joseph back to Fayette to board with the Whitmers while they finished the translation of the record.[34] After consulting with Father Whitmer, David was set to bring both Oliver and Joseph to Fayette, pending completion of the spring planting.

The request for David to leave Fayette for Harmony could not have come at a more inconvenient time. Fall harvest was dependent on a successful spring planting, and the Whitmers were depending on a successful fall harvest. With David's responsibility to prepare the soil for the spring planting, it would appear that his road to meet the Prophet Joseph would be delayed or canceled. But when David returned to his fields to resume plowing, he found that five to seven acres had been plowed during the night.[35] He was therefore able to complete the plowing in short order. What might have appeared as coincidence to some bore the mark of a "guiding hand above all things" the next day. When David went to spread the plaster of paris, a common soil preparation of the day, he found the work was already done. His sister said that her children had called her the day before to watch three strangers spread the plaster with remarkable skill. She assumed they had been hired by David or by Father Whitmer.[36] It seemed clear that the "guiding hand" of divine intervention would clear necessary roadblocks that would have impeded David Whitmer from completing his journey and connecting with the Prophet Joseph Smith. David drove the three-day journey of about one hundred miles to Harmony to bring Oliver and Joseph back to the Whitmer farm. They returned to Fayette around the first of June 1829.

The Whitmers received their new guests warmly. According to Joseph, Father Whitmer extended an invitation to stay with them, free of expense, for as long as was needed to complete the work.[37] In addition to the temporal support provided by the Whitmers, "David, John and Peter Whitmer, jun., became the Prophet's zealous friends and assistants in the work."[38] With David's road through the Palmyra region and his connection with the Prophet Joseph complete, he assisted in the restorative works that included his name on the charter of the newly established Church, which was organized in Peter Whitmer's home in 1830.

CONCLUSION

Fulfillment of Isaiah's prophecy of a marvelous work and wonder to come forth may have seemed implausible when he spoke it. Aligning all the factors necessary for a restorative effort is nearly incomprehensible to the logistical mind. But in June 1829, Joseph Smith, Martin Harris, Oliver Cowdery, and David Whitmer retired to the woods together and became forever known as witnesses of the foretold Restoration. In their testimony of the work to "all nations, kindreds, tongues, and people," Harris, Cowdery, and Whitmer testified that they "beheld and bear record that these things are true." They then stated, "And it is marvelous in our eyes" (Book of Mormon, "The Testimony of Three Witnesses").

When President Howard W. Hunter recalled the restorative efforts, he reminded the Saints that this marvelous work was the fruit of "the most humble beginnings."[39] Such beginnings began to take shape long before the First Vision in 1820. The prelude to such restorative events required individuals to be uprooted, endure the follies of their peers, be moved upon in unseen ways, and make connections with others that would yield a harvest beyond their mortal understanding and grasp. This prelude was not coincidence, nor was it mere fate. The divine arranging to bring the restorative work to pass was a wondrous work indeed. Elder Neal A. Maxwell reminds us that "His [God's] overseeing precision pertains not only to astrophysical orbits but to human orbits as well."[40] In such manner were the human orbits of Joseph Smith, Martin Harris, Oliver Cowdery, and David Whitmer aligned. Such alignment was a wondrous prelude to the marvelous Restoration.

NOTES

1. See Joseph Smith, *History of the Church of Jesus Christ of Latter-day Saints*, ed. B. H. Roberts, 2d ed. rev., 7 vols. (Salt Lake City: The Church of Jesus Christ of Latter-day Saints, 1932–51), 4:461.

2. Brigham Young, in *Journal of Discourses*, 26 vols. (London: Latter-day Saints' Book Depot, 1854–86), 7:289.

3. Thomas S. Monson, quoted in Joseph B. Wirthlin, "Lessons Learned in the Journey of Life," *Ensign*, December 2000, 9.

4. Lucy Mack Smith, *Biographical Sketches of Joseph Smith the Prophet and His Progenitors for Many Generations* (1853; reprint, Orem, Utah: Grandin Book, 1995), 15.

5. Richard Lloyd Anderson, *Joseph Smith's New England Heritage* (Salt Lake City: Deseret Book, 2003), 5–7.

6. Solomon Mack, *A Narraitve* [sic] *of the life of Solomon Mack Containing an Account of the Many Severe Accidents He Met with During a Long Series of Years, Together with the Extraordinary Manner in Which He Was Converted to the Christian Faith* (Windsor, Vt.: Solomon Mack, 1810), 10, in L. Tom Perry Special Collections, Harold B. Lee Library, Brigham Young University.

7. See Smith, *Biographical Sketches*, 36.

8. See Anderson, *Joseph Smith's New England Heritage*, 80.

9. See Anderson, *Joseph Smith's New England Heritage*, 117.

10. Ginseng, a root thought to prolong life and restore virility, grew wild in Vermont and was greatly valued in China.

11. Smith, *Biographical Sketches*, 66.

12. It was later proposed that the unusual weather pattern in 1816 was caused by the effects of a violent volcanic eruption in Indonesia (Henry Stommel and Elizabeth Stommel, *Volcano Weather* [Newport, R.I.: Henry and Elizabeth Stommel, 1983], 3, 11–12; cited in *Church History in the Fulness of Times* [Salt Lake City: The Church of Jesus Christ of Latter-day Saints, 2000], 24).

13. See Larry C. Porter, "A Study of the Origins of The Church of Jesus Christ of Latter-day Saints in the States of New York and Pennsylvania, 1816–1831" (Ph.D. diss., Brigham Young University, 1971), 10.

14. Larry Porter reports the move as "approximately 1818" because of contemporary accounts placing the Smiths in the area in 1818–19. Discussion as to

the actual location of the Smith's log home (whether in the Township of Palmyra or in Manchester) can also be found in Porter, "A Study of the Origins of The Church," 16–17.

15. What is now known as "Hill Cumorah" was also called "Mormon Hill," "Golden Bible Hill," and "Bible Hill" (Porter, "Study of the Origins of The Church," 25).

16. Young, in *Journal of Discourses,* 7:289–90.

17. See Richard Lloyd Anderson, *Investigating the Book of Mormon Witnesses* (Salt Lake City: Deseret Book, 1981), 95.

18. James Reeves, *Palmyra Courier,* May 24, 1872; James Reeves had known Martin Harris in Palmyra, New York.

19. See *Church History in the Fulness of Times,* 45.

20. See Anderson, *Investigating the Book of Mormon Witnesses,* 107.

21. See Smith, *Biographical Sketches,* 112–13.

22. Martin Harris sold one hundred and fifty-one acres at a public auction in April 1831 to pay Mr. E. B. Grandin (Wayne Cutler Gunnell, "Martin Harris— Witness and Benefactor to the Book of Mormon" [master's thesis, Brigham Young University, 1955], 38).

23. Stanley R. Gunn, *Oliver Cowdery: Second Elder and Scribe* (Salt Lake City: Bookcraft, 1962), 13.

24. Lucy Mack's mother was also a cousin of Mary Gates, who was married to Nathaniel Cowdery Jr. (Oliver Cowdery's second-great-granduncle); see Gunn, *Oliver Cowdery,* 14–15.

25. See Gunn, *Oliver Cowdery,* 14.

26. See Lucy Mack Smith, *Biographical Sketches,* 128; see also *Church History in the Fulness of Times,* 53.

27. See Gunn, *Oliver Cowdery,* 29.

28. Smith, *Biographical Sketches,* 128.

29. Smith, *Biographical Sketches,* 128.

30. Smith, *Biographical Sketches,* 129.

31. See Porter, "A Study of the Origins of The Church," 93.

32. See Lyndon W. Cook, ed. *David Whitmer Interviews: A Restoration Witness* (Orem, Utah: Grandin Book, 1993), 60.

33. See Cook, *David Whitmer Interviews,* 61.

34. See Andrew Jenson, *Latter-day Saint Biographical Encyclopedia,* 4 vols. (Salt Lake City: Western Epics, 1971), 1:265.

35. See David Whitmer interview, September 7–8, 1878, interviewed by Orson Pratt, cited in Cook, *David Whitmer Interviews,* 51.

36. See Smith, *Biographical Sketches,* 136–37.

37. See Smith, *History of the Church,* 1:49.

38. Jenson, *Latter-day Saint Biographical Encyclopedia,* 1:265.

39. Howard W. Hunter, "The Sixth Day of April, 1830," *Ensign,* May 1991, 63.

40. Neal A. Maxwell, "In Him All Things Hold Together," in *1990–91 Devotional and Fireside Speeches* (Provo, Utah: Brigham Young University Press, 1991), 108.

13

WORDS "FITLY SPOKEN"

TYNDALE'S ENGLISH TRANSLATION OF THE BIBLE

David Rolph Seely

*W*illiam Tyndale (1494–1536), reformer and translator, is the true father of the English Bible. His English translations of the Bible printed in 1526, 1530, and 1534 provided the basis for the King James Translation, and through his translations, Tyndale became one of the founders of the modern English language. In the process of translating the Bible from Hebrew and Greek into English, Tyndale coined several new English words—transforming older English words or in some cases inventing unique and striking new English words—that have since become central terms in religious discourse. From a study of just a few of these words, we can better understand Tyndale's genius for language, his methodology, and his theology, and we can gain insight into the complexity of translation. Most important, we can better appreciate the gift Tyndale gave to English speakers: the word of God in our own language. Truly, for Tyndale and for us, "a word fitly spoken is like apples of gold in pictures of silver" (Proverbs 25:11).

David Rolph Seely is a professor of ancient scripture at Brigham Young University.

Born in Gloucestershire, England, William Tyndale studied at Oxford and possibly Cambridge. He joined the reform movement there, and in 1524 he moved to Hamburg, Germany, never to return to his native country. The reformers all recognized the Bible as the authoritative voice of God that superseded the traditions of the Catholic Church. Foxe records Tyndale's early passion for the Bible. He recounts that Master Tyndale happened to be in the company of a learned man, and in communing and disputing with the learned man about the issue of the Bible and the Catholic Church, the learned man said: "We were better without God's law than the pope's. Maister Tyndall hearing that, answered him, I defy the Pope and all his laws, and said, if God spare my life ere many years, I will cause a boy that driveth the plough, shall know more of the Scripture than thou dost."[1]

In 1522, Tyndale, following the belief of the Reformers that it was necessary to make the scriptures available to people in their own language (a cause that was also championed by Martin Luther, his contemporary), conceived the plan of translating the Bible into English.

His translation was not the first. There is actually a long history of the translation of the word of God into English, beginning with a cowherd from Whitby named Caedmon who paraphrased some biblical passages into Old English in A.D. 670. Aldhelm, Bishop of Sherborne, translated the Psalter from the Vulgate into Anglo-Saxon in about A.D. 700, and the Venerable Bede (673–735) translated portions of the Vulgate into Old English. He died while translating the Gospel of John. King Alfred the Great (871–901) translated parts of Exodus and Acts into Old English, and the Lindisfarne Gospels (ca. 687) had an interlinear Anglo-Saxon translation between the Vulgate Latin lines. John Wycliffe was the first to translate the whole of the Bible into Middle English in 1380, a work that predated the printing press and was thus disseminated in manuscript form.[2]

But whereas Wycliffe's translation of the Bible was made from the Vulgate into Middle English, Tyndale was the first to translate the New Testament into Modern English from the original languages of Hebrew and Greek. He was a trailblazing pioneer among

English translators because there was no model translation from Hebrew or Greek to follow.[3] Because of increasing hostility against him and the other reformers, Tyndale realized it was impossible to do the translation in England, and thus he moved to the mainland of Europe. While working in Cologne, Worms, and Antwerp, he published his English translation of the New Testament in 1526 and his translation of the Pentateuch and the book of Jonah in 1530. He then published a revised version of his original New Testament translation and the Pentateuch in 1534, and he left behind a manuscript copy of his translation of Joshua through Chronicles.[4] Because he was wanted by the Catholic Church for his heretical views and his publication of the Bible into English, he was betrayed by an associate, kidnapped by authorities of the Church in Antwerp, and taken to Vilvorde (near Brussels), where he was tried for heresy and executed in 1536. His last words were, "Lord open the King of England's eyes."[5] Little did he know that just before his death King Henry VIII—as a part of his break with the Catholic Church—had granted permission for the circulation of the English Bible. The Bible that was circulated was produced by Matthew Coverdale and was largely based on Tyndale's work.

Because of the printing press, public demand, and financial incentive to publish his work, the Tyndale Bible was widely disseminated and had great impact on English speakers and the Bible itself. In 1604 the King James translators were commissioned to produce a new translation. It was to be based on previous translations and of all of the translations, Tyndale's was by far the most influential. For centuries the King James Bible has been rightfully praised as a "literary masterpiece," as the prime exemplar of the English language, and as a text that has shaped modern English. But in the last half of the twentieth century, scholars have discovered that much of the genius of the language of the King James Version was, in fact, originally the work of William Tyndale. The recent and definitive study by Jon Nielson and Royal Skousen has determined that a huge percentage of the familiar language of the King James Version comes from Tyndale. According to their study, about 76 percent of the Old Testament and 84 percent of the New Testament text of the King James Version are the retained words of Tyndale.[6]

The translation of the word of God into the modern spoken language of English, from the original languages of Hebrew and Greek, was an extraordinary achievement in the sixteenth century, not because scholars did not know Hebrew and Greek, but because English had not established itself as a language for serious matters. The educated elite—those trained in the classical languages of Greek and Latin—considered English a barbaric language without the complex grammatical nuances necessary to properly express the word of God. In fact, a debate was held in 1401 at Oxford between a man named Richard Ullerston and his critics as to whether English was an appropriate language for the translation of the Bible. The decision rendered by Thomas Arundel, the archbishop of Canterbury, effectively banned the English language from any aspect of English church life: "We therefore legislate and ordain that nobody shall from this day forth translate any text of the Holy Scriptures on his own authority into the English."[7] In addition, at the time of Tyndale the shift from Middle to Modern English had just begun. Tyndale's translation, along with Shakespeare and the King James Version, would establish Modern English as we know it today.

It is said that Tyndale was a master of seven foreign languages,[8] but most importantly, he was a master of his native language, English. Translators of the Bible before Tyndale relied on the Latin Vulgate (the official version of the Bible for the Catholic Church), but Tyndale believed that the original Hebrew and Greek of the scriptures were languages more suitably rendered into English than Latin: "Saint Jerome also translated the Bible into his mother tongue [i.e., the Latin Vulgate]: why may not we also? They will say it cannot be translated into our tongue, it is so rude. It is not so rude as they are false liars. For the Greek tongue agreeth more with the English than with the Latin. And the properties of the Hebrew tongue agreeth a thousand more times with the English than with the Latin."[9]

In the case of Hebrew, scholars have noted that Tyndale was

right in sensing the superiority of English to Latin in matters of rendering Hebrew syntax. One scholar has noted that Hebrew and English have similar word orders and that in his English translation Tyndale masterfully rendered the syntax of the original Hebrew into a fluid and rhythmical English prose that in turn influenced English writers.[10]

TYNDALE'S WORDS "FITLY SPOKEN"

In the process of his translation, Tyndale bequeathed much of the memorable English phraseology that we associate with the sacredness of the word of God. Consider the familiar cadences of the following phrases created by Tyndale: "let there be light, and there was light," "male and female created he them," "who told thee that thou wast naked?" "my brother's keeper," "the Lord bless thee, and keep thee: the Lord make his face shine upon thee," "thou shalt love the Lord thy God with all thine heart, with all thy soul and with all thy might," "the salt of the earth," "the powers that be," "a law unto themselves," "filthy lucre," and "fight the good fight." These phrases have become impressed in the English language both in religious discourse and proverbial expressions. One scholar thus assesses Tyndale's contribution to language: "It would be hard to overpraise the literary merits of what he had done. Much of his rendering would later be incorporated into the Authorized or King James Version, and the rhythmical beauty of his prose, skillful use of synonyms for freshness, variety, and point, and 'magical simplicity of phrase' imposed itself on all later versions, down to the present day."[11]

Tyndale faced a great challenge in rendering Hebrew and Greek words into his native English. Words are powerful instruments in the transfer of meaning, and thus the translation of words is very tricky. Within a language words develop complex semantic fields—that is, sets of meanings depending on context and usage. Thus any specific word is often very difficult, if not impossible, to accurately translate into another language since a corresponding term with the same semantic fields may not be found. As the old

Italian proverb goes, *tradutore traditore*—"a translator is a traitor." Any rendering of a text from one language to another inevitably involves interpretation and the changing of meaning.

The choice of words can also be theologically loaded. Since Tyndale was a Protestant, his translation was carefully phrased in order to state the viewpoints of the reformers. In several notable cases, Tyndale deliberately chose to render words that had a long legacy among Catholicism with new terms that Catholics found offensive. For example, he used "congregation" instead of "church," "elder" instead of "priest," "repentance" instead of "do penance," and "love" instead of "charity." Tyndale's English translations of these words were in many cases probably more accurate translations of the Greek terms, but they differed from the familiar Vulgate upon which much Christian theology had been based. These terms are loaded: "do penance" had sacramental implications rejected by many reformers—whereas "repentance" more closely reflected an act that could be done by an individual before God without the need of the church. And Tyndale preferred the term "love" as being more allusive to the Protestant understanding of grace and the term "charity" to be more in tune with the Catholic emphasis on works. These changes were offensive to Catholics and were heavily criticized by many, including Tyndale's countryman, Thomas More.[12] Interestingly enough, the King James translators chose to retain the traditional terms "church," "priest," and "charity," but nowhere does one find the word "penance" in the King James Version.

Like most translators, Tyndale sought to render the biblical text into plain and literal English and tried to capture the sense of each word in its original language and context. In many cases, particularly in the Old Testament, Tyndale came upon ancient words and phrases that did not have precise English counterparts. Tyndale studied the original Hebrew and/or Greek of the biblical text and then looked at the ancient translations in Greek and Latin—the Septuagint and the Vulgate—for help. He could also consult Wycliffe's translation—which was not very useful because it was in Middle English and rendered from the Vulgate. Tyndale apparently made great use of Luther's German translation of the New

Testament in 1522, for its grammar, vocabulary, and theology.[13] In several cases Tyndale solved translation problems by ingeniously coining new English words. Sometimes he simply transformed older English words, and sometimes he invented new and unique English words—some of which have become common vocabulary in religious discourse in English. Here we will look at six such "newly coined" words: *Jehovah, Passover, atonement, scapegoat, mercy seat,* and *shewbread.*

Jehovah. Perhaps the most significant of the "new" words that Tyndale bequeathed us is the name of God—*Jehovah.* Throughout the Hebrew Bible, the proper name of God is rendered with the tetragrammaton *YHWH*—which occurs, according to one count, 6,828 times.[14] The ancient vocalization of the four consonants of this name is not known, but scholars hypothesize that it was pronounced "Yahweh." Because of the sanctity of this name within Judaism, a tradition developed to call God not by His name but by the designation *Lord,* or *Adonai* in Hebrew. At the end of the fifth century after Christ, the Massoretes (who first put the vowels in the Hebrew text) reflected this tradition by putting the vowels for the Hebrew word *Adonai* below the consonants of the tetragrammaton, thereby directing the reader to read *Adonai* rather than the name of God contained in the tetragrammaton. The early Greek and Latin translators followed the Jewish tradition and simply rendered the tetragrammaton as Greek *kyrios* or Latin *Dominus.* In his Middle English translation, Wycliffe rendered *YHWH* as *Adonai,* and Luther translated the word into the German *HERR* ("Lord") using capital letters, presumably to distinguish it from the translation of the Hebrew word *Adonai* in the Bible into *Herr.*

Tyndale followed this tradition and used the English word LORDE throughout his translation, and apparently following Luther he put the word into capital letters. There are several times in scripture, however, when Tyndale deemed the name of God itself to be essential to the meaning of the text. For example, Tyndale rendered Exodus 6:3 as follows: "And God spake unto Moses saying unto him: I am the Lord, and I appeared unto Abraham, Isaac and

Jacob an almighty God: but in my name Jehovah was I not known unto them." Thus, Tyndale gave us the first occurrence of the word *Jehovah*—an anglicized form of the Hebrew *YHWH*—in English. The word "Jehovah" was formed by using the vowels of *Adonai* with the consonants *YHWH* producing YaHoWaH or YaHoVaH—since the Hebrew letter *w* can be pronounced as "w" or "v." Some have given Tyndale credit for actually inventing the word *Jehovah,* but scholars have found prior attestations of this word in a Latin theological text by Petrus Galatinus dating to A.D. 1520 and suspect that it might go back even further.[15] Whether a similar name already existed in Latin or not, according to the *Oxford English Dictionary* it was Tyndale who was responsible for coining this term in English. Tyndale also used *Jehovah* in titles such as *Jehovah Nissi* in Exodus 17:15 and *Jehovah Shalom* in Judges 6:24.

At the end of his translation of Genesis, Tyndale included a list of words explaining his translations of various Hebrew words. In these notes Tyndale explains the name *Jehovah:* "Jehovah is God's name, neither is any creature so called. And it is as much to say as one that is of himself, and dependeth of nothing. Moreover as oft as thou seest LORD in great letters (except there be an error in the printing) it is in Hebrew *Jehovah,* thou that art or he that is."[16]

The King James translators followed Tyndale and his predecessors in using the English word *Lord,* with the "L" as a full-sized capital and the "ORD" in small capital letters, to render the tetragrammaton. But in a few passages they also deemed it necessary to use the name *Jehovah.* For example, in the passage in Exodus 6:3 the King James Version follows Tyndale's rendering. The King James Version includes *Jehovah* in four other places in the Old Testament (Genesis 22:14; Psalm 83:18; Isaiah 12:2 and 26:4). Within the Restoration, the word *Jehovah* is the accepted word in English to represent Jesus Christ as the God of the Old Testament in the Book of Mormon, the Doctrine and Covenants, and the Pearl of Great Price.[17]

Passover. Throughout the Old Testament, Tyndale was faced with many legal and religious Hebrew terms that were difficult to find English equivalents for. The custom among previous translators was simply to render the Hebrew word into some form of the translation language. Tyndale met with the first of the Jewish festivals in Exodus—Passover. The translation of the Hebrew names of the Old Testament festivals posed an interesting challenge for translators. The Greek and Latin translators, along with Wycliffe and Luther, simply rendered Hebrew *Shabbath* with some form of the Hebrew word: Greek, *Sabbata;* Latin, *Sabbata;* Wycliffe, *Sabbath;* German, *Sabbatag.* Tyndale rendered it *sabbath day.* Then there were the three Hebrew pilgrimage festivals: *Pesach, Shavuoth,* and *Sukkoth.* Tyndale simply translated two of these words into English: *Shavuoth* as "weeks" and *Sukkoth,* meaning *tents,* as "tabernacles." However, there was not an English word for the Hebrew *Pesach.* Other translators simply transliterated the Hebrew letters in its place: Greek, *pesaq;* Latin as *phase* (using a different pronunciation of the Hebrew letters) or *pasqua;* Wycliffe used *Pasch;* and Luther, *Passa.*

Tyndale noted that the noun *pesach* in Hebrew was used to refer to the sacrifice itself—the paschal lamb—as well as to the festival itself. In addition, he noted that in Hebrew the noun *pesach* derived from a verb *P-S-CH* that meant "to pass over" or "jump over"—which was important in the story of the foundation of this festival in Exodus 12, where the Lord explains that the *pesach* lamb is a type of the fact that the Lord will "jump, skip, or pass" over the children of Israel and deliver them from death (Exodus 12:13). Tyndale may also have noted that Jerome, in his Latin translation, had attempted to render this same Hebrew wordplay. He used the term *transitus Domini* ("the passing over of the Lord") to describe the paschal sacrifice (Exodus 12:11), and the verb *transeo,* "to pass over," as it is used in Exodus 12:13 (*ac transibo vos,* "I will pass over you"). Elsewhere Jerome maintained *phase* or *pasqua* as the translation of Hebrew *pesach.*

Tyndale, determined to preserve the Hebrew wordplay in English, ingeniously invented the new English word *Passover* for the festival. Thus, in English the festival is called Passover, and the verbs of the Lord delivering Israel are "passed over." In the first biblical occurrence of the term *passover* in Exodus 12, "and ye shall eat it in haste: it is the Lord's passover" (v. 11), Tyndale added this pithy marginal note: "The lamb was called passover that the very name itself should put them in remembrance what it signified. For the signs that God ordained either signified the benefits done, or promises to come and were not dumb as are the signs of our dumb god the Pope."[18] Tyndale finishes his explanation of the Lord's *passover:* "for I will go about in the land of Egypt. . . . I will pass over you" (Exodus 12:12–13).

Oddly enough, Tyndale did not use his newly coined word in the New Testament but preferred the term *Easter*—which Christians of his time routinely used for the Christian festival. The term *Easter,* though derived from the name of a pagan goddess of the dawn, had in Tyndale's day become firmly attached to the Christian celebration of Passover. It is likely that by using the term by which all Christians who spoke English knew the Christian celebration of the Passover/Resurrection, Tyndale was attempting to communicate that the old festival of the law of Moses—Passover—had been fulfilled in Christ. Thus, in the Gospels Tyndale used *Easter* for the Last Supper (Matthew 26; see also Mark 14; Luke 22) and referred to the *Easter lamb* in 1 Corinthians 5:7 and Hebrews 11:28. Tyndale would likely have been amused that the King James translators would use his word *Passover* in all these Gospel passages, as well as throughout the Old Testament—using *Easter* only in Acts 12:4. Some have argued that Tyndale was influenced by Luther's use of the German *Oestern* in Acts 12:4, but everywhere else that Tyndale rendered the word *Easter,* Luther used *Passa.* The romance languages French (*paque*), Italian (*pasqua*), and Spanish (*pascua*) adopted a form of the original Hebrew—probably from the Vulgate—and in these countries the festival is known by a variation of its original Hebrew name *Pesach.* The term *Easter* prevailed among English-speaking Christians in reference to the Christian festival. But the Jewish festival, throughout the Bible and throughout Christian and Jewish discourse (in Christian Bible dictionaries and even in the *Encyclopedia Judaica*), is everywhere called by Tyndale's ingenious word *Passover.*

Atonement. Leviticus 16 contains a description of the most solemn of the festivals of the law of Moses called *Yom Kippur* in

Hebrew.[19] Tyndale coined three new English words in conjunction with this festival: *atonement, scapegoat,* and *mercy seat.* The Hebrew root behind *Kippur* is *K-P-R,* which has the sense of "to cover up" and occurs in contexts where it means "to appease, make amends, or reconcile."[20] Leviticus 16 contains many occurrences of this word in a verbal form describing the rituals of reconciliation between God and man. The Septuagint translates this word meaning "reconciliation" with various Greek words including *exilasmos* and *hilasterion,* which both mean "propitiation." The Vulgate uses *expiationum*—which has the sense of satisfying or appeasing.

Tyndale went in search of the perfect word that could be used as a noun or a verb and would describe the process by which man would offer sacrifices and offerings in order to cover over, appease, make amends, or reconcile with God. The word he coined was *atonement.* While many have stated that Tyndale invented this word, the *Oxford English Dictionary* lists several variations and combinations of "at" and "one," such as "to one," "at one," or "at once," "one ment" (used by Wycliffe), and "atonement," that were used in Tyndale's time. But Tyndale saw that this term was a very good match for the theological context of the relationship between God and man and put the verb *atone* and the noun *atonement* into his passages in the Old and New Testaments.

Tyndale used *atonement* in his 1526 New Testament in 2 Corinthians 5:18: "preaching of the atonement" (KJV "ministry of reconciliation"). While this term has become a common theological term in religious discussions, the King James translators continued to use this word in terms of the Old Testament usage but only actually used the term *atonement* in Romans 5:11. They preferred to use the words *reconciliation* and *propitiation* in the New Testament. Nevertheless, this term has become the common designation throughout Christianity for the saving acts of Jesus Christ on behalf of the children of men and the possibility of reconciliation and "at-one-ment" offered through His sacrifice.

Scapegoat. Leviticus 16 describes the ritual of the Day of Atonement in which two goats are selected—one for sacrifice and the other to set the sins on and to be sent out to the wilderness. The Hebrew word for this second goat is *Azazel,* a word that only occurs in this context in the Hebrew Bible. The early Greek and Latin translators presumed, probably incorrectly, that this word was made up of Hebrew *'ez 'ozel* meaning "a goat that goes away" (in Greek, *chimaros apopompaios,* "to be sent away," and in Latin, *caper emissarius*). Tyndale followed the Greek and Latin and invented a new English term for this entity. Using the English word *scape,* a variant of *escape* (Tyndale's use of *scape* in Matthew 15:18: "One tytle of the lawe shall not scape tyll all be fulfilled" [1526]) together with *goat* to get *scapegoat.*

Biblical scholars now believe that the term *Azazel* is most likely a proper name of a demon of some sort, and thus modern English translations usually render the term as *Azazel.* The term invented by Tyndale, however, is still accurate as a description of this goat that would be sent out to the wilderness bearing all of the sins of Israel, and the concept of the scapegoat has become a common proverbial expression in English.

Mercy seat. In the book of Exodus, the Lord commanded the children of Israel to construct the ark of the covenant. On the top of this ark was a covering of pure gold—in Hebrew called the *kapporeth*—cognate with *kippur,* rendered "atonement" (as discussed above). The Greek term used is *hilasterion,* and the Latin term is *propitiatoriaum.* Both terms refer to the function of the covering on the holy day of atonement when the high priest would come into the holy of holies and sprinkle the blood of the sacrifice on the cover. In his 1526 New Testament, Tyndale rendered this term as "the seate of grace" in Hebrews 9:5, but in his translation of the Old Testament, most likely influenced by Luther's *Gnadenstuhle* (literally "grace" or "mercy" with "chair" or "seat"), Tyndale coined the term "merciseate" (Exodus 25:17, 18). While Tyndale kept "seat of grace" in his 1524 New Testament, the King James translators used the term "mercie seat" throughout the Old and the New Testaments. The term "mercy seat" nicely links the idea of atonement implied by the Hebrew word *kapporeth* as it is linguistically linked with the host of terms dealing with repentance and forgiveness and the reconciliation offered to ancient Israel at this sacred covering. Thus, it became a common term in religious discourse. Modern translations often opt for less interpretative words. The New Revised Standard Version (NRSV) kept "mercy seat," while the New International Version (NIV) translated "atonement cover," and the New Jewish Publication Society Translation (NJPS) simply renders "cover."

Shewbread. In the description of the interior of the tabernacle, the Hebrew speaks of bread that is set out on a table before the Lord each week, described in Hebrew as *lechem panim*—literally "bread before the face" or "presence" of the Lord (Exodus 25:30). The Greek used *artoi enopioi* (literally "bread of the face") and Latin used *panes propositionis* (literally "bread setting forth for public view"). Luther used *schaubrot* (literally "display bread" or "shown bread"). Tyndale, perhaps influenced by Luther, invented a new English word literally translating the Hebrew by combining *shew* (pronounced "show") and *bread,* apparently meaning bread shown to the Lord. While this term is still used by those who read the King James Version, most modern translations have opted for a more literal translation such as "bread of the presence" (NIV, NRSV), or "bread of display" (NJPS).

CONCLUSION

Some of our six sample words are significant and essential in Restoration scripture. For example, the word *Jehovah* is the accepted rendering of the name of the Lord Jesus Christ in the Book of Mormon, the Doctrine and Covenants, the Pearl of Great Price, and throughout Latter-day Saint religious discourse. The words *atone* and *atonement* occur throughout the Book of Mormon, the Doctrine and Covenants, and the Pearl of Great Price as a description of the redemptive sacrifice of the Savior. The English word *atonement* is regularly used in explaining the nature of Christ's redemptive sacrifice and its ability to heal, make whole, and reconcile the broken relationship between God and humans caused by the Fall and by our sins. And who can imagine singing the hymn "I

Stand All Amazed" without the image of presenting oneself at the "mercy seat"?[21]

Tyndale realized that he was breaking new ground. In a touching introduction to the 1526 New Testament he wrote: "Them that are learned Christenly, I beseche: for as moche as I am sure, and my conscience beareth me recorde, that of a pure entent, singily and faythfully I have interpreted itt, as farre forth as god gave me the gyfte of knowledge, and understondynge: that the rudnes off the worke nowe at the fyrst tyme, offende them not: but that they consyder howe that I had no man to counterfet, nether was holpe with englysshe of eny that had intetpreted the same, or soche lyke thinge in the scripture before tyme."[22]

Tyndale's translation was carefully constructed with words "fitly spoken" (Proverbs 25:11). Throughout the ages his words, both in his translation and as they are preserved in the King James Translation, have brought and continue to bring many to Christ. Indeed, in his own words directed to the readers of his translation he invites us as follows: "Geve diligence Reder (I exhorte the) that thou come with a pure mynde, and as the scripture sayth with a syngle eye, unto the wordes of health, and of eternall lyfe: by the which (if we repent and beleve them) we are borne anewe, created afresshe, and enioye the frutes off the bloud of Christ."[23]

NOTES

1. John Foxe, *Book of Martyrs*, 1877, iv, 117, as cited in David Daniell, *The Bible in English: Its History and Influence* (New Haven, Conn.: Yale University Press, 2003), 142 (ref. 805 note 26).

2. For a succinct and readable review of English translations of the Bible before 1611, see Paul D. Wegner, *The Journey from Texts to Translations: The Origin and Development of the Bible* (Grand Rapids, Mich.: Baker Books, 1999), 271–304.

3. See Tyndale's introduction to the New Testament in *The New Testament 1526 Translated by William Tyndale, Original Spelling Edition*, ed. W. R. Cooper (London: The British Library, 2000), 554.

4. The translations of Tyndale are readily available for the modern reader in three editions: *Tyndale's Old Testament, Being the Pentateuch of 1530, Joshua to*

2 *Chronicles of 1537, and Jonah,* ed. David Daniell (New Haven, Conn.: Yale University Press, 1992); *Tyndale's New Testament, Translated from the Greek by William Tyndale 1534* (New Haven, Conn.: Yale University Press, 1989); William Tyndale, trans., *The New Testament 1526.*

5. As cited in Daniell, *Bible in English,* 156.

6. See Jon Nielson and Royal Skousen, "How Much of the King James Bible Is William Tyndale's? An Estimation Based on Sampling," in *Reformation* 3 (1998): 49–74.

7. As cited in Alister E. McGrath, *In the Beginning: The Story of the King James Bible and How It Changed a Nation, a Language, and a Culture* (New York: Doubleday, 2001), 33.

8. Hebrew, Greek, Latin, Italian, Spanish, French, and German. See Daniell, *Bible in English,* 142.

9. As cited in Daniell, *Tyndale's Old Testament,* xiv–xv.

10. Gerald Hammond has further noted: "Tyndale's claim for the superiority of English over Latin is, in essence, a matter of comparative syntax, and, broadly speaking, Tyndale is right. The only major variation between Hebrew and English word order is that in Hebrew the verb normally precedes the subject—as in "and said Moses"—and that the adjective often follows the noun. In all other respects, in particular the use of and disposition of qualifying clauses, the sixteenth-century translators followed Tyndale's lead in letting their renderings be governed by the syntax of the original. The result was the fluid and rhythmical prose which marks the narrative and prophetic books of the Hebrew Bible" (*The Making of the English Bible* [Manchester: Carcanet New Press, 1982], 45).

11. Benson Bobrick, *Wide As the Waters: The Story of the English Bible and the Revolution It Inspired* (New York: Simon & Schuster, 2001), 104–5.

12. The significance of Tyndale's translation in the Reformation can be measured by the vigorous opposition mounted against him by the Catholic Church. Thomas More, the Christian humanist and defender of the faith, criticized Tyndale's translation and theology extensively in *Dialogue Concerning Heresies*—to which Tyndale responded and defended himself in *An Answer unto Sir Thomas More's Dialogue of 1531*—and in the massive *Confutation of Tyndale's Answer,* a work that totaled almost two thousand pages (see Daniell, *Bible in English,* 149).

13. See Gerald Hammond, "William Tyndale's Pentateuch: Its Relation to Luther's German Bible and the Hebrew Original," in *Renaissance Quarterly* 33 (1980): 351–85.

14. See Ernst Jenni and Claus Westermann, *Theological Lexicon of the Old Testament,* trans. Mark E. Biddle, 3 vols. (Peabody, Mass.: Hendrickson, 1997), 2:524.

15. Catholic scholars have traced a Latin form of *Jehovah* back to the thirteenth

century (A. J. Maus, "Jehovah," in *The Catholic Encyclopedia,* 15 vols. [New York: Robert Appleton, 1909], 8:329–31).

16. Daniell, *Tyndale's Old Testament,* 82.

17. See 2 Nephi 22:2; Moroni 10:34; D&C 109:34, 42, 56, 68; 110:3; 128:9; Abraham 1:16.

18. Daniell, *Tyndale's Old Testament,* 105.

19. Yom Kippur is the common Jewish designation of the festival. The biblical name for this festival is *yom kippurim* (Leviticus 23:27; 25:9), but this designation does not occur in the description of the festival itself in Leviticus 16.

20. William L. Holladay, *A Concise Hebrew and Aramaic Lexicon of the Old Testament* (Grand Rapids, Mich.: Eerdmans, 1972), 163. Scholars debate the origin of the root *K-P-R.* Cognates in other Semitic language seem to be from two different roots, one meaning "to uproot, wipe away" and the other meaning "to cover, hide."

21. *Hymns of The Church of Jesus Christ of Latter-day Saints* (Salt Lake City: The Church of Jesus Christ of Latter-day Saints, 1985), no. 193.

22. Tyndale, trans. *New Testament 1526,* 554.

23. Tyndale, trans. *New Testament 1526,* 553.

14

"ALL THEIR CREEDS WERE AN ABOMINATION"

A BRIEF LOOK AT CREEDS AS PART OF THE APOSTASY

John W. Welch

On October 15, 1843, the Prophet Joseph Smith commented, "I cannot believe in any of the creeds of the different denominations, because they all have some things in them I cannot subscribe to, though all of them have some truth. I want to come up into the presence of God, and learn all things: but the creeds set up stakes, and say, 'Hitherto shalt thou come, and no further'; which I cannot subscribe to."[1] While Latter-day Saints gladly and gratefully recognize that all religious creeds contain some truth, the problem is that those formulations of doctrine also contain errors or impose limits that are "incompatible with the gospel's inclusive commitment to truth and continual revelation."[2] Such mixing of truth and error is reminiscent of the parable of the wheat and the tares, the Lord's most salient teaching on the nature of the Apostasy (Matthew 13:24–30, 37–43; JST Matthew 13; D&C 86:1–11).[3] Thus, the creeds themselves, as vessels of mixed qualities, become metaphors or manifestations of the Apostasy itself.

John W. Welch is a professor of law at Brigham Young University and editor-in-chief of BYU Studies.

With this observation in mind, let us consider the creeds as part of the Apostasy, as both cause and effect, symptom and result, of the disturbing religious conditions that plagued the mind and spirit of the youthful Joseph Smith, driving him to the silent grove to seek and receive a revealed solution and divine cure for his—and the world's—lack of wisdom. The accounts of the First Vision help us ascertain what the Lord communicated to Joseph in 1820 about the creeds and the problems they had created or reflected. We then follow the development of the creeds from the times of the New Testament into the main creeds of early Christianity and finally into the creeds of the Protestant churches in the early nineteenth century.

USING THE ACCOUNTS OF THE FIRST VISION AS A GUIDE

In the First Vision, Joseph Smith was plainly told that Christianity had fallen off the path most pleasing to God and that he should join none of its denominations. As he was told (and reports in his 1838/39 account), the main villain in this unfortunate ecclesiastical situation was the creeds. In response to his question "which of all the sects was right," Joseph was instructed by the Lord "that all their creeds were an abomination in his sight" (Joseph Smith–History 1:18–19).

This important disclosure by the Lord to Joseph Smith raises several questions: Which creeds might Jesus have had in mind? How many creeds existed in 1820, and which of those creeds had been adopted by which of the various "sects"? What did those creeds say, and what was it about them that made them so odious? Were they each individually an abomination, or was the problem that all of them together created a single abomination, due to the confusions, divisions, and contentions that they caused? How did the creeds of 1820 relate to the earlier creeds of Christianity, such as the Apostles' Creed, the Nicene Creed, the Symbol of Chalcedon, or the so-called Athanasian Creed? Was there something categorically wrong with these creeds in general, or only with certain creeds in particular?

We can begin to answer these questions about the history of creedalism in Christianity by combining and marshaling all of the information learned by Joseph Smith about this subject, as reported in the various accounts he gave of that seminal revelation. While the 1838/39 account of the First Vision (recorded by James Mulholland from dictation by Joseph Smith) is the only account of the First Vision to mention the "creeds" specifically by using that particular word, most of the Prophet's other surviving accounts of this vision contain equally unambiguous words to the effect that the people and churches of his day had departed from the gospel.

We learn three main things from this body of information: First, the accounts of the First Vision consistently make it clear that the gospel had been preached originally in truth and purity but that the world had strayed from it. Joseph's first account, handwritten in his journal in 1832, reports these words spoken by the Lord: "The world lieth in sin at this time and none doeth good no not one they have turned asside from the gospel and keep not <my> commandments they draw near to me with their lips while their hearts are far from me."[4] In 1843 Levi Richards reported that Joseph said that "none of them were right, that they were all wrong, & that the Everlasting covenant was broken."[5] Joseph's last known account, recorded by Alexander Neibaur in his 1844 journal, emphasizes this same point: "They are not my People, have gone astray there is none that doeth good no not one, but this is my Beloved son harken ye him."[6]

Second, in particular, errors of doctrine had been introduced into the beliefs of the people. "They teach for doctrines the commandments of men," we read in the 1838/39 account (Joseph Smith–History 1:19). In the Wentworth Letter in 1842, Joseph similarly declared that the two glorious personages who appeared before him told him that "all the religious denominations were believing in incorrect doctrines, and that none of them was acknowledged of God as his church and kingdom."[7] The early tracts by Orson Pratt in 1840 and by Orson Hyde in 1842 similarly emphasize that "all the religious demoninations were believing in incorrect doctrines"[8] and that "all of them erred in doctrine."[9]

Third, confusion, contention, and corruption had ensued in the lives of many who professed to be followers of Christ. This was the culminating and precipitating final blow. It is one thing for people to disagree using civility and kindness while pondering various inscrutable mysteries of divine truth. It is another thing for chaos and conflict to reign. At the age of twelve, Joseph was pierced to the soul by "the contentions and divi[si]ons the wicke[d]ness and abominations and the darkness which pervaded the minds of mankind."[10] In 1835 he similarly spoke of "being wrought up in my mind, respecting the subject of religion and looking at the different systems taught the children of men."[11] Being torn by the "tumult . . . so great and incessant," as various professors of religion "used all the powers of both reason and sophistry to prove their errors, or, at least to make the people think they were in error" (Joseph Smith–History 1:9), Joseph turned to the Lord for mercy and help. He was told that "those professors were all corrupt; that: 'they draw near to me with their lips, but their hearts are far from me'" (Joseph Smith–History 1:19).

Significantly, the historical record confirms this three-stage picture quite readily and thoroughly. Although it would require several volumes to examine and explore all of the questions posed above, this paper proposes to outline in broad strokes these three stages of creedal apostasy as brought to light in the First Vision accounts. From this three-stage overview, one may see how the emergence and evolution of these numerous creeds can be used to gauge the ascendancy and extent of the great Apostasy. Whether the adoption of these formal creeds should be seen primarily as a cause or as a mere symptom of apostasy is hard to say, but looking back on this quite staggering historical development from our vantage point today leaves little doubt that the crisis of the creeds had gone far enough by 1820 that the Lord's voice should be raised in disapproval and warning against it.[12]

NEW TESTAMENT PRE-CREEDAL STATEMENTS

Starting with the time of the New Testament, it is evident that original Christian declarations of faith began as genuinely simple statements of testimony. Several declarations of belief are found in the New Testament. Some of these actually begin with the words "we believe" (John 6:69) or "I believe" (Acts 8:37), words that the Latin Vulgate renders respectively as "credidimus" and "credo," from which Latin word the English term *creed* directly derives. Hence the basic idea of a creedal declaration of faith can be traced to these "pre-creedal" statements in the Bible. Interestingly and appropriately, these biblical statements are notably characterized by their spontaneous individuality and their succinct focus on testifying of the Savior's divine roles and powers. But ironically, and as so often happened in the Apostasy, seeds that were divine and good at the outset were corrupted and transformed into something far beyond what they were originally intended to be. In the case of the creeds, these biblical expressions of testimony may well have formed the root from which the later creeds would grow, but only after many wild branches had been grafted into this faithful stalk of believing declaration.

Pre-creedal statements of belief in the New Testament are short, varied, unrehearsed, and intensely personal. Consider three representative cases[13] from the words of Nathanael, Peter, and Paul.

Nathanael is the first reported disciple to verbally declare his inward recognition that Jesus of Nazareth was the Son of God. Nathanael, who was taken by Philip to see "him, of whom Moses in the law, and the prophets, did write," was greeted by Jesus, "Behold an Israelite indeed, in whom is no guile!" When Jesus said that he had seen Nathanael under the fig tree, this disciple broke forth in immediate testimony, "Rabbi, thou art the Son of God; thou art the King of Israel" (John 1:45–49). No one had told Nathanael what to say; his declaration is pure and unformulaic. Nor is there any compelling reason to believe that it was not historical, for what Christian community—Johannine or otherwise—would have called Jesus "Rabbi" or "the King of Israel" as a matter of institutional confession from which Nathanael's statement could otherwise have been derived? Nathanael's short statement fits especially into the Galilean context of Jesus' earliest ministry.

Peter's bold statements of belief in Jesus as the Christ are reported with flexibility in the four Gospels. In Mark, Peter's response to the question, "Whom do men say that I am?" is simple and matter-of-fact: "Thou art the Christ" (*su ei ho Christos,* Mark 8:29). In Luke, the answer is slightly longer: "The Christ of God" (*ton Christon tou theou,* Luke 9:20). In Matthew, the words *Son* and *living* are added to the expressions reported in Mark and Luke: "Thou art the Christ, the Son of the living God" (*su ei ho Christos ho huios tou theou tou zóntos,* Matthew 16:16). Finally, in John, following the Bread of Life Sermon, Peter responds to the question, "Will ye also go away?" by saying, "We believe and are sure [that is, 'we have come to know,' *egnókamen*] that thou art that Christ, the Son of the living God" (John 6:69). The earliest New Testament manuscripts actually present Peter's terminology here in varying terms, confessing Christ to be the following:

"The holy one of God" (*ho hagios tou theou,* Sinaiticus, Vaticanus, and other early manuscripts)

"The Christ the holy one of God" (Coptic)

"The Son of God" (Old Italian, Syriac)

"The Christ, the Son of God" (family 1, Vulgate)

"The Christ, the Son of the living God" (Matthew 16:16; family 13, Byzantine).

From this variance, one may conclude with confidence that rigidity was not the expected rule among the early Christians when it came to bearing personal testimony of Jesus Christ, although common key elements clearly run throughout these declarations.

Finally, among the New Testament writers, it was Paul who took the further step of articulating several specific dimensions or factors in the divinity of Jesus Christ—elements that in time would become staples in later, more elaborate creedal formulations. In his letter to Timothy, Paul called the following lyrical statement, confessedly (*homologoumenos*), the great mystery of worship—namely that "he (*hos*) or God (*theos*) was manifest in the flesh, justified in the spirit, seen of angels, preached in the nations, believed in the world, received in glory" (1 Timothy 3:16; author's translation).

On another occasion, writing to the Colossians, Paul declared, "All things were created by him, and for him. And he is before all things, and by him all things consist. And he is the head of the body, the church: who is the beginning, the firstborn from the dead; that in all things he might have preeminence. For it pleased the Father that in him should all fulness dwell; and, having made peace through the blood of his cross, by him to reconcile all things unto himself" (Colossians 1:16–20).

In these two confessions of faith, Paul encapsulates the main elements of his Christology: namely Jesus' incarnation (at birth), confirmation by the Spirit (at baptism), visitation by angels (at the Transfiguration), proclamation (by His Apostles), reception (by faithful followers), and exaltation (at the Ascension), together with His roles in creation, revelation, resurrection, perfection, crucifixion, and atoning reconciliation. Although Paul waxes eloquently expansive, his words in these statements remain in the sphere of personal expression. Nevertheless, it was the historical and theological assertions of these words and phrases that would eventually become key components of the Christian creeds.

THE EARLY CHRISTIAN CREEDS

As time progressed, the early Christian leaders and councils adopted creed after creed, slowly adding points of deviating doctrine until eventually a considerable number of odd and incorrect doctrines had been intermingled with the originally valid and truthful elements. Beginning around A.D. 200, Christians began to espouse and require of each other adherence to particular creeds, demonstrating and propagating their belief in Jesus Christ. Such creeds seemed needful because many people were teaching a wide range of doctrines about Jesus. Indeed, some of these heretical groups were way off the mark. Creeds functioned in many ways that, taken at face value, must have seemed salutary: They could serve as baptismal interview questions to be asked of an initiate before baptism; they could also serve as catechisms to prepare converts for baptism, as general guidelines for personal belief, as expressions of testimony, as collective declarations of belief, and as the texts for unifying speech acts that bound congregations together. At first, the main purpose of these creeds seems to have been more a matter of self-definition and admission, rather than anathematization or exclusion. Early Christians were mostly interested in encouraging and allowing people to join the church, and accordingly the variety and informality of the earliest creeds manifests little interest in imposing uniformity on all believers or in making exclusive truth claims that one formulation was orthodox and any other was heterodox.

But as these statements developed, the tendencies of creedal formulations went too far in the direction of definitive absolutism, taking away the liberty of the pure and simple spirit that had prevailed in the apostolic era (as seen above) and prescribing and imposing extensive definitions and boundaries on the faithful. Especially when Christianity became the state religion of the Roman Empire in the fourth century, the permissive and admitting roles of creedal statements became less relevant: Joining the church was taken for granted. Thus, the church changed its emphasis to regulating the internal affairs of the church and formulating rules that could be used to require consistency of belief among all members. As the following discussion demonstrates, this trajectory became increasingly extreme as time went on. What began in the second and third centuries as fairly straightforward and unproblematic declarations in the Old Roman, Apostles', and Caesarean Creeds became more and more arcane, philosophical, and delimiting as the fourth and fifth centuries played themselves out. This process of accretion, adding phrase on phrase, from creed to creed, is readily visible on the accompanying chart.

In the left-hand column, one of the earliest Christian creeds is given. It is brief and, for the most part, unproblematic. No one would object to its succinct opening statement in the Old Roman form of the Apostles' Creed, "I believe in God the Father Almighty, and in Jesus Christ his only begotten Son our Lord." One might wonder, however, about that creed's insertion of belief in "the holy Church." Understood in a proper sense as a declaration of authority to act in the name of God, this element is acceptable to Latter-day Saints; but as a claim that the Church itself is somehow holy or perfect or infallible, it would begin to raise concerns.

As we move to the right across the columns, we see elements in the creeds becoming observably more complicated. To the third-century declaration "I believe in God the Father Almighty" was added "Maker of heaven and earth," which then became in the early fourth-century "Maker of all things visible and invisible," which then evolved a few years later into "Ruler and Creator of all ages and creatures." As well intended as these embellishments might have been, they introduce unnecessary claims or descriptions that lay themselves open to error. For example, should the creed declare that God the Father is the Creator, or should that role be attributed to the Son (as in John 1:1–3 and Colossians 1:16)? The fourth-century Caesarean statement, along with the Nicene Creed, attempted to recognize both of these members of the Godhead as creators ("Jesus Christ . . . by whom *also* all things were made" or simply "by whom all things were made"), but this alternative was not embraced in the fifth-century Symbol of Chalcedon, by which time the inseparability of the Father and Son had come to prevail. Or again, what does it mean to create all things "visible and invisible"? What do these words add to the statement that God created "all things"? And how is the word *create* to be understood here? Why limit the declaration, tautologically, as in the Old Italian form of the Apostles' Creed, to being the "creator" of all "creatures"? One can easily see how the creeds would have been better off leaving such elements unstated rather than making such statements that would inevitably run the risk of being misunderstood or of being wrong.

Most controversial were the increasing attempts of the creeds to define the divine nature of Jesus Christ and His relationship to the Father. In the early years, it was sufficient to recognize Jesus Christ as the "only begotten Son." As time went on, elaborations moved from "Word of God, God of God, Light of Light" in the Caesarean formulation, to "Light of Light, very God of very God,

OLD ROMAN AND AFRICAN FORM OF THE APOSTLES' CREED (2d or 3d century)	THE APOSTLES' CREED (2d or 3d century)	THE CAESAREAN CREED according to Eusebius (A.D. 325)	AN OLD ITALIAN FORM OF THE APOSTLES' CREED (ca. A.D. 350)
I believe in God the Father Almighty.	I believe in God the Father Almighty; Maker of heaven and earth.	We believe in one God the Father Almighty, Maker of all things visible and invisible;	We believe in God the Father Almighty, Ruler and Creator of all ages and creatures.
And in Jesus Christ his only begotten Son our Lord,	And in Jesus Christ his only [begotten] Son our Lord;	And in one Lord Jesus Christ, the Word of God, God of God, Light of Light, Life of Life, the only-begotten Son, the first-born of every creature, begotten of God the Father before all ages, by whom also all things were made; who for our salvation was made flesh and made his home among men;	And in Jesus Christ, his only Son, our Lord;
who was born of the Holy Ghost and the Virgin Mary; crucified under Pontius Pilate, and buried; the third day he rose from the dead;	who was conceived by the Holy Ghost, born of the Virgin Mary; suffered under Pontius Pilate, was crucified, dead, and buried; he descended into hell; the third day he rose from the dead;	and suffered; and rose on the third day;	who was born of the Holy Ghost and from the Virgin Mary; who was crucified under Pontius Pilate, and buried; on the third day he rose from the dead;
he ascended into heaven, and sitteth at the right hand of the Father;	he ascended into heaven; and sitteth at the right hand of God the Father Almighty;	and ascended to the Father;	ascended into the heavens; sitteth on the right hand of God the Father;
from thence he shall come to judge the quick and the dead.	from thence he shall come to judge the quick and the dead.	and will come again in glory, to judge the quick and the dead.	from thence he shall come to judge the quick and the dead.
And in the Holy Ghost;	I believe in the Holy Ghost;	We believe also in one Holy Ghost.	And in the Holy Ghost;
the holy Church;	the holy Catholic Church; the communion of saints;		and the holy Catholic Church;
the forgiveness of sins;	the forgiveness of sins;		the remission of sins;
the resurrection of the body; [the life everlasting].	the resurrection of the body [flesh]; and the life everlasting. Amen.		the resurrection of the flesh.

I believe in one God the Father Almighty; Maker of heaven and earth, and of all things visible and invisible. And in one Lord Jesus Christ, the only-begotten Son of God,

begotten of the Father before all worlds [God of God], Light of Light, very God of very God, begotten, not made, being of one substance [essence] with the Father; by whom all things were made; who, for us men and for our salvation, came down from heaven,

and was incarnate by the Holy Ghost of the Virgin Mary, and was made man;

and was crucified also for us under Pontius Pilate; he suffered and was buried; and the third day he rose again, according to the Scriptures;

and ascended into heaven, and sitteth on the right hand of the Father;

and he shall come again, with glory, to judge both the quick and the dead; whose kingdom shall have no end.

And [I believe] in the Holy Ghost, the Lord and Giver of Life; who proceedeth from the Father [and the Son]; who with the Father and the Son together is worshiped and glorified; who spake by the Prophets.

And [I believe] one Holy Catholic and Apostolic Church.

I acknowledge one baptism for the remission of sins;

and I look for the resurrection of the dead, and the life of the world to come. Amen.

We, then, following the holy Fathers, all with one consent, teach men to confess one and the same Son, our Lord Jesus Christ, the same perfect in Godhead and also perfect in manhood; truly God and truly man, of a reasonable [rational] soul and body; consubstantial [coessential] with the Father according to the Godhead, and consubstantial with us according to the Manhood; in all things like unto us, without sin; begotten before all ages of the Father according to the Godhead, and in these latter days, for us and for our salvation,

born of the Virgin Mary, the Mother of God, according to the Manhood;

one and the same Christ, Son, Lord, Only-begotten, to be acknowledged in two natures, inconfusedly; unchangeably, indivisibly, inseparably, the distinction of natures being by no means taken away by the union, but rather the property of each nature being preserved, and concurring in one Person and one Subsistence, not parted or divided into two persons, but one and the same Son, and only begotten, God the Word, the Lord Jesus Christ; as the prophets from the beginning [have declared] concerning him, and the Lord Jesus Christ himself has taught us, and the Creed of the holy Fathers has handed down to us.

For the right Faith is, that we believe and confess: that our Lord Jesus Christ, the Son of God, is God and Man;

God, of the Substance [Essence] of the Father: begotten before the worlds and Man, of the Substance [Essence] of his Mother, born in the world.

Perfect God: and perfect Man, of a reasonable soul and human flesh subsisting.

Equal to the Father, as touching his Godhead: and inferior to the Father as touching his Manhood.

Who although he be God and Man; yet he is not two, but one Christ.

One; not by conversion of the Godhead into flesh: but by taking [assumption] of the Manhood into God.

One altogether; not by confusion of Substance [Essence]: but by unity of Person.

For as the reasonable soul and flesh is one man: so God and Man is one Christ;

Who suffered for our salvation: descended into hell: rose again the third day from the dead.

He ascended into heaven, he sitteth on the right hand of the Father God Almighty.

From whence he shall come to judge the quick and the dead.

At whose coming all men shall rise again with their bodies;

and shall give account for their own works.

And they that have done good shall go into life everlasting; and they that have done evil, into everlasting fire.

This is the Catholic Faith; which except a man believe faithfully [truly and firmly], he can not be saved.

begotten, not made, being of one substance [essence] with the Father" in the Nicene Creed, to "consubstantial [coessential] with the Father according to the Godhead, and consubstantial with us according to the Manhood; . . . in two natures, inconfusedly; unchangeably, indivisibly," as it is stated in the Symbol of Chalcedon. While it may be true that the Nicene Creed served an important purpose by defending the eternal divinity of Jesus Christ against the Arian doctrine that Jesus Himself was created ex nihilo by the Father,[14] it may also be true that the Nicene cure was as bad as the ailment, for neither Arius nor Athanasius seems to have understood the premortal existence of any of God's children, let alone that of His Firstborn Son.

Even more problematic, arcane, and obscure is the so-called Athanasian Creed, in the far right column of the chart. It was never adopted by any council and therefore is not truly a creed with any official status; indeed, it is of unknown authorship, but it probably dates to the seventh or eighth century. Even as an unofficial statement, it demonstrates how far things had progressed by that time in drafting statements of belief that were more statements of what one cannot comprehend than they were statements of what one can believe and testify of. If not erroneous, many of its declarations at least seem confusing and unscriptural, although intermingled with truth, such as the belief that "at [Christ's] coming all men shall rise again with their bodies; and shall give account for their own works."

My purpose in comparing these representative versions of early Christian creeds is not to attempt anything like a comprehensive discussion of the complex histories, philosophical debates, and ecclesiastical struggles that stand behind each of the formulations. That information can be readily found in several excellent and extensive studies of the early Christian creeds.[15] My purpose is simply to point out that the expansion of the creeds moved away from the simple declarations of faith that prevailed in first-century Christianity and that in that development one can clearly see increasing evidences of the incremental progression of the Apostasy. Latter-day Saints should not condemn all creeds equally, for all creeds were not created equal. Yet even the early creeds began to sow seeds that would in time spawn more debilitating problems. By the end of the ancient era, one may see in the creeds that the Apostasy was indeed in full array, harboring doctrinal problems and errors, sometimes as much by what they did not say as by what they did say.

THE PROTESTANT CREEDS

For many centuries, the work of the councils that produced these main creeds or symbols firmly remained within the unified realm of the "universal," or "catholic," church. Indeed, the main purpose of these early creeds was to create (or impose) uniformity of belief according to these standards of orthodoxy. But, inevitably, such superimposed uniformity would lead to protest and conflict, and with the Protestant Reformation, creeds reached the third, even more problematic stage.

Creeds now became statements of belief, formulated for the purpose of distinguishing and differentiating one religious group from another. Into the seventeenth and eighteenth centuries, the number of creeds climbed and the verbosity and complexity of these confessions soared. While all of this positioning may have been understandably necessitated by the political and rational forces that surrounded the various Protestant denominations or sects, the result was precisely as Joseph's experience depicts. Confusion, dissension, and self-serving manipulation characterized much of the religious fervor of his day, erupting in many cases (not only against the Mormons) in hostility, persecution, and violence.[16]

By 1820, numerous creeds of various denominations had been brought into existence. The main Protestant creeds are collected and translated conveniently in the works of Philip Schaff and of Jaroslav Pelikan and Valerie Hotchkiss. Chronologically listed here, along with a few Eastern and Catholic creeds, these formulations include the following[17]:

Synodical Tome (Eastern, 1341)
Synodical Tome (Eastern, 1351)
Confession of Faith (Mark of Ephesus, 1439)

Confession of Faith (Gennadius II of Constantinople,
 1455–56)
The Sixty-Seven Articles of Ulrich Zwingli (1523)
The Schleitheim Confession (1527)
The Ten Theses of Berne (1528)
Luther's Catechism (1529)
The Marburg Articles (1529)
The Augsburg Confession (1530)
The Tetrapolitan Confession (1530)
A Reckoning of the Faith (Zwingli, 1530)
The First Confession of Basel (1534)
The Wittenberg Concord (1536)
The Lausanne Articles (1536)
The Ten Articles (1536)
The Geneva Confession (1536)
The First Helvetic Confession (1536)
The Geneva Catechism (1541/1542)
Dogmatic Decrees of the Council of Trent (Catholic,
 1545–63)
The Zurich Agreement (Consensus Tigurinus, 1549)
The Anglican Catechism (1549)
The Gallican Confession (1559)
The First Scotch Confession (1560)
The Belgic Confession (1561)
The Heidelberg Catechism (1563)
The Thirty-Nine Articles of the Church of England (1563)
The Tridentine Profession of Faith (Catholic, 1564)
The Second Helvetic Confession (1566)
The Catechesis and Confession of Faith of the Polish
 Brethren (1574)
The Formula of Concord (1576)
The Reply to the Augsburg Confession (Ecumenical Patriarch
 Jeremias II, 1576)
The Transylvanian Confession of Faith (1579)
The King's Confession (1581)
The Second Scotch Confession (1581)

The Concept of Cologne (1591)

The Saxon Visitation Articles (1592)

The Lambeth Articles (1595)

A True Confession (English Separatists [Brownists], 1596)

The Arminian Articles (1610)

The Short Confession of Faith (1610)

The Irish Articles (1615)

The Canons of the Synod of Dort (1619)

Confession of Faith (Metrophanes Critopoulos, 1625)

The Eastern Confession of the Christian Faith (Cyril Lucar, 1629)

The Dordrecht Confession (1632)

The Orthodox Confession of the Eastern Church (1643)

The London Baptist Confession (1644)

The Westminster Confession of Faith (1647)

The Cambridge Platform (Congregationalists of New England, 1648)

The Faith and Practice of Thirty Congregations Gathered According to the Primitive Pattern (General Baptists, 1651)

The Confession of Waldennes (Presbyterian, 1655)

The Savoy Declaration (Congregationalist, 1658)

The Anglican Catechism, Revised (1662)

The Eighteen Decrees of the Synod of Jerusalem (Eastern, 1672)

The Confession of the Society of Friends (Quakers, 1675)

The Philadelphia Confession (Baptist, 1688)

The Easter Litany of the Moravian Church (1749)

Mennonite Articles of Faith by Cornelis Ris (1766)

The Methodist Articles of Religion (1784)

A Concise Statement of the Principles of the Only True Church (Shakers, 1790)

The Thirty-Nine Articles of the Church of England, American Revision (1801)

The Winchester Profession (Universalist Church, 1803)

Propositions from Declaration and Address (Thomas Campbell, 1809)

During Joseph Smith's lifetime, other creeds and confessions continued to be promulgated, especially in America. These included the following:

The Confession of the Cumberland Presbyterian Church (American, 1829)

The Declaration of the Congregational Union of England and Wales (1833)

The New Hampshire Confession (American, 1833)

The Auburn Declaration (Presbyterian, American, 1837)

One of the most salient features of these creeds is their length. They tended to be very long. The Belgic Confession of Faith, a Calvinist creed, runs about 9,000 words; the Westminster Confession of Faith contains approximately 12,500 words. The other creeds of that period all have thousands of words and numerous articles. The Calvinist Canons of the Synod of Dort, for example, has fifty-nine articles; the London Baptist Confession has fifty-three; the Belgic Confession, thirty-seven.

Another prominent feature of these creeds is their polemic stance. As important as saying what one believed was also saying what one did not believe and how the tenets of one denomination differed from those of another group. The Baptist Confession of 1688, for example, which is the most generally accepted Baptist confession in England and in the southern states in America, says the following about Catholicism: "The Lord Jesus Christ is the head of the Church; . . . neither can the Pope of Rome, in any sense, be head thereof, but is no other than Antichrist, that man of sin and son of perdition, that exalteth himself in the Church against Christ, and all that is called God: whom the Lord shall destroy with the brightness of his coming."[18] The Scotch Confession of Faith (1560), in Article 22, targets the "Papistical kirk [church]," or community of Catholics, as being false priests and criticizes specific practices and beliefs: "They have so adulterated both the one sacrament and the other with their own inventions, that no part of Christ's action abides in the original purity: for oil, salt, spittle, and suchlike in baptism, are but men's inventions. Adoration, veneration, bearing through streets and towns, and keeping of bread in boxes or buists [*chests*], are profanation of Christ's sacraments, and no use of the same."[19] Other creeds go out of their way to deal bluntly with what they consider to be specific heretical doctrines from Christian history. The Latter-day Saint Articles of Faith offer a much more conciliatory tone, "let them worship how, where, or what they may" (Articles of Faith 1:11).

The combative nature of the Protestant creeds is also evident by their dates. Many of these confessions coincide with the dates of Henry VIII and his schism from Rome, the Thirty Years' War in Europe (1618–48), the Cromwellian Revolution (1640–60), as well as the tumultuous times of the First and Second Awakenings in the mid-eighteenth and early nineteenth centuries.

Perhaps it was most of all in reference to these bloody battles, divisive contentions, and coercive tactics that the creeds of Christianity merited the term *abomination* in the words of the 1838/39 account of the First Vision. That word, of course, is offensive and jarring to our friends of other faiths. And indeed, it was a very strong word in the vocabulary of Joseph Smith's America. Webster's 1828 *Dictionary of the American Language* defines *abomination* as "1. extreme hatred; detestation. 2. The object of detestation, . . . 3. Hence, defilement, pollution, in a physical sense, or evil doctrines and practices, which are moral defilements."[20] Nevertheless, an *abomination* in the biblical sense can include anything that takes a person away from God or His righteousness. Obviously, the Bible uses the word *abomination* in connection with a wide range of sin or transgression, including idolatry (Deuteronomy 27:15), male homosexual conduct (Leviticus 18:22; 20:13), human sacrifice (Deuteronomy 12:31), eating ritually unclean animals (Leviticus 11:10–12; Deuteronomy 14:3–8), witchcraft and divination (Deuteronomy 18:9–14), and dishonest business dealings (Deuteronomy 25:13–16). Proverbs 6:17–19 gives a list of seven things that are an abomination unto God: "a proud look, a lying tongue, and hands that shed innocent blood, an heart that deviseth wicked imaginations, feet that be swift in running to mischief, a false witness that speaketh lies, and he that soweth discord among brethren." Thus, seeing the creeds as an abomination may readily be conflated with the problems that they had caused, as identified in the First Vision accounts, namely, turning people aside from the gospel, teaching incorrect doctrines of men, professing errors and corruptions, and inciting tumult.

Latter-day Saints typically hasten to say that the Articles of Faith, drawn from Joseph Smith's 1842 Wentworth Letter and canonized as an addition to the Pearl of Great Price at the Church's jubilee in 1880, do not constitute a creed: "Authoritative statements found in LDS literature are not viewed as elements in a creed. For example, although its thirteen Articles of Faith are scriptural, they are open-ended."[21] "They are not a creed in the traditional Christian sense. . . . Although not a formal creed, the Articles of Faith are a marvelously abridged summary (less than 400 words) of the basic beliefs of The Church of Jesus Christ of Latter-day Saints."[22] Nevertheless, the main topics covered in the Articles of Faith are commonly covered in most of these other confessions, although each expresses a considerably different point of view. Those topics typically include the nature of the Godhead, the fall of Adam and original sin, human responsibility, the atonement of Jesus Christ, baptism, communion through faith and repentance, belief in the Bible, and the empowerment of civil government to enforce orthodoxy. Rarely, however, will these confessions address the question of qualification for the ministry[23] and liberty of individual conscience insofar as the individual is making a good faith effort to follow Christian truths.[24] Absent from the typical traditional creed is virtually any mention of the numerous gifts of the Spirit (perhaps because Pentecostal spiritualism is by nature basically antithetical to rational verbal constraints), the Second Coming and the Millennium, the future restoration of the house of Israel, or, of course, a belief in the Book of Mormon as the word of God. These similarities and differences notwithstanding, the major problems caused by the traditional creeds are decisively nowhere visible in the Articles of Faith: those thirteen statements are short, clear, and simply declarative. They are also preventatively and generatively open ended: the inclusive words *all* or *and so forth* appear in

Articles of Faith 3, 6, 7, 9, and 13, most expansively in the assertion "We believe all that God has revealed, [and] all that He does now reveal" (Articles of Faith 1:9).

SUMMARY

This brief look at the creeds of Christianity has accomplished the following purposes:

First, we have seen that the accounts of the First Vision identify several problems raised by or in conjunction with the creeds. No specific malady was exclusively singled out.

Second, the problems were as much involved with content as with conflict. The concern was with not just what the creeds said but how they were used.

Third, a three-stage development from the New Testament to the early Christian creeds to the Protestant confessions is clearly visible. The loss of important truths of the gospel, of key covenants, and of plain and precious parts of the scriptures may well have happened in that order at a very early stage in Christian history (1 Nephi 13:26–28), but the profound effects of the Apostasy was not felt all at once but continued incrementally for years to come.

Fourth, the earliest Christian creeds were not as bad as one might have thought. In the first few centuries, Christian statements of belief remained largely unobjectionable from a Latter-day Saint point of view.

Fifth, as the centuries went on, the errors and complexities increased and predominated over the original seeds planted by the Lord and His Apostles. By the seventeenth and eighteenth centuries, numerous creeds were in existence. Many of them were extremely long, elaborate, controlling, and defining.

Sixth, with so many creeds in existence, it is unlikely that the Lord had any particular creed in mind when he spoke of them and their adherents as abominations of corruption. Thus, Latter-day Saints should not take issue so much with any single creed as with the whole concatenation of creedal formulations in general.

Joseph Smith, of course, was neither the first nor the last to raise objections to these problematic developments. There is a bold tradition of theological objectors who have spoken out from time to time against the creeds, fighting vigorously against the rising and raging tide of creedalism, and among whom may be counted such luminaries as John Milton, John Locke, John Taylor, Richard Price, John Simson, Francis Hutcheson, and others, who were openly branded as heretics. The history of these critics is engagingly reported by R. G. Crawford in the 1976 *Scottish Journal of Theology.*[25] But in the minds of most of these critics, the objection to creeds was based on the sufficiency of the Bible: "The Bible is the only religion of Protestants."[26] These objectors may have diagnosed the problem, but they prescribed the wrong cure. Closing the lid tighter on Christianity would not remove the lid that the creeds have imposed.[27] Only the restoration of the keys of continuing revelation could open the heavens and make the church a "living church" with which the Lord can be "well pleased" (D&C 1:30).

NOTES

1. Joseph Smith, *Teachings of the Prophet Joseph Smith,* sel. Joseph Fielding Smith (Salt Lake City: Deseret Book, 1976), 327.

2. Daniel H. Ludlow, ed., *Encyclopedia of Mormonism,* 5 vols. (New York: Macmillan, 1992), s.v. "Creeds." See also Bruce R. McConkie, *Mormon Doctrine,* 2d ed. (Salt Lake City: Bookcraft, 1979), 170–72.

3. Compared and analyzed in John W. Welch, "Modern Revelation: A Guide to Research about the Apostasy" (forthcoming from the Foundation for Ancient Research and Mormon Studies [FARMS], Provo, Utah).

4. Joseph Smith, *The Papers of Joseph Smith: Autobiographical and Historical Writings,* ed. Dean C. Jessee (Salt Lake City: Deseret Book, 1989), 1:6–7; first published in Dean C. Jessee, "The Early Accounts of Joseph Smith's First Vision," *BYU Studies* 9, no. 3 (1969): 275–96.

5. Levi Richards Journal, June 11, 1843, Church Archives.

6. Smith, *Papers of Joseph Smith,* 1:461.

7. Smith, *Papers of Joseph Smith,* 1:430.

8. Orson Pratt, "A Interesting Account," in *Papers of Joseph Smith,* 1:391.

9. Orson Hyde ("Ein Ruf aus der Wüste" ["A Cry from the Wilderness"], in *Papers of Joseph Smith,* 1:409) and Dan Jones (*History of the Latter-day Saints,* trans. Ronald D. Dennis [Provo, Utah: Religious Studies Center, Brigham Young

University, 2002], 16) hastened to place the blame on the fact that all "believed imperfect doctrines, to a greater or a lesser degree" and to exonerate many of these believers who "were zealous, conscientious, God-fearing men, fleeing evil, and worshiping him according to the light which they had." I appreciate James M. Reynolds for drawing my attention to this 1846 account by Dan Jones in this connection.

10. Smith, *Papers of Joseph Smith*, 1:5.

11. Joseph Smith, *The Papers of Joseph Smith: Journal, 1832–42*, ed. Dean C. Jessee (Salt Lake City: Deseret Book, 1992), 2:68–69.

12. Of course, it is possible that when Jesus said that "all their creeds are an abomination," he was not using the word "creeds" in a formal sense, but rather simply in reference to "any system of principles which are believed or professed," for the word *creed* had this meaning, as well as the formal meaning, in the American language in 1828, according to Webster's *Dictionary of the American Language*. I do not exclude this meaning, but neither do I think that this meaning should preclude the formal meaning. The following discussion outlines the development of the creedal crisis by looking at the official creeds, because they are indicative of the broader problems inherent in the belief systems they summarize and because they offer the best evidence of the main phenomena.

13. Several other biblical passages may reflect creedal declarations, including Deuteronomy 6:4; 1 Kings 18:39; John 20:28; Acts 8:37–38; 16:31; 1 Corinthians 8:6; Philippians 2:6–11; and 1 John 4:2. See also J. N. D. Kelly, *Early Christian Creeds* (London: Longmans, 1972), chapter 1, "Credal Elements in the New Testament."

14. For an excellent discussion of the positive features and helpful contributions of the early Christian Creeds, see Bijhan Nasser-Faili, "Early Christian Creeds and LDS Doctrine," *Journal of Latter Day Saint History* 12 (2000): 12–23; this article discusses the relationship between the Arian Controversy and the Nicene Creed on pages 16–17.

15. See, for example, Philip Schaff, *The Creeds of Christendom* (New York: Harper and Row, 1931); Kelly, *Early Christian Creeds;* Jaroslav Pelikan, *Credo: Historical and Theological Guide to Creeds and Confessions of Faith in the Christian Tradition* (New Haven, Conn.: Yale University Press, 2003), introductory volume to Jaroslav Pelikan and Valerie Hotchkiss, eds., *Creeds and Confessions in the Christian Tradition* (New Haven, Conn.: Yale University Press, 2003).

16. Such hostility and violence are graphically displayed and described in James H. Hutson, *Religion and the Founding of the American Republic* (Washington, D.C.: Library of Congress, 1998), chapters 1 and 2.

17. These lists are a selection of creeds included in Schaff, *Creeds of*

Christendom, and in Peliken and Hotchkiss, *Creeds and Confessions in the Christian Tradition.*

18. Schaff, *Creeds of Christendom,* 738–39.

19. Schaff, *Creeds of Christendom,* 471; spelling and capitalization modernized.

20. Noah Webster, *An American Dictionary of the English Language* (New York: Converse, 1828), s.v. "Abomination."

21. "Creeds," in Ludlow, *Encyclopedia of Mormonism,* 1:343.

22. David J. Whittaker, "Articles of Faith," in Ludlow, *Encyclopedia of Mormonism,* 1:67, 69; see also John W. Welch and David J. Whittaker, "'We Believe. . . . ': Development of the Articles of Faith," *Ensign,* September 1979, 51–55.

23. See Scotch Confession of Faith, Article 22, in Schaff, *Creeds of Christendom,* 471.

24. See Savoy Declaration, in Schaff, *Creeds of Christendom,* 720.

25. R. G. Crawford, "The Revolt against Creeds and Confessions of Faith," *Scottish Journal of Theology* 29 (1976): 13–25.

26. This statement is attributed to Chillingworth (Crawford, "Revolt against Creeds," 13).

27. Likewise, the recent attempt by popular Catholic theologian Luke Timothy Johnson, *The Creed: What Christians Believe and Why It Matters* (New York: Doubleday, 2003), is well worth reading, but ultimately it is a disappointing attempt to push Christians harder to use and study "the creed." While Johnson explains much about the origins and meanings of the words in one version of the creed, he leaves us to wonder which creed is right and why the use of it in the twenty-first century would actually have a more salutary effect than the questionable use of creeds has had over the past millennium and a half.

15

THOMAS BILNEY
A PRELUDE TO THE RESTORATION

David M. Whitchurch

*M*uch has been said about the Restoration and the coming forth of the Book of Mormon, and rightfully so. Joseph Smith had the faith and courage necessary to part the heavens, see the Father and the Son, and once again reconstitute the Church of Jesus Christ upon the earth. Persecution and opposition ensued. From the First Vision to the death of the Prophet Joseph, the very "elements" combined to "hedge up the way" (D&C 122:7). Even those within the newly restored Church struggled to retain their newfound way of life.

Just one year before his martyrdom, the Prophet Joseph Smith stated, "Many men will say, 'I will never forsake you, but will stand by you at all times.' But the moment you teach them some of the mysteries of the kingdom of God that are retained in the heavens and are to be revealed to the children of men when they are prepared for them, they will be the first to stone you and put you to death. It was this same principle that crucified the Lord Jesus

---

David M. Whitchurch is an associate professor of ancient scripture at Brigham Young University.

Christ, and will cause the people to kill the prophets in this generation."[1] In another sermon delivered to the Saints at Nauvoo, the
Prophet told the congregants: "But there has been a great difficulty
in getting anything into the heads of this generation. It has been like
splitting hemlock knots with a corn-dodger [hard-baked corn bread]
for a wedge, and a pumpkin for a beetle [hammer]. Even the Saints
are slow to understand."[2]

We rejoice at the dedication and strength of the early Saints
who remained faithful and feel sorrow for those who failed to stay
the course. Why did some fall short? Why so much persecution?
One answer may simply be that people resist change. The Lord
stated in a revelation to Joseph Smith, "And that wicked one cometh
and taketh away light and truth, through disobedience, from the
children of men, and *because of the tradition of their fathers*" (D&C
93:39; emphasis added). Opposition foments when people resist
change and allow seeds of discontent to be sown by the adversary.

Many individuals throughout earth's history felt the sting of persecution. Others encountered trials and tribulations similar to those
experienced by Joseph Smith long before the First Vision. Whether
we speak of Noah, Isaiah, Jeremiah, or the Savior Himself, persecution abounded throughout history. Jan Hus, John Wycliffe, Martin
Luther, Philipp Melanchthon, William Tyndale, John Calvin, Ulrich
Zwingli, and a host of others also endured tremendous suffering and
hardships. The pattern seems all too familiar—standing firm in one's
beliefs leads to persecution, betrayal, expulsion, and for some, martyrdom. The scriptures affirm the potential of discipleship: "For
unto you it is given in the behalf of Christ, not only to believe on
him, but also to suffer for his sake" (Philippians 1:29; see also
Matthew 5:10; 24:9, 13; Acts 5:41).

Latter-day prophets have commented on the significant role of
those reformers who helped prepare the way for the Restoration of
the gospel.[3] President Joseph F. Smith stated: "Calvin, Luther,
Melanchthon, and all the reformers, were inspired in thoughts,
words, and actions, to accomplish what they did for the ameliora-
tion, liberty and advancement of the human race. They paved the
way for the more perfect gospel of truth to come. Their inspiration,

as with that of the ancients, came from the Father, his Son Jesus Christ, and the Holy Ghost, the one true and living God."[4] We rightfully express gratitude for the strength and courage that these reformers displayed, but at the same time we often forget that as they broke from orthodoxy they did not do so with the intent to further any religious freedom other than their own. As early as 1531 Luther and Melanchthon "favor[ed] capital punishment for Anabaptist preachers and their unrepentant followers."[5] Henry VIII and Elizabeth I executed hundreds of Roman Catholics during their reigns. "From 1585, to be a Catholic priest in England was ipso facto treason."[6] Historical evidence from the fifteenth to seventeenth centuries demonstrates clearly that the reformers and counterreformers did all in their power to minimize and eliminate heterodoxy. Although church leaders, regardless of their religious affiliation, sought to reform religious deviancy, for those who refused, "executions were not only legitimate, but obligatory."[7]

Such being the case, consider the political and cultural climate required before Joseph Smith could publicly pronounce that "all their creeds were an abomination in [the Lord's] sight; that those professors were all corrupt; that: 'they draw near to me with their lips, but their hearts are far from me, they teach for doctrines the commandments of men, having a form of godliness, but they deny the power thereof'" (Joseph Smith–History 1:19). It took centuries and another continent before conditions allowed the gospel of Jesus Christ to take root in its fulness. From the Reformation to the Restoration, literally thousands of Protestants, Anabaptists, and Catholics died as religious martyrs.[8] Dedicated believers sought change. They desired something that society was not yet willing to give them: the ability to believe and worship as their own conscience and understanding dictated.

The story of one such martyr, Thomas Bilney, is little known, infrequently discussed, and rarely recognized for the effect he had on future generations. Bilney would likely have preferred it that way. From available sources, it appears he did not seek personal glory or notoriety. His life's mission, as he saw it, was to bring the word of God to the people. In so doing, he not only helped transform

England but, in some small way, the world. His story is a representative reminder to us all of the many who lost their lives holding fast
to what they believed and, in so doing, moved us closer to a time
when a young boy could earnestly implore God in a sacred grove,
receive a witness of the truth that exceeded all expectations, and
restore the gospel in its fulness.

BEFORE THOMAS BILNEY

To understand the sacrifice of Thomas Bilney it will help to
know something about the social and political climate of the late
fourteenth and early fifteenth centuries. Let us begin with John
Wycliffe. Born in Yorkshire, England, in about 1328, this Oxford-
educated priest recognized and began teaching the need for reform
within the Roman Catholic Church. During the Great Papal
Schism,[9] Wycliffe rejected the biblical basis of papal authority,
insisting on the primacy of scripture. He and his followers (later
known as Lollards) eventually traveled throughout the countryside
teaching his message of change. Wycliffe's determination to bring
about reform included the idea of translating scripture into the vernacular or common tongue. Wycliffe, or more likely those who
assisted him, produced the earliest complete English Bible sometime around 1382.[10]

Opposition to Reformation thought continued long after
Wycliffe's death. To help stem the tide, Henry IV of England
approved a petition against heretical teaching in 1401. A clause
within the petition known as *De Haertico Comburendo* (Concerning
the Burning of Heretics)[11] empowered bishops to arrest any unli-
censed preacher who taught, held meetings, or disseminated books
contrary to the rules of the Roman Catholic Church. John Foxe, the
sixteenth-century Protestant historian,[12] writes: "[Whoever] should
read the Scriptures in the mother-tongue (which was then called
Wickliff's learning), they should forfeit land, cattle, body, life, and
goods, from their heirs for ever, and so be condemned for heretics
to God, enemies to the crown, and most arrant traitors to the land.
Besides this, it was enacted, that never a sanctuary, nor privileged

ground within the realm, should hold them, though they were still permitted both to thieves and murderers. And if, in any case they would not give over, or were, after their pardon, relapsed, they should suffer death in two manner of kinds: that is; they should first be hanged for treason against the King, and then be burned for heresy against God."[13]

Thus, the punishment of death was introduced into English law for matters of opinion. Such aggressive efforts and partnership between the church and the monarchy helped quell—but not stop—expansion of religious diversity. Wycliffe's ideas and scriptures lived on. Even though he died in 1384—just two years after completing an English translation of the Bible—in the spring of 1428, forty-four years after his death, the Roman Catholic Church ordered his body disinterred, the remains burned, and the ashes scattered. Such efforts may have temporarily slowed the movement, but another wave of discontentment soon arose.

Desiderius Erasmus (1466?–1536), a Dutch scholar, theologian, humanist, and friend of Thomas More, Hugh Latimer, and other high-profile leaders of England, unknowingly instigated what was to become a lasting challenge to Roman orthodoxy. Erasmus's scholastic ability and popularity made him an eagerly sought-after guest of kings, emperors, popes, and cardinals. In 1509 he moved to Cambridge, England, where he would remain for the next five years. While there, Erasmus systematically prepared a parallel-column manuscript for a Greek-Latin New Testament (*Novum instrumentum*). Published in 1516, this Bible contained nearly four hundred marginal notes that identified and supported changes from Jerome's Latin Vulgate. Also included among the annotations were numerous comments on the ecclesiastical conditions of the day. Politically adept, Erasmus dedicated the book to Pope Leo X—who fully endorsed it—in spite of a number of statements in it that supported Reformation thought.[14] J. A. Wylie, a nineteenth-century Protestant historian, says of Erasmus: "Next to the heretics, the priests dreaded the scholars. Their instincts taught them that the new learning boded no good to their system.[15] Of all the learned men now in England the one whom they hated most was Erasmus, and with just reason. He stood confessedly at the head of the scholars, whether in England or on the Continent. He had great influence at court; he wielded a pungent wit, as they had occasion daily to experience—in short, he must be expelled [from] the kingdom. But Erasmus resolved to take ample compensation from those who had driven him out. He went straight to Basle, and . . . issued his Greek and Latin New Testament."[16]

From additional sources it seems that Erasmus intended to change the church rather than encourage people to break from it.[17] Nonetheless, the Roman Church at Cambridge and Oxford took a decidedly strong stance against Erasmus's Bible following its publication.[18] Yet, with the printing press and its ability to mass produce books, the Bible quickly made its way into the universities of England and Europe. In England, as elsewhere, it was received with great enthusiasm—"everywhere it was sought after and read" by Greek scholars and those learned in Latin.[19]

THOMAS BILNEY AND THE SCRIPTURES

Thomas Bilney has been recognized as the first at Cambridge to come to "the knowledge of Christ."[20] Little is known about his childhood other than that he was born around 1495 in the area of Norwich, Norfolk County, East Anglia, and that his parents sent him to Cambridge to study canon law while he was still very young. Sometime while at Cambridge, Bilney turned from canon law to theology and was ordained a priest in the summer of 1519.[21]

John Foxe describes Bilney as little in "stature and very slender of body, and of a strait and temperate diet, given to good letters and very fervent and studious in the Scriptures."[22] Furthermore, Bilney seems to have demonstrated tremendous discipline and compassion for those in need. Foxe states that "concerning his diet, . . . it was so strait, that for the space of a year and a half, he took commonly but one meal a day" so that he could give the remainder of his food to those in prison.[23] According to those who knew him, Bilney slept about four hours a night and "could abide no swearing nor singing."[24]

As Bilney struggled to know his standing and personal relationship before God, he turned to fasting, prolonged prayer, and acts of
penance through confession of his sins before a priest.[25] The sources
do not indicate how long he endured this inner struggle for peace,
but relief did not come until he discovered the scriptures. A change
of heart began when one day he overheard some friends talking
about Erasmus's New Testament.[26] Torn between personal curiosity and duty, he finally purchased a copy. "At last he took courage.
Urged, said he, by the hand of God, he walked out of the college,
slipped into the house where the volume was sold in secret, bought
it with fear and trembling, and then hastened back and shut himself
up in his room."[27] In a letter to Cuthbert Tunstal, bishop of London,
Bilney writes of his experience:

"But at last I heard speak of Jesus, even then when the New
Testament was first set forth by Erasmus. . . . I bought it even by
the providence of God, as I do now well understand and perceive:
and at the first reading (as I well remember), I chanced upon this
sentence of St. Paul (O most sweet and comfortable sentence to my
soul!) in 1 Tim. i., 'It is a true saying, and worthy of all men to be
embraced, that Christ Jesus came into the world to save sinners; of
whom I am the chief and principal.' This one sentence, through
God's instruction and inward working, which I did not then perceive, did so exhilarate my heart, being before wounded with the
guilt of my sins, and being almost in despair, that immediately I felt
a marvellous comfort and quietness, insomuch 'that my bruised
bones leaped for joy.'"[28]

From this point on, Bilney immersed himself in the scriptures.[29]
They were, he says, "more pleasant unto me than the honey or the
honey-comb."[30] As his pursuit of truth continued, Bilney states, "At
last I desired nothing more, than that I, being so comforted by him,
might be strengthened by his Holy Spirit and grace from above, that
I might teach the wicked his ways, which are mercy and truth; and
that the wicked might be converted unto him by me."[31] Others soon
joined Thomas Bilney in Cambridge, where they formed a private
group to discuss the scriptures. As a note of interest, one of those

who joined Bilney was William Tyndale.[32] Precisely what their relationship was remains unknown. Nonetheless, each of these early reformers, in his own way, would affect all of England.

While still at Oxford, Tyndale "increased as well in the knowledge of tongues, and other liberal arts, as especially in the knowledge of the Scriptures."[33] In time Tyndale would achieve mastery in eight languages.[34] No doubt such linguistic talent aided him as he translated the New Testament and portions of the Old Testament into English. His determination to make the scriptures available to the public is evident from a verbal exchange he had while working as a schoolmaster for an English knight. During a heated discussion with a visiting "divine" (theologian), Tyndale remarked that "if God spared him life, ere many years he would cause a boy that driveth the plough, to know more of the Scripture than he did."[35] Such a prophetic statement can be seen in the fact that over 80 percent of the language Tyndale used in his translations of the Bible (1526, 1530, and 1534) is retained in the King James Bible we use today.[36]

Bilney's impact on the Reformation can also be seen in the conversion of Hugh Latimer. Latimer, recognized for his keen mind, powerful oratory skills, and early devotion to the Roman Catholic Church, describes his conversion to reformist ideas in a speech he gave to Katherine Grey, Duchess of Suffolk, during the reign of Edward VI:

"Here I have occasion to tell you a story which happened at Cambridge [in 1524]. Master Bilney . . . that suffered death for God's word sake; the same Bilney was the instrument whereby God called me to knowledge. . . . For I was as obstinate a papist as any was in England, insomuch that when I should be made bachelor of divinity, my whole oration went against Philip Melancthon and against his opinions. Bilney heard me at that time, and perceived that I was zealous without knowledge: and he came to me afterward in my study, and desired me, for God's sake, to hear his confession. I did so; and, to say the truth, by his confession I learned more than before in many years. So from that time forward I began to smell the word of God, and forsook the school-doctors and such fooleries."[37]

Bilney and Latimer fast became friends, parting ways when Bilney left Cambridge to preach throughout the countryside. Latimer went on to gain favor with Henry VIII and his son Edward VI. His influence on these kings and among the general populace was a significant factor in England's eventual break from the Roman Catholic Church.

On July 23, 1525, Bilney received a license to preach in public at parishes outside Cambridge.[38] At about this same time, Thomas Wolsey (cardinal in the Catholic Church and lord chancellor to Henry VIII) determined he must forcefully confront those who promoted heretical ideas, for the spreading of heresy was "worse than multiple murderers, because their victims lived on to harm others in turn."[39] Bilney's preaching did not escape Wolsey's attention. He summoned Bilney, who appeared before him sometime during the year 1526, the same year William Tyndale published his English New Testament. Published in Worms, Germany, copies were quickly smuggled into England and "for the first time the whole New Testament . . . could be read by anyone."[40] English authorities banned Tyndale's Bible but to no avail. Reformist ideas were now spreading on the Continent and in England. Martin Luther had translated and published his German New Testament just four years previously (1522) and, in his own right, had taken on the established church. As Bilney appeared before Wolsey, the latter demanded and received from Bilney an oath that he did not believe and would not teach Martin Luther's doctrines.

The following year (1527) Bilney and a Cambridge associate, Thomas Arthur, preached a series of sermons at a number of parishes, including some in and near London. Their lectures raised the ire of several priests. After gathering evidence against them, the bishop of London, Cuthbert Tunstal, arranged for their arrest and imprisonment.[41] On November 27, 1527, Arthur and Bilney appeared in London before Cardinal Wolsey and a sizable group of bishops, lawyers, and divines.[42]

Cardinal Wolsey began his inquiry by asking Bilney about the oath he had taken to "not preach, rehearse, or defend any of Luther's opinions."[43] Bilney replied that he had made such an oath and, during further questioning, repudiated Luther, admitting that Luther and his teachings were heretical.[44] Such a statement benefited Bilney in two ways. First, it let his accusers know that his sympathies did not lie with Martin Luther and his teachers per se; and second, by rejecting Luther and his ideas it removed the subject from the judiciary docket. Wolsey, unable to remain for the entire trial due to other responsibilities within his realm, turned the proceedings over to Tunstal. Before leaving, he gave explicit instructions that the defendants were either to abjure or to be delivered to the civil authorities for execution.[45] Wolsey's instructions emanated from a view that duplicitous interpretation of the scriptures contradicted Christ and His divine church. Calvin and others held similar beliefs and "ridiculed those who would permit people to read and understand the Bible as they pleased."[46]

Written questions (called interrogatories) were then issued to Arthur and Bilney. "Far from yearning to kill heretics, members of the clergy frequently strained to save them."[47] Such careful proceedings intended, if possible, to reclaim the wayward by securing formal recantation. In addition, bringing errant persons back to the fold helped to reinforce the existing order within the church. Some of the primary issues centered on such matters as the pope's authority, praying and reading scriptures in English, and the selling of indulgences—all of which challenged the orthodoxy of Bilney's day.

According to Foxe, throughout the trial Bilney never countered the authority of the church or openly rejected the authority of the pope.[48] In his view, "he would not be a slander to the gospel, trusting that he was not separate from the church."[49] It seems that Bilney desired to effectively change the church from within. Like many religious leaders of his day, he recognized a need to limit access to the scriptures. He held that the scriptures could be translated into the vernacular, but for the most part they should be read and explained by clergy, who would minimize misunderstandings and wrongful interpretations of doctrine. For unstated reasons, Bilney felt inclined that the people should have the Lord's Prayer in their own tongue and "wished that the gospels and epistles . . . might be read in English." Regarding indulgences, he said "it were better that they should be restrained, than that they should be any longer used as they have been, to the injury of Christ's passion."[50] Such views must have brought enormous concerns as they eroded and undermined the solidarity of the church.

The trial lasted eleven days, and Tunstal made deliberate efforts throughout the time to get Bilney to recant. It seems that Tunstal's strategy in part was to give Bilney unprecedented opportunities to abjure in order to "secure a public demonstration of the fairness of the trial and a public renunciation of heresy from Bilney."[51] There is some suggestion that the church was also concerned about the spread of ideas from the universities to the general populace. Such an outward movement of reformist thoughts would wreak havoc for Cardinal Wolsey and the church. Bilney had already proved his persuasiveness among scholars, parish clergy, and laity in the conversions of Hugh Latimer and other high-profile scholars.[52] If Tunstal could get Bilney to recant it might be a major step in slowing down, or even stopping, the spread of heretical ideas. Besides, he firmly believed that "eternal damnation was no mere symbol: it was *literally* what happened to heretics who died at odds with Christ and his mystical body, the one Church."[53]

Throughout the trial Tunstal gave Bilney considerable opportunity to carefully consider his position. Bilney, however, remained steadfast to his beliefs. Finally, Tunstal declared: "Thomas Bilney, I pronounce thee convicted of heresy."[54] Just before announcing Bilney's punishment, he decided to give him one last chance to abjure by granting him "two nights' respite to deliberate" on the matter and to consult with his friends. Foxe tells us the result: "On the 7th of December . . . the bishop of London with the other bishops being assembled, Bilney also personally appeared; whom the bishop of London asked, whether he would now return to the unity of the church, and revoke the errors and heresies whereof he stood accused, detected, and convicted. He answered, that now he was persuaded by Master Dancaster and others his friends, he would submit himself, trusting that they would deal gently with him, both in his abjuration and penance."[55] Tunstal and the other clergy must have felt a sense of relief. Bilney finally agreed to abjure, having been convinced by his friends that if his life was spared he would be of greater service to the Lord. Bilney would later lament his decision to recant.

Latimer writes of Bilney's abjuration: "I will advise you first, and above all things, to abjure all your friends, all your friendships; leave not one unabjured. It is they that shall undo you, and not your enemies. It was his very friends that brought Bilney to it."[56] After Bilney read his abjuration before the plaintiffs, Bishop Tunstal absolved him and then announced his penance. The next day (Sunday) he was to walk before the procession at St. Paul's Church bareheaded, carrying faggots (a bundle of sticks used as fuel) on his shoulder, and stand before the preacher at Paul's cross where he was exhorted to repent. He was then sent to the Tower of London where he spent the next year in prison before returning to Cambridge.[57] The purpose for such public display and humiliation sent a clear message of warning to others who might have held similar views to Bilney's.

Returning to Cambridge brought Bilney no relief. John Foxe writes that "he was in such an anguish and agony, that nothing did him good, neither eating nor drinking, nor even any other communication of God's word."[58] Latimer also recounted the torment he felt: "[He] had such conflicts within himself, beholding this image of death, that his friends were afraid to let him be alone: they were fain to be with him day and night, and comforted him as they could, but no comforts would serve. As for the comfortable places of scripture, to bring them unto him it was as though a man would run him through the heart with a sword."[59] More than two years passed before Bilney determined that he must be faithful to his convictions and once again preach what he knew to be true. Foxe writes of his departure from Cambridge: "And thus, being fully determined in his mind, and setting his time, he took his leave in Trinity Hall, at ten o'clock at night, of certain of his friends, and said, that he would go to Jerusalem; alluding belike to the words and examples of Christ in the gospel."[60]

Bilney returned to Norfolk, where he had taught years earlier. Without a license to preach, however, he no longer had access to local parishes. He therefore entered households, reaffirming the truthfulness of his message to those he had taught previously. Later he preached more openly. While in Norwich one day he visited an elderly anchoress (nun) "whom he had converted to Christ" and gave her one of Tyndale's English New Testaments.[61] She in turn lent the scriptures to others who visited her. Information soon reached Thomas More, the new chancellor of England who had replaced Thomas Wolsey in October 1529. More immediately had Bilney arrested and imprisoned at the Tower of London. As a relapsed heretic, Bilney had no chance of defense.

The bishop of Norwich requested that the trial be moved to his diocese so as to set an example for those who espoused heretical ideas.[62] A public execution would also serve to deter "would-be criminals [and] to reinforce the existing authority."[63] Many priests visited Bilney in Norwich while he was in prison at Guildhall. Once again they sought for him to recant so as "not to die in his opinions, saying, he should be damned body and soul if he so continued."[64] This time Bilney remained unmoved. In the early part of August 1531, his fate being decided, he was degraded by his priestly order and handed over to civil authorities for execution.[65]

The night before his execution, several of his friends from Cambridge visited him in prison. The records indicate that Bilney greeted them with a "cheerful heart and quiet mind."[66] The following episode is best told by John Foxe:

"Sitting with his said friends in godly talk to their edification, some put him in mind, that though the fire, which he should suffer the next day, should be of great heat unto his body, yet the comfort of God's Spirit should cool it to his everlasting refreshing. At this word the said Thomas Bilney, putting his hand toward the flame of the candle burning before them . . . and feeling the heat thereof, . . . 'I feel by experience, and have known it long by philosophy, that fire, by God's ordinance, is naturally hot: but yet I am persuaded by God's holy word, and by the experience of some, spoken of in the same, that in the flame they felt no heat, and in the fire they felt no consumption: and I constantly believe, that howsoever the stubble of this my body shall be wasted by it, yet my soul and spirit shall be purged thereby; a pain for the time, whereon notwithstanding followeth joy unspeakable.' And here he much treated of this place of scripture. 'Fear not, for I have redeemed thee, and called thee by thy name; thou art mine own. When thou goest through the water I will be with thee, and the strong floods shall not overflow thee. When thou walkest in the fire, it shall not burn thee, and the flame shall not kindle upon thee, for I am the Lord thy God, the holy One of Israel.'"[67]

The horrors of martyrdom seem almost unfathomable in our day and age; yet for Bilney and others, martydom demonstrated "conformity to an ancient course of action, grounded in scripture and epitomized in the crucifixion of Christ himself."[68] The manner of death verified the martyrs' inner conviction of what they believed. To die well displayed faith in Christ and fidelity to Him and His word.

The next day Bilney was taken by the guards to the place of execution (called Lollards' Pit) located just outside the city gate about a mile from Guildhall. As he left the prison and walked to the place of martyrdom, his friends came to him and prayed that he take his death patiently. Bilney responded: "Ye see when the mariner is entered his ship to sail on the troublous sea, how he for a while is tossed in the billows of the same, but yet, in hope that he shall once come to the quiet haven, he beareth in better comfort the perils which he feeleth: so am I now toward this sailing; and whatsoever storms I shall feel, yet shortly after shall my ship be in the haven, as I doubt not thereof, by the grace of God, desiring you to help me with your prayers to the same effect."[69] After arriving at Lollards' Pit, he offered a prayer quoting a portion from Psalm 143:1–2: "Hear my prayer, O Lord give ear to my supplications. . . . And enter not into judgment with thy servant: for in thy sight shall no man living be justified." When he had finished his prayer, the officers chained him to a stake, placed reeds and faggots about him, and lit the fire that ended the life of Thomas Bilney.

Conclusion

Thomas Bilney was not the first and would certainly not be the last to die for his convictions. Many suffered a similar fate for their beliefs, including Hugh Latimer, William Tyndale, and in centuries to come, Joseph Smith. Yet, the lives and deaths of these early martyrs combined to ignite a fire not to be extinguished. Within just a few short years following Bilney's death, English Parliament would stop all contributions to the Roman Catholic Church and give Henry VIII supreme control over the Church of England. Although England's move toward independence is seen as more of a political maneuver, it nonetheless opened the door a bit wider for the possibility of greater religious diversity. It also brought the availability and accessibility of the scriptures to the common person one step closer to reality. By 1539 efforts were under way to place the first *authorized* English Bible in every church throughout England. In time, Bible reading would not only be legal but mandatory.[70]

Within the ensuing years, others seeking their own religious freedoms would flee England, eventually making their way to America. The centuries that followed brought new generations of people—people with Bibles in hand—seeking a new place to worship. Christian pluralism eventually "emerged de facto, much to the chagrin of all the parties involved"; so much so, that "God's truth remained the subject of heated disagreement."[71] Such would be the case in upstate New York in 1820 when a young Joseph Smith sought not to break away from a particular faith but to know which one held the truth. With scriptures in hand—written in English— he would read from James, "If any of you lack wisdom, let him ask of God, that giveth to all men liberally, and upbraideth not; and it shall be given him" (James 1:5), and thus began the latter-day restoration of the gospel of Jesus Christ.

Notes

1. Joseph Smith, *History of The Church of Jesus Christ of Latter-day Saints*, ed. B. H. Roberts, 2d ed. rev., 7 vols. (Salt Lake City: The Church of Jesus Christ of Latter-day Saints, 1932–51), 5:424.

2. Smith, *History of the Church,* 6:184.

3. For additional statements from Latter-day Saint leaders about the reformers, see the following: Spencer W. Kimball, *The Teachings of Spencer W. Kimball,* ed. Edward L. Kimball (Salt Lake City: Deseret Book, 1982), 426; Gordon B. Hinckley, in Conference Report, October 2002, 85; Bruce R. McConkie, *Brigham Young University Speeches of the Year* (Provo, Utah: Brigham Young University Press, 1984), 45.

4. Joseph F. Smith, "Fountain of Truth," *Improvement Era,* June 1907, 629.

5. Brad S. Gregory, *Salvation at Stake: Christian Martyrdom in Early Modern Europe* (Cambridge, Mass.: Harvard University Press, 1999), 95.

6. Gregory, *Salvation at Stake,* 92.

7. Gregory, *Salvation at Stake,* 79.

8. It has been estimated that roughly five thousand Protestants, Anabaptists, and Catholics were killed as religious martyrs from 1523 to 1680; see Gregory, *Salvation at Stake,* 6.

9. Between 1378 and 1418 two popes each claimed leadership of the Roman Church—one from Rome and the other from Avignon. At one point the feud went so far that each pope excommunicated the other. See David Daniell, *The Bible in English: Its History and Influence* (New Haven, Conn.: Yale University Press, 2003), 71–72.

10. See Daniell, *Bible in English,* 66, 73.

11. See Bobrick Benson, *Wide As the Waters: The Story of the English Bible and the Revolution It Inspired* (New York: Simon and Schuster, 2001), 67.

12. Much has been said about John Foxe's *Book of Martyrs* (also known as *Acts and Monuments of These Latter and Perillous Days, Touching Matters of the Church*). Recognized as a partisan historian, Foxe provides a passionate and comprehensive history of those who died to defend and establish Christ's church through the ages. Attacks and defenses were made on Foxe and his book from the time it was first published in 1563. In the early 1830s, S. R. Maitland successfully began a campaign to discredit *Acts and Monuments* through a scholarly examination of sixteenth-century English documents. In 1940, J. F. Mozley defended Foxe's book by reexamining documentation available in the British Museum. The charges of Foxe's willful misrepresentation were largely cleared by Mozley, so much so that modern historians no longer feel constrained to apologize when citing from *Acts and Monuments.* For more details regarding the historical accuracy of John Foxe's *Acts and Monuments,* see Warren W. Wooden, *John Foxe* (Boston, Mass.: Twayne, 1983). In addition, a more recent Reformation historian writes, "The wider point is clear and very significant: even where specific corroboration is impossible, we can use the sympathetic description of martyrs' public words and actions with a high degree of confidence" (Gregory, *Salvation at Stake,* 21).

13. John Foxe, *Foxe's Book of Martyrs,* ed. W. Grinton Berry (Grand Rapids, Mich.: Baker Book House, 2000), 86–87.

14. See Daniell, *Bible in English,* 116–17.

15. The historian David Daniell stated that "Protestantism was an intellectual movement in English, powered by university men, dependent on free discussion at all levels" (*Bible in English,* 130).

16. J. A. Wylie, *The History of Protestantism,* 3 vols. (New York: Cassell Petter & Galpin, 1874–77), 3:358.

17. Even today, the Roman Catholic Church recognizes Erasmus as one who "laboured for a reform of the Church that would not be antagonistic to the pope and the bishops, nor productive of a violent rupture, but which, through the dissemination of a larger enlightenment, would eventually but gradually result in the wished-for reorganization" (*The Catholic Encyclopedia,* 15 vols. [New York: Robert Appleton, 1909], 5:512).

18. See J. H. Merle d'Aubigné, *The Reformation in England,* ed. S. M. Houghton, 2 vols. (London: Banner of Truth Trust, 1962), 1:154.

19. Wylie, *History of Protestantism,* 3:358.

20. John Foxe, *The Acts and Monuments of John Foxe,* ed. Stephen Reed Cattley, 8 vols. (London: R. B. Seeley and W. Burnside, 1837), 4:651.

21. See Sir Leslie Stephen and Sir Sidney Lee, eds., *Dictionary of National Biography* (London: Oxford University Press, 1959–60), 2:502.

22. Foxe, *Acts and Monuments,* 4:620.

23. Foxe, *Acts and Monuments,* 4:621.

24. Foxe, *Acts and Monuments,* 4:621.

25. See d'Aubigne, *Reformation in England,* 1:154.

26. See Wylie, *History of Protestantism,* 3:359.

27. D'Aubigné, *Reformation in England,* 1:154–55.

28. Foxe, *Acts and Monuments,* 4:635.

29. A Bible with numerous marginal notes that once belonged to Bilney now resides in the Corpus College library at Cambridge. See Stephen and Lee, *Dictionary of National Biography,* 2:502.

30. Foxe, *Acts and Monuments,* 4:635.

31. Foxe, *Acts and Monuments,* 4:635–36.

32. See Wylie, *History of Protestantism,* 3:359.

33. Foxe, *Acts and Monuments,* 5:115.

34. See Daniell, *Bible in English,* 142.

35. Foxe, *Acts and Monuments,* 5:117.

36. See Daniell, *Bible in English,* 136.

37. George Elwes Corrie, ed., *Sermons by Hugh Latimer, Sometime Bishop of Worcester* (Cambridge: University Press, 1844), 334–35. Latimer gave the speech in 1552. Philipp Melanchthon was a friend of Martin Luther and professor of Greek at a university in Wittenberg, Germany. While Martin Luther was in hiding at Wartburg Castle (after being convicted at the Diet of Worms), Melanchthon took over his lectures, proving himself a powerful proponent of reformation thought.

38. Stephen and Lee, *Dictionary of National Biography*, 2:503.

39. Gregory, *Salvation at Stake*, 86.

40. Daniell, *Bible in English*, 144.

41. See Stephen and Lee, *Dictionary of National Biography*, 2:503–4.

42. See Foxe, *Acts and Monuments*, 4:621–22.

43. Foxe, *Acts and Monuments*, 4:622.

44. See Foxe, *Acts and Monuments*, 4:622, 625.

45. See Foxe, *Acts and Monuments*, 4:622, 624–26.

46. Gregory, *Salvation at Stake*, 89.

47. Gregory, *Salvation at Stake*, 80.

48. See Foxe, *Acts and Monuments*, 4:625–26.

49. Foxe, *Acts and Monuments*, 4:631.

50. Foxe, *Acts and Monuments*, 4:626.

51. Greg Walker, "Saint or Schemer? The 1527 Heresy Trial of Thomas Bilney Reconsidered," *Journal of Ecclesiastical History* 40, no. 1 (January 1989): 224.

52. See Walker, "Saint or Schemer?" 227.

53. Gregory, *Salvation at Stake*, 85; emphasis in original.

54. D'Aubigné, *Reformation in England*, 1:294.

55. Foxe, *Acts and Monuments*, 4:632.

56. Corrie, *Sermons by Hugh Latimer*, 222.

57. See Stephen and Lee, *Dictionary of National Biography*, 2:504.

58. Foxe, *Acts and Monuments*, 4:641.

59. Corrie, *Sermons by Hugh Latimer*, 222.

60. Foxe, *Acts and Monuments*, 4:642; see also Matthew 16:21; Mark 10:33; Luke 9:51.

61. Foxe, *Acts and Monuments*, 4:642.

62. See d'Aubigné, *Reformation in England*, 2:72–73.

63. Gregory, *Salvation at Stake*, 77.

64. Foxe, *Acts and Monuments*, 4:642.

65. Bilney was placed in Guildhall in Norwich. The prison where he was held still exists today.

66. Foxe, *Acts and Monuments,* 4:653.

67. Foxe, *Acts and Monuments,* 4:653. See Isaiah 43:1–3 for scripture reference.

68. Gregory, *Salvation at Stake,* 119.

69. Foxe, *Acts and Monuments,* 4:654. Bilney's words while going to Lollards' Pit are somewhat reminiscent of those of Joseph Smith, who said as he traveled to Carthage in the summer of 1844, "I am going like a lamb to the slaughter; but I am calm as a summer's morning; I have a conscience void of offense towards God, and towards all men" (D&C 135:4).

70. See John Stevens Kerr, *Ancient Texts Alive Today: The Story of the English Bible,* ed. Charles Houser (New York: American Bible Society, 1999), 72.

71. Gregory, *Salvation at Stake,* 348.

16

FROM GUTENBERG TO GRANDIN

TRACING THE DEVELOPMENT OF THE PRINTING PRESS

Keith J. Wilson

Late in March 1830, a notice in the Palmyra, New York, newspaper appeared announcing the recent publication of the Book of Mormon. It was the culmination of a three-year translating and printing process that would ultimately stamp Palmyra as the birthplace of Mormonism. Producing this book in the small town along the Erie Canal was an event of unusual proportion as well as portent. In many ways this physical event occurred because of a stream of individuals and inventions that stretched over a four-hundred-year period. The result of this quiet process was an available printing press and competent personnel who in 1830 delivered a book that was anciently described as "a marvellous work and a wonder" (Isaiah 29:14). The story of the physical printing developments that culminated that memorable day of March 26, 1830, in Palmyra, New York, is a fascinating one.

Keith J. Wilson is an associate professor of ancient scripture at Brigham Young University.

A Brief History of Printing

Printing actually began hundreds of years before the development of the printing press in fifteenth-century Europe. The Chinese are credited with first carving wooden blocks and using them to print symbols and images as early as A.D. 175. Their insurmountable challenge was the sheer number of characters that they had to create in order to have just one complete set of images. By about A.D. 300 the modern codex book form was introduced and became the standard format. In time, the wooden blocks gave way to earthenware and then eventually to bronze reliefs. This technology gradually spread from the Chinese to the Japanese, the Koreans, and finally the Turks. Even so, in the year 1400, after more than a thousand years of hand-carved letter printing, the process of creating a book was more of an art than a science. But this process was about to change as a result of one gifted inventor.

The Gutenberg breakthrough. Johann Gansfleisch zum Gutenberg was a goldsmith by trade and began experimenting with printing in the 1430s. He faced four technical challenges to mechanical printing. The first was the need for durable metal type that could be uniformly mass produced. He applied his metalworking acumen to this challenge and successfully devised a new mixture of lead, antimony, and tin suitable for inexpensive castings. His second obstacle might have been his most technical hurdle.[1] Even though he was well versed in the use of molds, he now had to design a reusable mold that could cast different sized letters with identical length and dimensions. After much perseverance he refined and produced a type-casting mold that gave printers uniform, durable metal type. Yet another task was to reformulate ink so it would transfer from his metal type to the existing paper without smudging or smearing. Borrowing from oil painters, he was able to modify their paint with linseed oil and carbon lampblack to produce a suitable printer's ink.[2] And finally he had to construct a press that would uniformly transfer inked letters onto paper. Many suggest that he borrowed his design from German winepresses, and others believe it must have come from a cheese or a papermaker's press. History is silent concerning his impetus, even though his eventual design did closely resemble a common winepress.

Gutenberg's prodigious invention arrived in a world hungry for mental stimulation. His press was replicated, and his technology spread quickly. Within just fifty years of his first press, over twelve million books had been printed in more than one thousand print shops.[3] Scholars have titled this period "The Incunabula," or cradle of printing. Ironically, Gutenberg did not see the impact of his work during his lifetime. Five years after his invention, he was forced into bankruptcy. Even though he was befriended in his poverty, he died in relative obscurity about ten years later. Recently, some five hundred years later, this man whose grave no longer even exists was honored as "The Man of the Millennium."[4]

One of the first pieces of printed material that Gutenberg published was his famed Gutenberg Bible. Almost four hundred years later, the Book of Mormon was printed using technology that Gutenberg himself would have readily recognized. What were the changes that occurred from the Gutenberg press in the fifteenth century to the Grandin in the nineteenth? Print historians have codified these four hundred years into three distinctive periods of printing developments: the creative period, 1450–1550; the refining period, 1550–1800; and the mechanization period, 1800–1900.[5]

The creative period, 1450–1550. The creative period immersed the world in printing and books in the short span of just one hundred years. By 1550 Gutenberg's technology was everywhere. A few institutions tried in vain to suppress it, supposing that an educated populous would threaten traditional structures. But their efforts proved completely inconsequential and failed to stem a deluge of printed materials. By the middle of the sixteenth century, as one writer summarized, "the experiment was over."[6]

The refining period, 1550–1800. The period that followed Gutenberg's era was really just a prolonged pause in printing technology. The printing pundits have titled it the refining period, but in reality the refinements were only minor adjustments. Some of these adjustments occurred in 1620 through the Dutchman William Blaeu. His changes consisted of stabilizing the platen (or printing surface) to avoid smearing, installing an iron hand lever for greater leverage, devising a rolling bed to position the form into printing position, and designing springs to more quickly release the platen.[7] The second significant modification occurred late in this refining period. In 1772 William Haas of Switzerland introduced metal replacement parts in the stressful components of the wooden press. Even though this represented a great step forward, it went largely unnoticed until Adam Ramage incorporated it into his popular wooden presses in the early 1800s.[8]

Thus, the refining period of some 250 years concluded with a few improvements, but the press remained realistically a Gutenberg press. Because this press was so widespread and universal, it became known as the "common press." It was a large frame press, usually built out of oak or mahogany. In America it was the press that produced Benjamin Franklin's *Poor Richard's Almanac* and Thomas Payne's *Common Sense*. This press required two people to operate, and at top speed they could produce about two hundred sheets per hour. Their output would frequently slow to as few as twenty sheets per hour.[9] The work required to physically operate a common press was so strenuous and repetitive that observers claimed one could recognize a printer on the street because "the right shoulder and foot became enlarged, the left shoulder sunken; the body moved sideways, crablike when walking."[10]

While printing technology remained at a standstill, nations and cultures continued their forward march. The Industrial Revolution created wealth and a middle class. Philosophers such as Imanuel Kant, John Locke, and David Hume taught the value of rational thought and reason, ideas that seemed to fan the flames of the American Revolutionary War (some have even suggested that the war was won as much by lead type as by lead bullets). Democracy demanded a literate and mentally active public, so while reading had once been the domain of the clergy or the gentleman, it now emerged as the business of the middle class. In America the common press became the working partner of the common man.

The mechanization period, 1800–1900. The year 1800 ushered in a new century. It also brought the cusp of a technological tidal wave in the field of printing. One historian called this amazing surge "a wholesale alteration . . . beyond the wildest dreams of earlier printers . . . [and] beyond the most extravagant hopes of earlier publishers and book-buyers."[11]

One of the first salvos of change occurred in an overlapping industry. Prior to 1800, paper was produced by hand in slow and costly paper mills. In 1787 only ninety mills existed in all of America.[12] Paper was expensive, in short supply, and of poor quality. Finer book-quality paper usually came from England and was hard to come by. In some of his correspondences, Benjamin Franklin complained about frequent paper shortages.[13] The British were also quick to exploit this situation. In 1767 as they tried to maintain control of the thirteen colonies, England imposed the infamous Townshed Act. A central feature of this measure was a punitive tax on rags that were needed to manufacture paper. With these limitations the cost of paper alone constituted over 20 percent of the total price of printing a book. The situation was stifling for the American printing industry.

Two years prior to 1800, a French inventor named Nicolas Robert built a mechanical paper machine. Within five years English paper mills were producing ten times more paper than they had previously produced. By 1810 the number of paper mills in America had more than doubled. Not only was paper in ample supply but the cost tumbled by as much as 30 percent in a twenty-five year span.[14] What had been a severe restriction for American printers all but vanished overnight.

Ironically, most of the innovations and advances had been suggested previously, but inertia and institutions had completely stymied them. Within the space of twenty-five years, a resurgence occurred that could only be compared to the incunabula of printing itself. Scholars have labeled this time as the period of mechanization. Upon closer examination, perhaps it merits the title of the "reincunabula" because so much occurred in such a brief time span in the American printing industry.

NINETEENTH-CENTURY IRON HANDPRESSES IN AMERICA

The Stanhope press. At the onset of the nineteenth century, England provided the perfect climate for the invention of the first iron handpress. The industrial revolution was in full swing, and England was home to an ambitious inventor named Charles, the third Earl Stanhope. About the year 1800 he cast and built the first all-metal handpress. Others had previously used metal parts and even metal frames, but he was the first to put it all together. His second great innovation came in his use of compound levers to drive the contact surfaces of his press. A third advancement involved the efficiency of the press. Common (wooden) presses printed at about the same speed as a Stanhope press: two hundred sheets per hour. However, the iron press generally tripled the size of the platen or printing surface. Also, the common press required the pressman to make two pulls with the printing lever. The new iron press utilized just one motion. It was a big step forward in print efficiency.[15]

The Columbian press. The first iron handpress to be built in America was designed and manufactured by George Clymer in Philadelphia, the heartland of America's printing industry. In 1813 he built a press that abandoned the screw drive that had been the central feature of Gutenberg's modified winepress. Clymer replaced this mechanism with a large pivoting crossbeam and lever. The distinguishing visual feature of this press, nicknamed "The Columbian," was its ornately decorated headpiece and flatware. One observer referred to this press as both a technical and an artistic advancement.[16] Because of its weight and cost, only a few were manufactured and sold in America. Yet by 1820 the Columbian press had established itself in England and Europe as the leading machine.

The Ruthven press. A second foreign-built handpress arrived in America in 1818. Called the Ruthven press after its Scottish inventor, John Ruthven, this press featured a very different design and print mechanism. Standing just three feet high (compared to five to eight feet for other presses), the Ruthven maintained a stationary printing plate. The benefits of this press were reduced cost, weight, and size. But this press never really established itself in the United States and was primarily found only in the catalogs of the day.

The Wells press. The second American-built iron handpress arrived courtesy of inventor John Wells in 1819.[17] His biggest innovation involved the use of offset toggle levers. Unfortunately for Wells, his design moved faster than his presses. Two years later, unpatented presses from rival manufacturers began selling his trademark toggle lever apparatus. Wells bitterly complained, "In 1820 several of my [patented] presses were in the Bible office in N. York; and after Peter Smith had commenced the manufacture of presses, I was informed that he had examined them many times. His patent is dated '29th Dec. 1821.'"[18] Wells confronted Mr. Smith, but patent laws provided him little recourse.[19] He continued to market his press until his death in 1833, but he was a much better designer than salesman. In retrospect, he facilitated an important advance in iron handpresses in America, but, unfortunately, others reaped the benefits.

The Stansbury iron press. The Stansbury iron press emerged in 1821. Adam Stansbury constructed a press similar to the Wells model of 1819, yet different in two ways. It employed a unique transfer mechanism, and it was manufactured in Cincinnati rather than New York. In spite of these changes, this press also failed to sweep the printing market.

The Smith press. Perhaps the most controversial press of this technology deluge was the Smith press of 1821. History incriminates Mr. Peter Smith as marketing his press with pilfered technology long before he had any legal patents. On the other hand, it appears that Mr. Smith legitimately invented and introduced the distinctive acorn shape into the American printing industry. This shape became the symbol of American handpresses during the 1820s and 1830s. (Ironically, the Wells press changed the shape of its frame in 1822 to conform to the Smith acorn press.) Purchased in 1823 by the aggressive Robert Hoe and Company, the Smith press quickly became one of America's most popular machines. It was not unusually fast, exceptionally reliable, or substantially cheaper. It was simply the model that Robert Hoe owned, advertised, and sold. Thus, for a brief period this acorn press came to visually symbolize the handpress in America.[20]

The Washington press. The last of the iron handpresses prior to 1830 arguably became America's most popular press of the nineteenth century. The Washington press was developed by Samuel Rust in 1821. This press was most noted for its light weight, its toggle technology, and its component frame,[21] though what really popularized this press in America was the purchase of the patent by Robert Hoe in 1835. Hoe was known as the Henry Ford of the printing industry, and the Washington press became the Model T of the nineteenth century. Hoe and Company produced over six thousand of these units before they were outdated, but the Washington press would not have been readily available before 1835.

The seven previous iron handpresses would have been the only models in printer's catalogs prior to 1830 in America. Each had modified or improved slightly on its progenitor. To be sure, there were other metal presses in England and Europe, but they had not yet made their way to America. When Joseph Smith, Oliver Cowdery, and Martin Harris commenced looking for a book printer in 1829, these presses would have constituted the field of possibilities.

PRINTING IN AMERICA, 1829

By 1829 approximately four hundred years had elapsed since Gutenberg first introduced the wooden handpress. His press had undergone some cosmetic changes, but its design was basically intact. From its onset, the Gutenberg press could produce about two hundred sheets per hour if conditions were right and two experienced pressmen were at the controls.[22]

By the early 1800s the wooden press was still the press of choice in America for all but the larger newspaper printers. Prior to 1800, however, presses in America were difficult to purchase without long delays or required inside contacts.[23] For this reason almost all book printing prior to 1820 occurred in England. Suddenly all this began to change.

Concomitant with the rise of metal presses was a parallel surge of reliable wooden presses. Manufacturer Adam Ramage answered America's need for inexpensive wooden presses. Between 1800 and 1827 he built more than twelve hundred presses with a sticker price of only $130.[24] Importation of presses ceased almost overnight.[25] New as well as used presses helped smaller shops and newspapers to proliferate. The result was a surge in printed materials and in a literate public. Americans became voracious readers. Nowhere was this more obvious than in the newspaper industry. By 1830 Bulwer-Lytton calculated that one in thirty-six people bought newspapers in England, while in Pennsylvania one in four purchased them.[26] Rather quickly an appetite for reading was answered with an amazing further proliferation of printing. The printing scholar S. H. Steinberg summarized these amazing times best when he noted, "Within a generation . . . these inventions [went] . . . beyond the wildest dreams of earlier printers."[27]

Printing possibilities in Palmyra in 1829. On June 11, 1829, Joseph Smith secured the copyright for the Book of Mormon. Shortly thereafter records indicate that he and Oliver Cowdery began their efforts to secure a printer for the manuscript. Their first recorded attempt was at Egbert Grandin's printing shop in Palmyra.

Palmyra in 1829 was a bustling little city of four thousand people. Just four years earlier, the Erie Canal had opened with great fanfare and promise. The canal cut right through Palmyra and was ideal for the economical shipping of heavier loads such as a 1500-pound iron press. Palmyra had swelled by 30 percent in just ten years, and many projected it as a key business center between Rochester and Albany.[28] One of the eager entrepreneurs of frontier Palmyra was Egbert Grandin. In his late teens, Grandin had apprenticed at Palmyra's newspaper, the *Wayne Sentinel* (formerly *Palmyra Herald* and *Canal Advertizer*). About four years later, he bought the newspaper and became its editor at the young age of twenty-one. The following year, in the fall of 1828, he moved into a new building on Main Street.[29] Finally, in early 1829 he purchased a state-of-the-art iron handpress. This Smith press was manufactured by Robert Hoe & Company in New York City and was transported along the Erie Canal to rural Palmyra.[30] In the spring of 1829, a hoist was constructed, and the new press was lifted into position on the third floor of the Grandin printing shop. Thus, a daring twenty-one-year-old with little more than a dream purchased a printing shop, moved the business and a costly press into a new and spacious location, and ventured heavily into the printing industry. Some would view these events as providential, others as mere historical coincidences. What is certain is that all this occurred without Grandin's foreknowledge of the imminent printing of the Book of Mormon.

As these events converged, Joseph and Oliver set out to find a printer. They approached Grandin and were politely refused. He cited as his reasons both the religious implications and the fear that his friend Martin Harris was being duped and exploited.[31] This set-back pointed them in the direction of Rochester, some twenty-five miles away. While there, Joseph and Martin twice approached Thurlow Weed, publisher of the *Rochester Anti-Masonic Enquirer.* In his diary Mr. Weed recorded, "I thought the man either crazed or a very shallow imposter, and therefore declined to become a pub-lisher."[32] At another shop, Elihu Marshall agreed to print the book, albeit at an inflated price. Joseph and Martin returned to Palmyra with only one option in hand: Send someone back to Rochester and then shuttle the manuscript copy each day to the printer in order to ensure its safety.

In late June 1829, Martin Harris approached his printer friend Grandin one last time. Martin resolutely stated that the book was going to press. If Grandin stood by his refusal, it would still be printed in Rochester.[33] In a rather abrupt reversal, Grandin recon-sidered. According to his grandson, "after consulting friends who felt that it was merely a business matter and that he would be in no way related to the religion, he consented."[34] Perhaps Grandin's decision was influenced also by his recent acquisition of the expen-sive Smith press. Furthermore, he did not seem to have any major printing orders occupying his equipment or schedule. Once Grandin agreed in principle, he moved quickly to expand his print-ing team. In June 1829 he enlisted the help of the former *Wayne Sentinel* owner John Gilbert to set the type and estimate the printing order. Together they estimated that they could produce five thousand books for three thousand dollars by the following February. The size of the order did not seem to worry either Grandin or Gilbert, even though Pomeroy Tucker (Palmyra's first newspaper printer) was quoted as saying that "the largest printing job ever done in it [Wayne County] was the first edition of Jo Smith's . . . Golden Bible."[35] Other observers have suggested that this order was perhaps ten times larger than the normal book orders of that day.[36] Undaunted, Grandin accepted a promissory note on Harris's farm for three thousand dollars payable in eighteen months. The mortgage deed was recorded on August 25, 1829, and with a new set of pica type the printing commenced.[37]

The printing commences. The printing of the Book of Mormon stretched from late August 1829 until March 26, 1830.[38] The days were long and relentless. One account indicates that the printing work continued for eleven hours per day, six days a week, for seven months.[39] Using this as a guide, Grandin's printing crew had 184 total days available for the project.[40] However, in January printing ceased. The townspeople had begun to worry Grandin about an announced boycott of the book. At this point Grandin had an immense financial stake in the feasibility of the project. There is no record of any prepayments he might have received, and it appears that he was carrying all of the risk with only the promissory note on Martin Harris's farm. With the potential boycott looming, Grandin stopped work and Joseph was summoned from Harmony, Pennsylvania. He and Martin allayed Grandin's concerns and the printing resumed.[41] Finally on March 26, 1830, the *Wayne Sentinel* printed the title page of the Book of Mormon with the notice that "the above work, containing about 600 pages, large Duodecimo, is now for sale, wholesale and retail, at the Palmyra bookstore." What had occurred during these seven months was remarkable. The existing records identify nine individuals who worked with Grandin during these months, even though the actual number was probably much higher.[42] The Smith press, known for its quality book printing and its strong frame, was well suited for the mammoth job of the first edition printing.[43] Even the phrase "mammoth job" might be an understatement. The Smith press had a platen of about 21 by 30 inches. Sixteen pages were typeset and printed with each pull of the press lever. This meant that for a 592-page book with a run of 5,000 copies, approximately 2,960,000 pages had to be printed. In layman's terms, the printing lever on this rugged Smith press would have been pulled at least 185,000 times during this seven-month period. It would have necessitated more than a thousand pulls per day.

But this was not all. To print each sheet of paper, two skilled pressmen had to quickly perform nine other separate tasks. After the printing pull, these other nine steps were as follows: crank the bed back to its original position, lift up the frisket assembly, lift the frisket bracket and remove the sheet, hand ink all sixteen pages in the composite layout, lift the frisket bracket, register the sheet on the timpan bracket, lower the frisket bracket back into place, swing the frisket basket down on the inked layout, and crank the removable bed under the platen. Completing these tasks meant that one of the 185,000 pulls had been completed. On a daily basis, these tasks had to be repeated more than one thousand times.[44] However, this printing procedure constituted only a fraction of the effort to actually produce the book. The type and spacers, which totaled over 42,500 individual pieces for each form, had to be typeset thirty-seven different times. (The total number of pieces set during the seven months was more than 1.5 million.) The entire manuscript also had to be punctuated by the typesetter.[45] Next, the printed sheets had to be hung and dried, after which the thirty-seven signatures were folded, cut apart, and stitched together for each book. Finally, a binding was applied to the 592 pages.[46] For a small frontier newspaper, this 184-day process was nothing short of phenomenal.[47]

Grandin: a postscript. As a postscript to this virtuoso performance by a country printing shop, Grandin grew restless with printing and in the following year turned to other civic pursuits outside his printing shop. By 1833 he was forced to sell his business. He then tried his hand at a number of unsuccessful ventures. He became ill and died in 1845 at the young age of thirty-nine. In retrospect, he controlled and worked his printing business for just four brief years, from 1827 to 1831. On his tombstone was carved the epitaph "An honest man, the noblest work of God."[48] To those who sense the truthfulness of the Book of Mormon, this statement could be rephrased, "An honest man who nobly assisted the work of God."

Summary

Using March 26, 1830, as a printing benchmark, the following developments represent significant trends or events that culminated in the printing of the Book of Mormon:

1. Printing had an incredibly auspicious start (twelve million books in fifty years) with Gutenberg's press.

2. The Gutenberg wooden press, or the common press, remained virtually the same from 1450 to 1800. It could print about two hundred sheets, or about three hundred square feet of surface printing, per hour.

3. The Industrial Revolution introduced the first iron handpress in England in 1798.

4. By 1800 America had developed an insatiable appetite for reading, and the printing industry responded with a proliferation of presses and materials.

5. Seven iron handpresses of different designs surfaced in America from 1815 to 1830. They became available only in the mid to late 1820s.

6. These iron presses printed three to four times the amount of printed material as the common wooden press and were well-suited for book printing. One drawback, however, was that iron presses were heavy—fifteen hundred pounds.

7. The Erie Canal opened in 1825 and was available for shipping heavier items.

8. The cost of paper fell by 30 percent in just thirty years, and the availability increased due to the mechanization of paper factories.

9. E. B. Grandin apprenticed for four years in a printing shop in rural Palmyra, New York. In 1827, at age twenty-one, he purchased the same printing shop.

10. Between one and two years later, Grandin bought a new iron press, which was three to four times more efficient than his other wooden press.

11. Grandin hired his former master printer as typesetter and contracted to print the largest book order to that time in Wayne County: the Book of Mormon.

12. The pace of 1.5 sheets per minute in 184 days was a near-Herculean printing feat in rural New York.

In sum, it took just seven months to print 5,000 copies of a 592-page book in Palmyra. There were two brief stoppages but no vandalism or maliciousness. In contrast, the translation of the Book of Mormon had to be moved three times to carve out just sixty-five working days within a two-year period. This salient observation remains: it would have been highly disruptive to move the printing once it began. Unlike the translation work, unless the book was completely printed in one shop, considerable time would have been lost in trying to relocate the printing process.

In addition to uninterrupted press time, a final perspective to consider involves the historical timing of this 1829 printing job. What difference would a twenty-year time shift have meant to the Book of Mormon printing? If Joseph had been born earlier and had sought a printer in 1809 in Palmyra, he would have found none. Had he been able to locate a willing printer in Rochester (25 miles west), the printing shop would have had a common press with the typical printing surface of 12 by 18 inches. This machine would have required at least three times as much time to print five thousand copies of the Book of Mormon at only newspaper quality. Instead of seven months it would have required twenty-one months, or almost two years. Undoubtedly there would have also been paper shortages, persecution, and sundry delays. Considering all these obstacles, it is apparent that the general timing of the printing of the Book of Mormon was very significant.

Anciently the Lord, through the prophet Isaiah, foretold the day when He would "do a marvellous work among this people, even a marvellous work and a wonder" (Isaiah 29:14). Often the Latter-day Saint interpretation of this passage points to the Book of Mormon in its entirety, a marvelous manifestation in this last dispensation. But what if Isaiah was also foretelling the marvelous physical manner in which this marvelous work would be brought forth? To those who have come to believe, the timely events from Gutenberg to Grandin that facilitated the printing of the Book of Mormon might be yet another evidence of God's hand in this marvelous work and a wonder.

NOTES

1. See Victor Scholderer, *Johann Gutenberg: The Inventor of Printing* (London: Trustees of the British Museum, 1963), 23; see also Warren Chappell, *A Short History of the Printed Word* (New York: Alfred A. Knopf, 1970), 48.

2. See James Moran, *Printing Presses: History & Development from the Fifteenth Century to Modern Times* (Berkeley: University of California Press, 1973), 18; see also Edmund C. Arnold, *Ink on Paper 2: A Handbook of the Graphic Arts* (New York: Harper & Row, 1972), 238.

3. See Chappell, *Short History of the Printed Word*, 84.

4. "Who Mattered Most in This Millennium," *USA Today*, December 23, 1999, sec. A, 17.

5. See S. H. Steinberg, *Five Hundred Years of Printing* (New Castle, Del.: The British Library & Oak Knoll Press, 1996), I.

6. Philip Gaskell, *A New Introduction to Bibliography* (London: Oxford University Press, 1972), 2.

7. See Robert Hoe, *A Short History of the Printing Press* (New York: Gilliss Press, 1902), 6; see also Frank E. Comparato, *Chronicles of Genius and Folly* (Culver City, Calif.: Labyrinthos, 1979), 2.

8. See Moran, *Printing Presses*, 41.

9. See Arnold, *Ink on Paper 2*, 127.

10. Comparato, *Chronicles of Genius and Folly*, 31.

11. Steinberg, *Five Hundred Years of Printing*, 137.

12. See Lawrence C. Wroth, *The Colonial Printer* (Charlottesville, Va.: Dominion Books, 1964), 129, 134.

13. See Wroth, *Colonial Printer*, 129, 134.

14. See Steinberg, *Five Hundred Years of Printing*, 138.

15. See Stephen O. Saxe, *American Iron Hand Presses* (New Castle, Del.: Oak Knoll Books, 1992), 4.

16. See James Moran, "The Columbian Press," *Journal of the Printing Historical Society* 5 (1969): 14–15.

17. See Rollo G. Silver, *The American Printer* (Charlottesville, Va.: University Press of Virginia, 1967), 50.

18. An abridgment of "Johnson's Typographia" (Boston 1828), 302–4, quoted in Silver, *American Printer,* 51.

19. See Saxe, *American Hand Presses,* 24.

20. See Ralph Green, *The Iron Hand Press in America* (Rowayton, Conn.: The Press, 1948), 13.

21. See Saxe, *American Iron Hand Presses,* 44.

22. See Moran, *Printing Presses,* 44.

23. See Silver, *American Printer,* 37.

24. See Milton W. Hamilton, *Adam Ramage and His Presses* (Portland Me.: Southworth-Anthoensen Press, 1942), 3; see also Comparato, *Chronicles of Genius and Folly,* 31.

25. See Hamilton, *Adam Ramage and His Presses,* 11.

26. See Chappell, *Short History of the Printed Word,* 199.

27. Steinberg, *Five Hundred Years of Printing,* 137.

28. See Larry C. Porter, Milton V. Backman Jr., and Susan Easton Black, eds., *Regional Studies in Latter-day Saint Church History: New York* (Provo, Utah: Department of Church History and Doctrine, 1992), 2–3.

29. See Larry C. Porter, *New York and Pennsylvania,* vol. 2 of *Sacred Places,* ed. LaMar C. Berrett (Salt Lake City: Deseret Book, 2000), 169.

30. See Larry C. Porter, "Book of Mormon, Printing and Publication," in *Book of Mormon Reference Companion,* ed. Dennis L. Largey (Salt Lake City: Deseret Book, 2003), 136; see also Larry C. Porter, "Grandin, Egbert Bratt," in *Book of Mormon Reference Companion,* 307; "Press That Printed the First Copy of the Book of Mormon," *Deseret News,* November 5, 1998, sec. A, 18.

31. See Susan Easton Black and Charles D. Tate Jr., eds., *Joseph Smith: The Prophet, The Man* (Provo, Utah: Religious Studies Center, 1993), 5; see also Porter, "Grandin, Egbert Bratt," 309.

32. Black and Tate, *Joseph Smith,* 52; see also Richard L. Bushman, *Joseph Smith and the Beginnings of Mormonism* (Urbana, Ill.: University of Illinois Press, 1988), 107.

33. See John H. Gilbert, Esq., Memorandum, September 8, 1892, Palmyra.

34. Henry Allen to "The Librarian of the Palmyra Library"; cited in *BYU Studies* 10, no. 3 (Spring 1970): 252.

35. Porter, "Book of Mormon, Printing and Publication," 134.

36. See Hellmut Lehmann-Haupt, W. Lawrence Roth, and Ruth S. Grannis, *The Book in America*, 2d ed. (New York: R. R. Bowker, 1951), 40; Louis E. Crandall, "The Printing of the Original Book of Mormon" (unpublished paper).

37. See Gilbert, Memorandum; see also Porter, "Book of Mormon, Printing and Publication," 134; Don Enders, unpublished manuscript in possession of the author, 3.

38. See Porter, "Book of Mormon, Printing and Publication," 138.

39. See Gayle Goble Ord, "The Book of Mormon Goes to Press," *Ensign*, December 1972, 69.

40. A period of 184 days was the maximum time available for printing the Book of Mormon within the seven-month period. There is one piece of extant evidence that indicates Grandin's crew was able to work faster than the maximum 184 working days. John Gilbert claimed that they were able to completely print one form every three days (Memorandum, 3). If they were somehow able to sustain this speed, the total printing time (including typesetting) would have been incredibly reduced to just 111 days. This also means they would have pulled the press not 1,000 times per day but upwards of 1,600 times per day, or 2.5 times per minute. Work on the project was halted once in November, and the second delay came in January. The November stoppage resulted from a need for more type (Porter, "Book of Mormon, Printing and Publication," 135).

41. See Bushman, *Joseph Smith and the Beginnings of Mormonism*, 110; Lucy Smith, *Biographical Sketches of Joseph Smith the Prophet and His Progenitors for Many Generations* (Independence, Mo.: Herald Publishing House, 1969), 180.

42. Porter, "Book of Mormon, Printing and Publication," 138.

43. See Silver, *American Printer*, 51.

44. See Crandall, "Printing of the Original Book of Mormon."

45. See Gilbert, Memorandum.

46. Not all of these processes of binding and folding were completely finished by March 26, 1830. Enough were finished, however, to advertise the book for sale.

47. See Crandall, "Printing of the Original Book of Mormon," 261.

48. Porter, "Grandin, Egbert Bratt," 310.

INDEX